The Earth Mother:

Legends, Goddesses, and Ritual Arts of India

Other Books by Pupul Jayakar

God Is Not a Full Stop

Indira Gandhi: A Photographic Tribute

The Buddha

J. Krishnamurti: A Biography

The EARTH MOTHER

Legends, Goddesses, and Ritual Arts of India

Pupul Jayakar

1817

Harper & Row, Publishers, San Francisco
New York, Grand Rapids, Philadelphia, St. Louis
London, Singapore, Sydney, Tokyo, Toronto

First published as *The Earthen Drum* by the National Museum in India in 1980.
Published in a revised, updated edition as *The Earth Mother* by Penguin Books India, Ltd. in 1989.

FIRST HARPER & ROW EDITION, REPRINTED BY ARRANGEMENT WITH PENGUIN BOOKS INDIA, LTD.

Library of Congress Cataloging-in-Publication Data

Jayakar, Pupul.
The earth mother : legends, goddesses, and ritual arts of India / by Pupul Jayakar.
p. cm.
Rev. and updated ed. of: The earthen drum. 1980.
Includes bibliographical references (p.).
ISBN 0-06-250405-3
1. Art, Indic. 2. Mother-goddesses in art. 3. Art and society—India. I. Jayakar, Pupul. Earthen drum. II. Title.
(N8191.I4J39 1990)
700'.954—dc20 89-46434
CIP

---

90 91 92 93 94 HAD 10 9 8 7 6 5 4 3 2 1

This edition is printed on acid-free paper that meets the American National Standards Institute Z39.48 Standard.

To

Nanda Gowri
Ratan Gowri
Iravata
Radhika
Sunanda
Maya

Contents

Acknowledgments

I am greatly indebted to Shri B. K. Thapar, ex-Director General of the Archaeological Survey of India and his department, the National Museum, the British Museum, the Victoria and Albert Museum, the India House Library, the Deccan College, the Prince of Wales Museum, the Ashutosh Museum, the West Bengal Department of Archaeology and the innumerable private and public owners who have permitted their objects to be reproduced in this book. I owe a special debt of gratitude to Dr. Sivaramamurti, who, while he was Director of the National Museum, persuaded me to write this book and who, with his scholarship and total dedication, deepened my understanding. I am also indebted to:

Rai Krishnadasji, whose erudition, passion, and perception arise out of a unique awareness of the interdependence between the classical and a peoples' art.

The late Dr. Motichandra for the valuable time he spent in discussion with me helping to unravel some of the knots of this still untrodden path.

Dr. N. R. Banerjee, former Director, National Museum, for his valuable help and advice.

Dr. Kapila Vatsyayan for her sensitivity and understanding of this subject.

The late W. G. Archer for the delightful evening I spent in his home discussing the broad spectrum of rural painting. It is a matter of sadness for me that he is not with us to see the book in print.

John Irwin with whom I carried on a dialogue for many years.

The late Dr. Verrier Elwin, whose insights into the tribal mind provided the key to many of my investigations.

Shri Sankho Choudhary, Shri Haku Shah, and Shri J. Swaminathan for their unique understanding of the ambience within which these arts have flowered.

Dr. P. Banerjee, former Assistant Director, and Dr. C. B. Pandey, former Keeper (Publications), of the National Museum, for their scholarship and interest.

Shri Benoy Sarkar of the Handicrafts and Handlooms Exports Corporation of India, Ltd., New Delhi, for the excellence of the design and layout.

The All India Handicrafts Board, the Handicrafts and Handlooms Exports Corporation of India, Ltd., the Weavers' Service Centre, All India Handloom Board, the National Institute of Design, and Government of India for the help they have provided.

The late Shri Maharathi, the late Shri Kulkarni, Smt. Geeti Sen, and Smt. Mohna Iyengar of the Office of the Development Commissioner for Handicrafts for their valuable assistance.

Lance Dane for the infinite care and interest in taking many of the photographs.

(The dates given in the captions of photos 15 and 41 are tentative.)

Preface

A revised and updated edition of *The Earthen Drum* (under which title this book was first published) was long overdue. It was in the early '70s that the late Dr. C. Sivaramamurti, an eminent scholar of Indian art and then Director of the National Museum in India, suggested that I write a book for the museum on the art and ritual of the "Little Tradition." Fragmentary studies on the subject existed, but no overarching view was available.

It was during a period of intense inquiry that I, with the hesitant mind of a pilgrim, approached the book. I was touring villages and small towns in India, entering into dialogue with women and men from the craft ambience, listening to the myths and songs that carried the history of their race, closely observing their skills and their links to heritage, their insights into seasons and their relationship to creation. It was a period of search and inquiry into the nature of myth, into symbol and its inner resonances, its ways of revelation; into the mystery of color and its vocabulary of tone within tone.

Simultaneously, I was delving into self-knowing, into an unexplored universe of space, sound, color, and word picture. This descent into depth and density brought to the surface traces of a long forgotten childhood erased by time; and beyond the personal to those energies, those inchoate and expanding mysteries of color, sound, word that are the repository of the senses undifferentiated, the raw material of the racial unconscious. It is out of this altogetherness of seeing and listening that insight arose into the nature of the goddess and her primal links to energy, to the earth, and to manifestation. With these perceptions I examined the artifacts of history, of the living present, and scholarship, to find support for what was revealed. The word pictures, the resonances, the direct research into original sources, and the garnering of the studies on the subject come together in *The Earthen Drum,* published and released by the National Museum in October 1980.

In the last decade new discoveries of archaeology and studies of cultural anthropology have pushed back the frontiers of prehistory and with it the perceptions of the primordial Earth Mother. The further you extend the frontiers of the past, and so the frontiers of the mind, the further recede the primal insights into the goddess. For this reason I have found it necessary to update and revise *The Earthen Drum* which finds new form in the present edition. Reviewing the book, I felt the title *The Earth Mother* would be more appropriate. For the book deals with that germ of female energy from which all manifestations—nature, the arts, ritual, and symbol—emerge.

The discovery of a bone image of the Mother in cave shelters in Mirzapur, Uttar Pradesh, carbon dated to 20,000 BC, bears witness to the antiquity of the goddess and the energy and imagery that coalesced to endow her with form.

Two vast anonymous rivers of the creative flow in parallel streams over the landmass of India. One is based on a male-oriented artisan tradition where craftsmen are organized into guilds or *śrenis.* Craftsmen within these guilds trace their source to Viśwakarma, the first creator. Within this tradition, the transmission of skill, knowledge of material, and the quickening of insight is from guru to disciple, from father to son. The other is based on the recognition of woman as the original creator. A heritage that traces its origins to Adi Śakti, the first woman, who spins the threads of creation. She creates, she conceives, and she destroys in a simultaneity of time, for in her is alive the wisdom that in *srishti* or creation is the seed of *samhara* or destruction. In such a scenario of ending and beginning, death is an ending and yet a passage to a beginning. In *srishti* is *samhara,* in *samhara* is *srishti.*

A substratum of female memories of power and energy has existed from the primordial past. Within this stream, women were the holders and sustainers of heritage. Integral to this was an understanding of the nature of cyclic time, and the rites of passage, of seasons entering creation. All transmission of myth, the contacting of energy sources and the initiating of rites of the auspicious, flowed from mother to daughter, through poesy, art, skill, ritual, the unspoken word, and gesture. When asked as to the source of her skill and her visual and aural vocabulary, a woman from the rural areas of Bihar said, "It is from a *parampara,* a time without beginning. We hold this knowing in our wombs."

In recent years geologists drilling for oil found evidence of a vast resource of water that lay about 2.5 kilometers below the Ganges riverbed. Deep in the racial unconscious of India is the knowledge of a lost river which nurtures the soil of India, is sacred, is the river of creation, of insight. As it flows underground, in the heart of the earth, so it flows within woman. To touch it is not to go back in historical time, it is not a sequential movement, it is to give breath to seed.

A concern with the altogetherness of perception and the resonances of the earth, that made possible the transmission of millennia, is under assault. Sensibilities and rhythms that took centuries to mature take a few decades to destroy. A material culture and its values clog transmission, the capacity to enter depth and the within of nature and manifestation.

As the energy of transformation disappears, as spaces close in, the Earth Mother can no longer arise, stride forth, transform, and renew herself. Her habitat, the earth, the air, the waters, are polluted, her forests and groves ravaged. We witness her dissipation at our peril.

I owe a debt of gratitude to Dr. Stella Kramrisch for permitting me to use a modified version of her review of my book *The Earthen Drum* as a foreword to *The Earth Mother*. I would like to thank my granddaughter, Sunanda Herzberger, for editing the book afresh, for the sensitivity with which she approached the subject, for the ear that listened to her grandmother's words. Perhaps here too was a transmission, from a grandmother to a granddaughter. May she drink of the rivers.

April 1989 *Pupul Jayakar*
New Delhi

Foreword

The Earth Mother is a work of singular importance. It does not treat of the great Indian monuments in stone or bronze, but uncovers the rich soil of manifold though coherent texture on which they came to be. The iconic as well as abstract forms created within the traditions of ritual practice in rural India as much as the diminutive reliefs found in the ancient cities of the Harappan civilization contribute essentially to the meaning of the book, which does not offer a conspectus of Indian art under royal or other patronage from the third millennium BC to the present, but treats of practically all the varieties of visual art created and used by the rural, tribal, and other people of the vast country through the millennia.

The Earth Mother is a metaphor for the creative energy of India that quickens and reverberates in widely different forms. Where similarity is striking, as for example in the clay figurines of Zhob and Kulli in Afghanistan of the third millennium BC and in the ritual clay figurines of Bengal today, this paradoxically shows an immediacy that defies definition, while it convinces by its documentation.

Each of the small objects discussed and illustrated side by side is a token of a world of magic, myth, and transformation, of alchemy and *yoga* power. It is a world of will and creative energy that throbs deep below the high altitudes where Indian sages sought and attained liberation. Into this world of the Earth Mother and her creative energy Pupul Jayakar is an eloquent guide. She leads with knowledge, intuition, and imagination.

The sixteen chapters of the book read easily, while the structure of the text links several approaches. A summary of each section will map out the vast territory covered.

"The Rural Roots," the first chapter, touches upon the complexity of the rural situation. It speaks of settled villages where *purāṇic* gods are worshipped and coexist with household and fertility rites, the *vratas,* removed from Vedic ritual; it tells of nomadic people at times forming settled communities, and of aboriginals living in forests and mountains and having no recorded history.

These three types, it is shown, are not static, for history has recorded the withdrawal from cities in repeated retreats to villages and to the mountains. The first was that of the Harappan civilization to the Deccan, followed by the Aryan invaders, a conquest which caused an "archaic people's culture based on the primacy of the female principle" to "survive in secret women's rites and fertility rituals."

These introductory remarks lead the author to the pervading theme of her book, the *vratas.* The author sees the "*vrātyas,* magicians and masters of breath control" who "have practiced sexual rites linked to agricultural magic and fertility," as having provided the name to the *vrata* rituals that have permeated the countryside north of the Vindhyas and that are "the ritual-bound base that conditions the life of the Hindu householder."

Woman was the main participant and actor of the *vratas,* "which connected her to the furthermost limits of human memories when woman as priestess and seer guarded the mysteries, the ways of the numinous female." "It was around the *vratas,* thousands of variations of which existed in city, settled village, and forest that the rural arts found significant expression." "The *vrata* tradition freed the participant from the inflexible hold of the great (i.e. *Brahmanic*) tradition." *Brahmanic* worship was available only to the *Brahmin;* "the *vrata pūjā* and observances were available to the woman, the non-*Brahmin,* the *Śūdra,* and rural tribes. They brought into operation song, dance, the visual arts of picture- and image-making, magical formulae of incantation and gesture." The *vrata* rites provided the channels through which contact with nature and life was maintained and renewed by the worship of the earth, sun, and water and by invoking of the energy of growing things—trees, plants, and animals. The demands of sex and fertility, wealth and prosperity, were translated into minutely detailed rituals which gave to the vast country a common bond and vision. *Vrata* provided a living storehouse of the archaic past continually transformed into the contemporary moment through group action. The *vrata* rites through the centuries were to maintain their integrity independent of and parallel to the orthodox *Brahmin*-dominated culture. Having drawn this picture of the *vrata* tradition, itself "ritual bound" though vital as against the "inflexible hold" of the *Brahmin* Aryan tradition, the author sees "two movements that emerged out of the fusion of Aryans and autochthons" and that "both these streams in their vernacular form found expression in the rural tradition."

Whether the *vrātyas* were renegades from the Vedic fold, as some think, or came from the outside, their rites were admitted or readmitted within the Vedic tradition. A whole book of the *Atharva Veda* treats of the *vrātya* ritual; our knowledge of its stems from this source. *Vrata* tradition and rural tradition are not identical. Variations of the *vratas* existed in the city, settled village, and forest. Though it was around the *vratas* that thousands of rural arts found significant expression, two movements emerged out of the fusion of Aryan (*mārgī*) and autochthonous (*deśī*). The creativity within the autochthonous is the paramount factor in the rural tradition.

It was *vrata* tradition that pointed the way back to the origins when the Earth Mother—virgin and mother in one—held sway. It was only after the fusion of races and the crystallization of agricultural communities that the participation of the male god in the rituals enacted around the cycle of fertility was recognized. But this leads us into another consideration, that of tribal art.

Before leaving the Aryan, Vedic, Brahmin tradition on the one hand and the *vratya* tradition on the other and also the Harappan past, attention may be drawn to "a stark, headless, sightless icon of the Earth Mother" (illus. 9) in contrast to a female with eyes, facial features, and ornaments articulate and prominent. Illustration 9 from Bhilwalli, Madhya Pradesh, of the aftermath of the Harappan culture 1500–1000 BC, is to illustrate the contrast with a work (illus. 1) of "the protected culture" of Harappa (third millennium BC); the other being the "product of an unsettled people that were concerned only with the protective and the essential."

The Bhilwalli figurine terminates at its upper end with three short stumplike projections, the two lateral ones standing for the arms, the upper in the middle, a rounded triangular shape, for the faceless head; it may be pointed out that the three protuberances are similar to those of chalcolithic figurines from Asia Minor and Greece.

The author describes tribal art like that of the Bhils, which in their *pithoras* ensures fertility by including a copulating couple in their pictures. We now find ourselves in the domain of *tantra,* where the act of union became the focal point. Agricultural magic was fused with alchemy and *tantra.* The earliest treatise on alchemy, the *Rasaratnakara* of Nāgārjuna, is a work of the second or third century AD. It must have been preceded by a practice of alchemy. Mrs. Jayakar speaks of the tribal origins of *tantra*—which in Orissa is known as *savarī vidyā* after the Śavara tribe—and of its lowly homes. The *kubjikā tantra* originated in the homes of potters. However, "while the women operated in the magical religious domain of *maṇḍala* and *vrata* ritual, they played no part in the artistic tradition. This lay in the hands of the craftsmen, who also were the link between the monumental forms of the great tradition and the rural gods and the tribal deities of forest and mountain. It was the artisan tradition that produced the great temples of the *purāṇic* gods and also the artifacts for the tribal people."

"In *tantric* art the body of the goddess was geometric abstraction as well as color." Mrs. Jayakar considers the circle, double-spiral, the cross, square, triangle, *svastika*, and the "mystical diagram" at the sites of the Indus Valley and in the cave art of India as establishing an ancient worship of the female divinity. This association of the feminine principle with pictorial abstraction is so deeply embodied in the Indian consciousness that the anthropomorphic form of the goddess never replaces the diagram, but continues through the centuries to coexist with it.

A short chapter following the fundamental first chapter is called "The Legends of Integration" and exemplifies the Dravidization of the country in historical times. The incorporation of Hindu gods among tribal, local, and village divinities is shown by tribal legends; one of the most striking instances of transformation is that of Durgā Kātyāyanī and Mahisasura. The descent into autochthonous depths, from the sky- and heaven-oriented *Brahmanic* vision to earth, firmly rests on "the *Veda* of the rural tradition," this being the name of the third section. It is also the name most aptly given to the *Atharva Veda,* a record of the religion of the autochthonous people living in settled agricultural communities. The magic conjured by the hymns of the *Atharva Veda* comprises the making of figures and effigies, the invocation of deified plants, animals, and bird-faced "mothers"; the *Atharva Veda* speaks of the power of transforming a woman into a forest tree providing healing sap for curing disease. These *mantras* of the *Atharva Veda* required accompanying ritual practices, the preparation of a sacred site delimited in shape, a *yantra* surcharged with energy and power, and a *maṇḍala* as "sensitized object that is the manifest form of the incarnation." The world of the Atharva Veda is infested by *yaksas* and *pisacas,* haunted by *apsaras,* a world of magic and seeing that makes manifest the form of things, a world of awareness of the sap of trees and the smell of flowers, earth, and death. This is the world of *kama*, sensual love.

In this chapter, the author firmly establishes the roots of autochthonous Indian art, its power of transformation made visible in the form of sculpture and painting, where tree and woman are not only an iconographic theme but a seen continuity and oneness of limb, be it that of the tree's or the woman's shape. Mrs. Jayakar here also proves the context of nonfigurative abstract art, that of the *maṇḍala* as cognate with Indian figurative art, the two kinds of form—as the next chapter shows—being perennial from the Harappan civilization to the present.

In the fourth chapter, "The Ritual Art of the Harappan Civilization," the transforming quality of Indian form is exemplified by the propinquity and assimilation of anthropomorphic figure and tree and of plant and animal shape. An unmistakable style of the diminutive relief results which however—it has to be said here—is also conditioned by the "withes" technique of closely set parallel ridges, to which the author herself refers. A circular shape like "the transverse form of a sea shell," whence issue long-necked animal heads, unicorn, bull, stag, and tiger in dynamic rotation is interpreted by the author as implying forces of birth, life, and movement—conveying also that "from the sea-forms have been born the animals of the land." This circular device we observe on the other hand is of the same kind as one extended from the feathered horns of a tiger to its lower jaw, which continues the serrated circular device. Because the circular movement in the figure runs counterclockwise, against the course of the sun, it is seen to link this ancient amulet to magical rites, aimed at controlling and directing the laws of nature.

Mrs. Jayakar is excellent in her descriptions and eloquent in her deductions. Still, as long as the Harappan script remains undeciphered, her seductively imaginative inferences have to await confirmation. This includes the identification of the Harappan *yogi* figure as that of a *vrātya.*

Some of the connected and/or recurrent themes tempt an interpretation, like the figure of the upside-down woman giving birth to a plant, and on the reverse of the same tablet a scene of decapitation, both representations showing the same undeciphered inscription; the versions of the tree-woman-tiger composition are most vividly interpreted in their relation to amulets of near recent date. On the other hand, the manner in which the woman of the tree-woman-tiger scheme is shown abstract in one relief and voluptuously fleshed out in the other, though not further commented upon, makes it clear that within one theme and one particular composition the most contrasting styles could be used, each of great power. The tiger shows both styles, the full-bodied naturalism which is overlaid and combined with the "withes" style. It may also be noticed that the heads of the tiger and woman in the figure are graced with horns—"the sacred buffalo horns of magic"—while both tiger and woman are without them in another relief.

Whether most sensitively abstract or equally sensitively naturalistic, the theme involving tree, tiger, and woman is rendered with equal immediacy, whether using the linear and feathery "plant style" or the opulent, naturalistic "animal style." Most of the bulls, buffaloes, and unicorns—not considered in this book—in other Harappan reliefs excel in the "animal style."

The interpretation of the Harappan reliefs as long as their inscriptions remain undeciphered cannot but be tentative, though they may be less tentative than any of the interpretations of the script. While the latter has no analogy in any other script, figures and scenes of the clay reliefs and their rendering have their analogies and continuity in equally diminutive representations, though in a different technique. The silver amulets of recent centuries from Maharashtra representing the goddess are as suggestive of plant symbolism as are her feathery, mimosa-like lineaments in the Harappan tablets. To what extent this transformation of the anthropomorphic goddess into forms of vegetation is transmitted by the respective relief techniques may not be left out of consideration. In both types, the Harappan clay amulets and the silver amulets, the assimilation to and transformation into vegetation shapes is visually compelling.

The first chapter of the book attempts to reveal the rural roots by projecting back into the far distant past the heritage of later ages collected in the hymns of the *Atharva Veda,* as also in the *tantric* tradition and the flowering of alchemy.

This ahistoric method has its justification, for some of the hymns collected in the *Atharva Veda* might have preexisted this collection, just as *tantric* practices must have preceded *tantric* doctrines and terminology. A bond of magic links the *Atharva Veda,* the *tantras,* and alchemy to their autochthonous roots.

Similarly, while tribal legends show the transformation of Hindu gods and their incorporation in local village deities, the latter are autochthonous, more ancient than the Hindu gods, who became transposed into their likeness. By backward projection the *grāma devatās* seem to be at the root of the *purāṇic* Hindu god who, once more transformed, returns to his point of origin. The numerous Harappan reliefs of buffalo and the appearance of buffalo horns on many of the theriomorphic and anthropomorphic figures of the Harappan amulets show the mythical importance of the buffalo. The buffalo demon, antagonist of the great goddess as Durgā in the *purāṇas,* is known as an incarnation of Siva, in Maharashtra and Himachal Pradesh.

In the third chapter, one of the most significant chapters of the book, Mrs. Jayakar shows how in the *Atharva Veda* the focus of the earlier *vedas* shifted from sky to earth, how the plants in their sacred presence on earth were praised, as healers having magic powers and "deified make manifest the forms of things." This is the world of the *vrātya,* a fusion of magic and vision. Mrs. Jayakar sees the figure of the *vrātya* as the arch *yogi* who had the power to awaken the earth in the solstice rites where the bard and the prostitute in his retinue performed ritual intercourse to make fertile the earth.

The magical rites necessitated tools to make them effective. These were the *yantras* by which the powers were confined in geometrical closed forms accompanied by spells and incantations. The geometrical shape—the triangle being the simplest—by confining the power, defined it and became its symbol. The rites of magic and witchcraft, on the other hand, if directed against a person required an image or effigy of the person against whom they were directed. *Yantra* and *maṇḍala,* accompanied by *mantra* and *mudrā,* uttered sound forms and significant hand gestures (*mudrā*), can be traced back to the *Atharva Veda,* as also the images made of the animal-faced goddess and the effigies in human shape of the destined victim, the adversary in human shape. It is the *yantra/maṇḍala,* the enclosed sacred space that holds the surcharged energy and power "that is the pivot of the rural arts of India." Mrs. Jayakar sees some of their forms represented on the Harappan amulets and in backward projection sees the figure of the *yogi* on these amulets as prefiguring the *vrātya.* Worn on the body the amulet was a portable shrine, drawing the wearer of the amulet within the field of protection.

It is by "the oral tradition" (fifth chapter) that the vocabulary of the knowledge was disseminated, by Vedic bards, by court minstrels, and by wandering holy men. The Aryan *vrātya* priests were disseminators of the magical knowledge that *yogis* practiced. These were—we must mention—not the *yogis* seeking release. The *yogis* in question sought and had the powers of the magician-sorcerer; they summoned this power by means of their own otherwise dormant energy. They sought and projected this energy with the help of the magic diagrams. With these they evoked the power of the dormant goddess, the *kuṇḍalinī.* Her worship is through her *yantra,* a triangle, a mathematical abstraction. It is in this way that the goddess is invoked and acquires the shape of woman. Although "the goddess has no image," once conjured she may be seen in that likeness. The *tantric* elaborations of the forms of the goddess are explicit. Her supremacy in the *tantras* rest on her felt presence—in the spells of the *Atharva Veda*—in trees, plants, and animals who contribute to her shape or that of her incarnations as village goddesses, or *grāma devatās*. The presence of the goddess reverberates in the pages of *The Earth Mother*—a metaphor of the body of the young woman who offers her body to her singer to play on her so as to bring out her music.

The rural traditions, popularized by bards and conveyed in the vernacular, by the tenth century had become subjacent to the lyricism of songs which by that time celebrated Kāma, the god of love, in his incarnation as Kṛṣṇa, the dark, aboriginal hero and phallic god, and his male role in his love for Rādhā. The "Rādhā-Kṛṣṇa" consciousness is expressed in Jayadeva's *Gīta Govinda* of the twelfth century. Mrs. Jayakar attributes the ascension of the male god in the rural consciousness through the assertion of the male principle deified in the Aryan mind. The flood of emotion released in vernacular poetry, "the *apabhraṁśa* and *deśī*" (sixth chapter) also coincides with the slow integration of Hindu and Muslim culture on the village level.

During the centuries of Muslim invasions and supremacy, traditional Indian cultural life withdrew into the interior of the country, to rural societies where the Ahīr, Gond, Baiga, and Śavara tribes added to the Kṛṣṇa legend their own ecstatic expressions. All the time, however, settled village society had followed the annual rhythm of the sun and the monthly course of the moon in rites that celebrated and cooperated with the movement of the luminaries.

In the seventh chapter, "The Paintings of Settled Village Societies," *yantras* are an essential part of the rituals of agricultural seasons and of the rites of passage, like the initiation and the rites for the dead. Spells and ritual diagrams to ensure the fertility of crops, the potency of the bridegroom, the destruction of witches, the protection from tigers have each their own form: dot, triangle, square, hexagon, circle, spirals, etc. These function as power centers. Ultimately these power centers are seats of the active presence of the goddess whether they are employed by peasant householders, *yogis,* alchemists, or *tantric* adepts.

The first eight chapters are fundamental for understanding the extant types of rural art preserved and practiced today. Foremost among them are the *bhitti chitras* or wall paintings of Mithila. Their vitality, range, and perfectedness is a miracle witnessed. Mrs. Jayakar was personally instrumental in bringing about the prodigious efflorescence of a village tradition that nearly had died out by 1950. When, as a relief measure after the drought of 1968, Mrs. Jayakar provided the women with means to paint and communicated to them her enthusiasm, they began to remember and continue a tradition that had survived in but a few paintings or their mere traces. The *madhubani* paintings are celebrations of fertility that were to transform the bleak, dried-out countryside. They worked their magic through a wealth of pictorial control, and an inexhaustible range of creative power awakened in the women of Mithila. The surety of line in which symbols and mythical figures enliven at ritually given occasions the walls of the houses—and by now also paintings on cloth and paper—is constant irrespective of the unmistakable, individual quality of the work of each of the painters. By now, a second, young generation of women painters enriches the *madhubani* tradition. It has not become mannered nor lost its integrity. The several phases of the reawakened tradition are described by Mrs. Jayakar. At the back of the miraculously reawakened creativity and confidence of the *madhubani* women painters lies the rich historical past of the region which contributed to and did not break the ritual context of life in Mithila.

The ninth chapter, "The *Maṇḍalas* and Magical Drawings," discusses the *maṇḍalas* of *yogic* inner experience and magical tools, such as those by which the dead are freed from their ghost state and become ancestors (*pitṛ*). This type of *yantra* is placed below the anthropomorphic image of the goddess invoked. In current practice the magic *maṇḍalas* of invoked power and its anthropomorphic image of deity coexist as a result of the mobility and commingling of tribal and rural traditions.

The tenth chapter considers the *vrata maṇḍalas* in particular. These are liturgical drawings serving rites described in the *Kauśika Sūtra* several centuries after the *Atharva Veda.* There are over two thousand *vratas,* some common to the whole of India, others "local receptacles of autochthonous rites." No priest participates. Women draw the diagrams on walls and floor. Incantations in a secret, initiatory language accompany the drawings. "The archetypal diagram is the channel through which the energy of living things can be tapped and made operative in rites of transformation." The root of *vrata* rituals lies in the belief that desire when visualized and made concrete through *maṇḍala* and activated through spell and ritual gesture generates an energy that ensures its own fulfillment.

Through the *maṇḍalas* the participants seek protection from the malignant forces of nature. These magical practices pervade Hinduism. They were according to *gṛhya sūtras* and *manu smṛti* obligatory for the Hindu householder.

The *vrata maṇḍalas,* considered as a kind of writing are an extreme type of rural art. The other end of its range is the narrative painting (see "Paintings as *Kathā,* or Story"). Their varieties in the several rural centers of India show the lively—at times banal—work of painters, some of whom are tribal converts to Hinduism, while others work on different levels of magic and/or communication. The exhibition of these paintings—all by men—is accompanied by recitations and songs. Mrs. Jayakar never falters in characterizing each regional type of painting and performance.

When turning in the twelfth chapter to the pictographs of tribal people—the Warlis, the Bhils, the Gonds, the Śavaras—Mrs. Jayakar shows how their magical character and high visual competence work together to promote fertility, avert disease, propitiate the dead, and fulfill the demands of ghosts and spirits. By painting the picture and including the object desired, the result is achieved and the spirit is satisfied. Women of the tribe do not participate in the paintings of the mysteries. The artists, as with the Śavaras, are magician-priests.

In the final four chapters, devoted to sculpture, Mrs. Jayakar admits that it is impossible to ascertain when cult images of *grāma devatās* appeared first in rural shrines, as the tribal population had been exposed for centuries to the culture of settled villages. Of greater importance than this statement is the question of when the earliest movement toward form caused a turning away from the unhewn piece of stone smeared with vermilion and worshiped, to a recognizable likeness of divinity. Plaques cast in metal, showing the face of a deity, would be placed over the aniconic stone.

It is well to remember that the tribal people had no craftsmen of their own and that their needs for tools and ritual objects were met by rural craftsmen who lived within the tribal environment where they absorbed the rhythms, ideas, dreams, and visions of the tribal painters—who painted but were not makers of objects. The same crafts tradition supplied also the need of the villagers. "In the hands of the image-maker the gods of the tribe and village fused." There is hardly a type of rural image whose Hindu genealogy is left untraced and whose rural transformations are left unrecorded.

Of greatest significance, however, in the context of the book are Mrs. Jayakar's deeply felt chapters on the images of the "Mothers," whom she observes assuming various shapes and names as they migrate from the Vindhyas to Afghanistan, undergoing continuous transformations as they absorb the ancient types of the goddess who is virgin, yet mother. The *apsaras* are spirits of water and vegetation, enchanters and magicians, "incandescent with power and mystery, linked with the earth and the secrets of fertility and death." If the *Atharva Veda* equates plants with the goddess, she says of herself in the *Mārkaṇḍeya Purāṇa:* "I shall support the whole world with the life-giving vegetables I shall grow out of my body." The life of vegetation was identified with the energy of the goddess, who exacted animal sacrifice. The goddess is also worshiped as a bundle of flowering plants, while underneath her altar a square diagram marks her seat. Reference has already been made to images of the goddess holding her weapons and attributes, while her body is formed of leaves (as on amulets from the tribal areas of Maharashtra). The animal-headed human bodies of the goddess in sculptures of the school of Mathura in the beginning of the present era trace their ancestry to the animal-headed goddesses of the *Atharva Veda.* The goddess, a composite of human, plant, and animal, features the power to heal and to transform, whatever her shape. Essentially she is the virgin Earth Mother—as long as the male image is not made to join her, as protector first and then as consort.

The goddess herself also is subject to change. The terrible Mothers may change their nature and change from devourers into protectors. But whatever her manifestations in anthropomorphic-zoomorphic shapes, her *yantra* remains the same, the *Śrī Chakra.*

Mrs. Jayakar sees the sacred female form represented in the clay images of the deathly figurines of the food-cultivating communities of Zhob and Kulli; in the mystical sorceress identified as *yogan* (*yoginī*) of the urban, Harappan civilization; and in the abbreviated versions of the female shapes of the chalcolithic culture of the Deccan, in contemporary hamlets throughout India. They are the holders of the secret of the earth; they also hold in one hand a cup of blood to fecundate the earth; this may correspond to Viṣṇu's blood that filled the skull-cup of Śiva Bhairava. The cup is held by the young girl's bronze figurine from Mohenjo-daro, wrongly considered by others as a dancer.

There is not much left untold by Mrs. Jayakar of what she calls the ritual art of rural India. Her language is bold and fiery, her vision is comprehensive, her understanding goes to the roots. She writes from direct experience.

The sixteen chapters of the book form one organic whole, like the petals of the *aṣṭadala,* the eight-petaled lotus *maṇḍala. The Earth Mother* supplements my earlier *Unknown India: Ritual Art in Tribe and Village* and exceeds its scope. It is an indispensable and stimulating guide for artists and scholars who will draw sustenance from *The Earth Mother.*

May 1989
Philadelphia Museum of Art *Stella Kramrisch*

The Earth Mother:

Legends, Goddesses, and Ritual Arts of India

Introduction

This book does not attempt to be a definitive study of the rural arts, nor does it attempt to provide a chronological time sequence for such a study. The subject attempted is vast and the existing research fragmentary. Social anthropology, art history, and the study of oral traditions, of vernacular, literary, and visual forms will have to coalesce to give future research content and meaning. This book seeks only to explore and to open windows, to link myth and ritual to ageless art forms and to place the rural arts in the right perspective. It attempts to reveal that the rural arts of India have, through the centuries, established a unity, an ambience of mood and direction, that transcends and bridges the geographical fragmentation of the land.

These arts are grounded in the consciousness that the earth is structured on the landmass of India. Arising out of a primordial vision that reaches out towards the cardinal directions, observes the sacred contours of the land, delineates the sanctity of enclosed spaces, names the guardians of the cardinal points of direction, and establishes the sacred altars, or *pīthas* of the goddess at the extremities of the country, these arts are infused with insights charged with delight, insights that have established holy places at the confluence of rivers, on the peaks of mountains, on the seashore, and in the midst of dense forests.

"History is to be seen displayed in full detail in the villages of India—provided one has the vision and insight required to read that history,"[1] said D. D. Kosambi. I wish to acknowledge a debt to his work and to that of Ananda Coomaraswamy. The complex contemporary Indian scene is only understood when the important nature of prehistorical survival is grasped. By realizing that Indian history is not linear, one becomes aware of the way the rural tradition develops: like a spiral, it uncoils and coils. Within this movement nothing is totally rejected, nothing discarded, no issues polarized. The alien and the heretical are neither confronted nor destroyed; instead they are transformed. The rural tradition has a skill of genius, in inventing myths and reinterpreting texts, that reduces the alien to familiar symbols and metaphors.

The gap between orthodox dogma and heretical belief is never unbridgeable. Deities and systems maligned and ostracized in one age become benevolent and respectable in another. Durgā Kātyāyanī, the dark, fierce aboriginal goddess of earth and forest grove, is eulogized in the *Devī Upaniṣad,* when the *purāṇic* male gods sing her praises in verses derived from the sacred *Gāyatrī.*[2] In Orissa and Bengal, Varunai and Karunai, the Buddhist deities that disappeared with Buddhism from the shrines of the great tradition, reappear in interior villages as the Thakurāins—the beloved village mothers.

Aboriginal gods are adopted by the great tradition; genealogies are created; homelands altered. Ayanār (a forest god with the sign of the peacock), originally a god of the Śavara tribe, appears in the *purāṇas* as the son of Śiva, as the *yogī,* and as Viṣṇu in his form as Mohinī, the incandescent temptress who awakens and seduces Śiva, seated silent in meditation. Out of the seed of Śiva, the god of the autochthons, conceived on the body of the Aryan godhead, is born Śāstā, Hariharputra, the protective deity of the village people of Tamil Nadu and Kerala, whose shrine at Śabari Malai in Kerala retains its primitive Śavara origins in its name.

The process of assimilation is continuous. The *devatās* of the forest and tribe, largely regarded as malevolent and exorcized in the *Atharva Veda,* later fused with the *purāṇic* gods, and emerged to be invoked and propitiated as the *gṛha devatās,* the household gods. The gods of the great tradition assume vernacular forms as the guardians, the *kṣetrapālas,* at village shrines.

"India is a country of tremendous survivals," and she carries her stone age along with her. The atomic age exists beside the chalcolithic. To trace the survival of the life-patterns of another age, and to witness their transformation and operation within village societies today, is to grasp the true significance of the Indian scene. There is perhaps no other country where these prehistoric elements are so clearly discernible or so important, and nowhere is this as apparent as in the art and ritual of village and tribe. The refusal to reject, and the capacity to transform, archaic myth and ritual into the living present, is surely a characteristic peculiar to the Indian ethos.

Today rural India is in a state of flux. It finds itself challenged at all levels of life, ritual, art, and function. Exploding population, an indiscriminate destruction of the environment, a continuing revolution in communications, and the accelerated penetration of technology and artifacts of urban industrial societies into isolated villages have generated enormous pressures and brought into the rural situation new challenges and tensions. Everywhere we turn, we see the whisper of the new technological culture— bullock carts with rubber tires, transistors in village squares, mass-produced Kṛṣṇa sculptures in painted plaster sold at village fairs.

The myths, symbols, rituals, and *grāma devatās,* the village godlings, described in this book will disappear, to be replaced by new village gods with their attributes. The primal danger to the rural ethos is not the change of godhead; it is the linear time-stream, integral to a technological culture, taking over rural India's cyclic sense of time, where the transitory and the eternal exist simultaneously within a myth-richened perspective, where the past is constantly transformed and recreated in the immediacy of group ritual. A challenge is posed to the perception and approach of the artisan, a challenge not only of tool, technique, and resources of power, but of human values, attitudes, and directions, a challenge to those attributes of the human situation that are integral to the creative process.

The danger to rural India lies in its accepting the values and norms of a technological culture and of a consumer-oriented society and, in doing so, losing communion with nature and its inexhaustible resources of energy. The danger is of losing a sense of the mysterious sacredness of the earth, the "life-giving, tranquil, fragrant, auspicious Mother," whom the Atharvan poet invokes: "To breathe upon us, place us at the centre of the forces that have issued from thy body, unite us with the splendid energy of maidens, with the light that is in males, in heroes, in horses and the beasts of the forests."[3]

The Rural Roots

The rural arts of India are the arts of the settled villages and countryside, of people with lives tuned to the rhythm of nature and its laws of cyclical change, an art with a central concern with the earth and with harvesting. It is the art of fairs and festivals and pilgrimages, of song, dance, and epic performance; an art of a people whose memories of ancient migrations forced by war, epidemic, hunger, and memories of live myths make the archaic *purāṇic* gods and legends contemporary. It is an art involved with household and fertility rituals, the *vratas,* far removed from the Vedic pantheon and observances. It is an art involving the rites that invoke and establish the goddess, an art that quickens the kernel of energy and power within the hut and the village community.

The rural arts of India are the visual expression and technological processes of people living at several cultural, religious, and sociological levels. They are based on archaic technological processes and skills created by the artisan communities to fulfill the functional needs of village societies. They are processes that, until recently, had remained static for over two thousand years.

Rural arts include the visual expressions of nomadic people, the culture of wanderers, people exposed to changing landscapes, who traveled over the valleys and highlands of India, at times forming settled communities, establishing kingdoms, carrying with them the traditions and memories of vast spaces and of an original home on the bank of the river Yamunā. Rural arts include the arts of people whose transient art forms must move with the moving tribe. The energy of these people is tuned to the life cycle of cattle; they create and sing ballads of love and elopement and create gods in their own likeness.

Rural arts are also the arts of people living in forests and mountains, the ancient inheritors of this land, who claim to be the first-born of the earth; people with a remote past but no recorded history. It is also the art of the people who hunted wild beasts, collected wild products from the dark and pathless forests, established kingdoms and ruled large tracts of the heartlands of India, then disappeared into caves and mountains. Rural arts include the arts of these people whose religion gives every instant of their life a sense of mysterious sacredness; people potent with magic, with knowledge of incantation and ritual, with an intense awareness born of man's earliest concern to combat and propitiate the unseen, the terrible; people with power over and intimate kinship with animals, with trees, with stones, and with water; people with a central concern with fertility, with their ears close to the earth who whispers to them her secrets so long as they do not wound her breasts with the plough. Forest and mountain dwellers speak of themselves as *har, hara, ho,* and *horo*—"man." Their minds are quickened with epic myth and legend, with multitudinous gods, born of dream, of magic, borrowed from people living in the fertile cultivated plains. The rural arts are born of a people with a passionate involvement in the uninhibited loveplay of man and woman, free of the moral confines of settled societies, with wild and tender love songs and dances evoked by the coming together of boy and girl, songs that are never written down, but constantly created in the act of love and courtship.

My Singer
From that earthen drum
What sweet music you bring
From the earthen drum of my body
Who can bring such music
As you, my Singer?
Take, take me in your arms,
Sling me about your neck,
Play on me, on my body till I give the drum's
Sweet note.[1]

An inquiry into the structure of worship in interior rural societies reveals a fragile and at times nonexistent line that divides the quick and the dead, the today and the yesterday, the historical, the mythological, the dim past of prehistory. A recent government of India census publication documenting village festivals, gods, and rituals of Andhra Pradesh illustrates the living reality in the making of myth, legend, and village deities in rural India. In the detailed maps of districts and villages, one sees that the worship of *siddhas,* the ancient magician-alchemists, the deified *yogīs* with their supporting myths and enshrined images, coexists with the bloodthirsty rites to the *grāma devatās,* the village mothers. In the village of Mudumala in Cuddapah district, Śiva Mahādeva, the great god of the Hindus, is born in the home of a Muslim householder as Siddha, the alchemist saint.[2] Bāsavannā, the historical founder of the *vīra śaiva* cult, fuses with the ancient *yakṣa* cult of Nandikeśvara and is enshrined and worshiped in the form of a stone bull.

Gods take form out of the fusion of the autochthon deities with the *brahmanic* divinities. Skanda or Subramaniam, the son of Śiva and the wild untamed mothers, is manifest as Subraya Devaru or Nāga Devaru, the serpent-god. His image is carved in stone as a seven-headed cobra with the hood raised to strike or as two rampant cobras intertwined. Nṛsiṁha, the lion incarnation of Viṣṇu, appears with a fierce lion face.

In the Jillellamudi village of the Guntur district of Andhra Pradesh, the main object of worship is a living *grāma devatā,* a village goddess, a woman named Jillellamudi Ammā. She is married, has children, yet she is worshiped, with yellow turmeric, vermilion powder, ***kum kum,*** and wild flowers. Myths of her miraculous powers are in the making. Legends have gathered around her mysterious arrival in the village, and an annual festival celebrates the day. Besides the living, deified *Ammā,* no other shrines or gods exist in the village. A devotee writes, "Twenty-five years ago, on a bright day, when the sun was shining above the row of dark clouds in the sky, a small bullock cart brought a young couple into this village. This seeming insignificant incident was probably the beginning of a new beginning in human history, a new leaf in the book of eternity, a new chapter with a thousand wonders. The young housewife was none other than the Universal Mother."[3] The sacred lady of compassion sits in smiling equipoise to receive her devotees, be they rich or poor, Harijan or Brahmin. The worship of the Mother, the *Ammā,* is free of all divisions of caste, creed, race, or economic status.

Behind the living *grāma devatā* of Jillellamudi stretches a hinterland, peopled with countless images of the sacred female. We find grim *grāma mātṛkās,* the village mothers, manifest in stone, tree, animal, or fierce human form—deified female saints enshrined in stone. In some areas the goddesses of *tantric* Buddhism merge with the sacred lady of the Vindhya Mountain and with the local *grāma devatās,* to create the many Durgās of Andhra. Images of the nurturing Universal Mother carved in painted wood exist in juxtaposition with the bloodthirsty rites to Pellammā, the terrible Mother. The vocabulary and the worship of the living, the dead, and the enshrined is often identical.

There are, in the archaic Gond legend of Lingo Pen, intimations of an age when Mahādeva or Śiva, the wild and wondrous god of the autochthons, had no human form but was a rounded stone, a *lingam,* washed by the waters of the Narmada. Even to this day there are areas of the Narmada river basin where every stone in the waters is said to be a Śiva *lingam.*

> There the God Mahādev was ruling from the upper sea to the lower sea. What was Mahādev doing? He was swimming like a rolling stone, he had no hands, no feet.
>
> He remained like the trunk [of a tree]. Then Mahādev performed austerities for twelve months.
>
> And Bhagwan [god] came and stood close to Mahādev and called to him.
>
> "Thy devotion is finished, emerge out of the water," he said.
>
> "How shall I emerge? I have no hands, no feet, no eyes." Then Mahādev received Man's form. Thus Man's form complete was made in the luminous world.[4]

The antiquity of the worship of the *lingam,* the phallus, and the *yoni,* the female sex organ, and their active rituals are evident from the presence of a large number of phallic stones and circular ring stones found at Harappan culture sites. Through the centuries primitive man has sought the phallic symbol of divinity in river-smoothed pebbles alive with color in water—in the *bāṇa lingams*—in fragments of ancient stone carvings, and in rocks with suggestive forms rising immovable from the earth.

A curious legend from the village Achant, in the Guntur district of Andhra Pradesh, surrounds the worship of a stone *lingam* in the form of a woman's breast. The sage Achyuta was guilty of breaking a vow of celibacy and was born on the earth as Oduyanambi, a devotee of Lord Śiva. His wife, Gaṅgā, was born as a dancing girl and named Paramañchī. Oduyanambi took a vow that he would worship a Śiva *lingam* every three hours. But as ordained he met and fell in love with Paramañchī. After a night of love Oduyanambi awoke and saw that the hour of worship was upon him, and he was unprepared. His heart filled with love and despair, his eyes fell on the naked left breast of his love, and he saw in it the form of the Śiva *lingam*. Taking the sandalwood paste used by the lovers in their love rites, Oduyanambi smeared the breast of his beloved with sandalwood paste and offered betel leaves to the living *lingam*. The breast, worshiped as the Lord, was transformed into stone and enshrined as the *chanti lingam,* the *lingam* of the breast. The Śiva *lingam* on Achant has no pedestal but emanates from the ground, it is said, as the remaining portion of the body of the dancing girl, while the *yoni,* on which the *lingam* rests, lies buried within the ground. The Śiva *lingam* of Achant has three natural holes to suggest the three eyes of Lord Śiva.[5]

Modern Hinduism carries much of its prehistory with it. The sacredness of sites survives the changing of gods. A primordial sense of the sanctity of places, of the *sthala,* and an ancient knowing of the living, pervading presence of the divinity of the Earth Mother, establishes her worship at crossroads and in aniconic stones. It is this element that was invoked when at the instant of enlightenment the Buddha touched the earth with his hand and called the primordial Earth Mother to witness; for the site of the Buddha's enlightenment, the earth and the *bodhi* tree, were already holy and ancient. The earth under the *bodhi* tree was the abode of a *nāga,* a cobra, the sacred protector of the site, who appeared and placed his hood over the Buddha's head to shelter the Holy One; an archetypal image that recalls the Indus Valley seal in which a cross-legged *yogī* is delineated, seated silent in ecstatic meditation, guarded and flanked by two serpents with upraised hoods.[6] The moment of revelation, that still second of the birth of the unmanifest, is the mystery that, with the holy site, has to be guarded and protected.

D. D. Kosambi, in *Myth and Reality,* has unraveled, with rare insight, empirical evidence to show that the sites in Maharashtra of the local *grāma devatās,* the village mothers, and their cults are identical to the sites on the Western Ghats where the Buddhist monks built their *stūpas.* At the Junnar caves, the goddess Manmodi (jaw-breaker) was present before the Buddhist caves were carved, and returns to be worshiped without change of name a thousand years later.[7] In Maharashtra, sites of the numinous lady lie on the crossroads of neolithic tracks that abound in microliths and macroliths. The memory of the originally displaced bloodthirsty deities is still extant.

The primordial sense of the sacredness of sites, a sacredness that survives the changing gods, is evident also in tribal people, the main servitors of important holy Hindu shrines. At Jagannath Puri in Orissa, the Śavaras tribe have free entry to the *garbha gṛha,* the sanctum sanctorum, where the Śavara deity Nilbandha, the blue god, is worshiped as Jagannātha, the lord of the world; and at the temple of Śri Śailam, in Andhra Pradesh, the tribal Chenchus are the main attendants of the Śiva shrine, and pull the chariot of the great god. That the Śiva of Śri Śailam has autochthonous origins is established by his name, Chenchu Malliah, the lord of the

Chenchus tribe. At the ancient Guruvāyur temple in Kerala, there is a very small Śakti shrine beyond the temple walls. The shrine consists of four walls around an *aśoka* tree, at the base of which the goddess, as an aniconic stone, is installed. The shrine is open to the sky and is believed to be of great antiquity. Nayar women circumambulate the tree and shrine before they enter the precincts of the Guruvayur Kṛṣṇa temple.

One of the factors that adds complexity to the rural situation is that in its memories are a fusion of the sophisticated and the naive, the sublime and the shamanistic, classical equilibrium and savage distortion, the cosmic appreciation and the demoniac ritual.

These seemingly inexplicable contradictions arise out of the manner in which sources of intellectual and cultural life, centered in cities and anchored within the framework of the great tradition, have faced the savage onslaughts of invasion and the threatened annihilation of the postulates, the roots of mind and heart. The Indian answer, a solution for survival recurrent in the history of the country, has been the great retreats, a movement of withdrawal away from the cities and the main migration routes to the forest, mountain, and village—a migration from the life and sophistication that permeates the city, to the countryside, to fertilize, absorb, and be absorbed. The vast hinterland makes pursuit and annihilation impossible. This has led to the secret growth of isolated centers of cultural life that retain elements of great antiquity. This has made possible powerful mutations and emergences from the rural background of passionate streams of vernacular language and art that have illuminated and transformed the countryside and that, in turn, have given life and sustenance to the great tradition.

The earliest known of these retreats was at the time of the great Aryan invasions from the northwest, around 1750 BC, when the cities of the Harappan culture were destroyed, and the patriarchal Aryans had their first confrontation with the matriarchal Harappans. A hymn from the *Ṛg Veda,* first of the Vedic books, addresses God: "Through fear of thee, the dark-colored inhabitants fled, not waiting for battle, abandoning their possessions" and "Strike down, O Maghavan (Indra), the host of sorceresses in the ruined city of Vailasthanaka." In a later text: "The people to whom these ruined sites belong, these many settlements widely distributed, they, O Agni (fire), having been expelled by thee, have migrated to another land."[8] In the frantic escape from the waves of storming invaders, in the following centuries of persistent pressure, much that was identifiable in the Harappan culture disappeared. The vast storehouses of art and technology, magic and ritual, merged into the surrounding agricultural societies or reappeared transformed in the icons and artifacts of the dwellers along the river valleys, on the Deccan plateau, or in the faces of the *grāma devatās* of the autochthons of the south. In the Deccan, later, chalcolithic sites show a continuity in the technology and art of icon and image. Headless, earthbound, massive abstractions of the numinous female have been found at Bhilwalli and Inamgaon in Madhya Pradesh and Maharashtra. The sophisticated culture of the Harappan cities that had molded the sacral female form with seeing eyes, with faces and features pinched into shape, with elaborate headdress and girdle, was replaced by faceless, sightless abstractions, images of the Great Mother emerging from the earth, with arms outstretched in the primal gesture of epiphany and affirmation.[9] The one was the product of a protected culture that had the leisure and security to delineate and ornament, the other the product of an unsettled people who were concerned only with the protective and the essential.

Similar migrations took place in Orissa, Bengal, and Bihar in the ninth and tenth centuries, when, with the persecution of the Buddhists, entire Buddhist communities left the deltaic region and sought refuge in the remote countryside. The undercurrents of the rural arts in Orissa bear the massive impact of this retreat and are rich in *tantric* Buddhist imagery. Migrations occurred again at the time of the Muslim invasions, between the eleventh and thirteenth centuries, when vast numbers of philosophers, writers, painters, and musicians migrated to Mithila, Sarai Khela, and to the isolated valleys of the Himalayan ranges. In Magadha, with the sacking of the Vikramaśilā monastery, Buddhist *siddhas, gurus* of breath control and alchemy, sought refuge in the villages of Andhra Pradesh. It is from them that the south Indian tradition of the *sittars,* magician alchemists and poets, has its origins.[10]

Cataclysmic changes were inevitable when the nomadic cattle-rearing Aryans met and fused with the autochthonous agricultural communities. Myth and epic legend reveal subtleties and nuances with which the ancient races absorbed and negated the power of the invader. By the time of the Mauryas, a landscape emerged along the northern river valleys of cities supported by a vast countryside divided into innumerable self-sufficient villages. The Janapadas, ancient tribal groups, were slowly and deliberately broken up, and the tribal people settled on the land in isolated agricultural village societies. The breakup and the assimilation of these Janapadas led to a surface disappearance of ancient mother rights among vast masses of the population, but an archaic peoples' culture based on the primacy of the female principle survived in secret women's rites and fertility rituals. The

Aryan invaders, who sought to destroy this ancient culture, were, instead, assimilated.

Early indications are available of the desire of the Aryan tribes to absorb the local inhabitants through conversion, through marriage, and through acceptance of artisan skills. The Aryan rulers prescribed the *vrata stoma* ceremony to purify the ritual-bound nonsacrificer and introduce him into the Aryan fold. This ceremony was named after the ancient *vrātyas,* magicians and masters of breath control, familiar from the *Atharva Veda,* who were also known to have practiced sexual rites linked to agricultural magic and fertility. The *vrātyas* were to provide the name to the *vratas*—rituals, homeopathic magic, and alchemy that have permeated the countryside north of the Vindhyas—providing the ritual-bound base that conditions the life of the Hindu householder. For the woman, as the main participant and actor of the ritual, the *vratas* were the umbilical cord which connected her to the furthermost limits of human memories, when woman as priestess and seer guarded the mysteries, the ways of the numinous female. It was around these *vratas,* thousands of variations of which existed in the cities, settled villages, and forests, that the rural arts found significant expression. Free of the *brahmanic* canons which demanded discipline and conformity in art and ritual, the *vrata* tradition freed the participant from the inflexible hold of the great tradition. Unlike the *brahmanic* worship of *mantra* and sacrifice, which was available only to the *Brahmin,* the *vrata pūjā* and observances were open to the woman, to the non-*Brahmin,* to the Śūdra and the tribesman. Multi-dimensional in approach, the *vratas* brought into operation song, dance, the visual arts of picture and image-making, magical formulae of incantation and gesture. Many urgencies mingled in the *vrata* rites, providing the channels through which contact with nature and life was maintained and renewed through the worship of the earth, sun, and water and the invoking of the energy of growing things, of trees, plants, and animals. The demands of sex and fertility, wealth and prosperity, were translated in minutely detailed rituals which gave to the vast country a common ritual and a vision. It provided a living storehouse of the archaic past continually transformed into the contemporary moment, through group action. The *vrata* rites were, through the centuries, to maintain their integrity and existence, independent and parallel to the orthodox *Brahmin*-dominated culture.

Two movements emerged out of the fusion of the Aryans and the autochthons: the Vedic, or *mārgī,* directed to ritual, incantations, and sacrifice, intended to propitiate the gods; and the non-Vedic or *deśī,* propelled by magic and alchemy, concerned with *vrata* and *tantric* ritual, acts to control and change the course of things. Both these streams find expression in the rural tradition in their vernacular form.

The Pañchāyatana worship of the five main deities—Sūrya, Viṣṇu, Śiva, Gaṇeśa, and Gaurī—integral to orthodox ritual Hindu worship also represents a fusion of many streams: the earth-worshipers and the sun-worshipers, the worshipers of the male gods and the worshipers of the indigenous female divinities. The symbols of the gods give some indication of the sources of their origin. Śiva is worshiped in the form of a *bāṇa lingam,* a river pebble from the waters of the Narmada, the banks of which are the homeland of tribal peoples. Gaṇeśa, originally an aboriginal deity to be propitiated as the cause of obstacles, later admitted into the orthodoxy as the remover of obstacles, is worshiped in the form of a smooth, glowing, red pebble, also found in the waters of the river Narmada. The symbol for the goddess Gaurī is a lump of crude iron ore mined from the mountains situated in the heart of the tribal country, the homeland of the iron-smelting *asuras*. Viṣṇu is symbolized by a *śāligrāma,* a fossil with double spiral-like convolutions, the *chakra,* a form of fossil found only in the waters of the Gaṇḍaki River in Nepal. Sūrya is represented by a rock crystal found in the mines of Rajasthan and Gujarat, lands where the Huns and Gujars had wandered, carrying with them from the plains of Central Asia their worship of the sun.

The interaction with the earth, fertility, and food, and the primitive wonder at the transformation of seed into living life-giving plant triggered in ancient man the search for the explosive energy resources that generate life and change. The earliest primordial images of the Earth Mother glorified a female fecundating principle that held within itself the secret of birth and death. The dark, earthbound goddess was a virgin, yet a mother, for "no father seemed necessary to the society in which she originated."[11] It was only after the fusion of races and the crystallization of settled agricultural communities, with the resultant destruction of ancient mother rights, that the participation of the male god in rituals enacted around the cycle of fertility was recognized. Inevitably this fundamental change in the nature of the numinous one transformed ritual and priesthood. Based on the belief that fertility could be ensured by enacting the functions of reproduction, rituals and magical rites were evolved to accommodate the male god. In the ancient *mahāvrata,* the solstice rites to ensure fertility, the woman engages in ritual intercourse with the bard. Today, among the Oraon tribe, before the sowing of seed, when the earth is virgin and the *śāla* tree is in bloom, a symbolic marriage of the earth goddess to Sūraj Deotā, the sun god, is performed. The village priest, the *baiga,* and his wife enact the sacred rites. Before the wedding of the gods is solemnized Oraons can neither gather vegetables, fruits, or flowers of the new season, nor can they perform weddings. When the Bhils, primitive people of western India, paint their sacred *pithoras,* they include in an obscure corner a copulating man and woman. When asked to explain, they say, "without this where would the world be?"[12]

With the emergence of the male gods in the rural pantheon, new god relationships were evolved. The potent male divinity emerged as the *kṣetrapāla*—protector and fecundator of the body of the goddess, the earth, and the field. The search for transformation and transmutation continued, with the archetypal image of *mithuna,* the two made one, replacing the image of the one. The act of union became the focal point of experimentation. Agricultural magic fused with alchemy and *tantra.*

The secrets of alchemy, in which gross metal is transmuted to gold, was felt to be of the same nature as the psychophysical process involved in the mutation of the human mind and body which makes them free of the ravages of time and the processes of decay. The earliest treatise on alchemy was the *Rasaratnākara* by Nāgārjuna, the Buddhist sage, written in the second or third century AD.[13] This text propounds the ultimate secret of alchemy—the fixation of mercury. *Pārada,* mercury, was described in the *Rasārṇava,* a Śaivite text of the twelfth century, as the seed of Hara; mica was the ovum of Gaurī. The union of the two, mercury and mica, Śiva and Śakti, man and woman, through *yoga,* through ritual intercourse or through the alchemy of chemical mutation created the *rasa siddhas,* the masters of alchemy and *tantra,* gurus who had minds and bodies that were eternally young. All *mantras* were at the service of the *rasa siddhas.* Liberation, wealth, prosperity, eternal youth were obtainable through the mastery of *yoga,* ritual, and mercury. The laboratory and the mythical, magical ritual became integral to the chemistry of physical and psychological mutation.

Tantra became the repository of ancient chemical knowledge. In later centuries, the birth and manifestation of eternal youth, through the fixation of mercury, came to be symbolized in the myth of Kumāra, the magical boy and the secret doctrine of *kumāra vidyā.* Kumāra, born of the seed of Śiva, held in the womb of Agni and cast into the waters (the womb of the six mothers) was held to be identical with the timeless state of mind and body, born of the union of mercury and mica.[14] The *Rasa-ratna-sammuchchaya,* written in the sixteenth century, gives details of the rites of *tantric* initiation in which the pupil was initiated into rites of mercurial lore. As mercury supplanted archaic plant alchemy and magic, so, in time, the word *rasa,* originally synonymous with mercury, gained new dimensions of meaning till it included, and became identical with, the nature of fluid or the elixir of life. A vast literature and secret ritual surrounded the *tantric* doctrine of *rasa* and the release of the waters within the sea of ecstasy. The word *rasa* gained many nuances of meaning. In aesthetics it was the tincture, the essence, and the ecstasy. Overflowing, moving, filling, it became synonymous with the activity of heightened sensory perception, integral to art. *Rasa* was the very nature of color and energy. Without it the object of art, however perfect, remained inert. The quickening, the pulsation, was the fluid movement of *rasa.* The holders of the essence were the passion-intoxicated *rasadharis,* the enlightened ones of *tantra,* the Rādhā-Kṛṣṇa-maddened devotees of Mathura, the poet, painter, and madman.

One of the sources in *tantra* for the comprehension of the nature and chemistry of color was alchemy. *Tantra* took the active transforming principles of color chemistry and added a dimension, that of direct perception of the "interiority" of human consciousness. The unity of color, form, sound, and energy was perceived, and through this germinal source was projected the cosmic energy-filled image of the goddess as color, sound, and geometric form. An intense involvement with color is visible in much of the alchemic writing. The colors emanating from different kinds of metals when burned are carefully observed. The burning of copper produces a blue-green flame; tin, a pigeon-colored flame; lead, a pale, muted flame; iron, the flame of a peacock's throat.

Eight *rasas* were distinguished and each was given an individual color. Mica was white, red, yellow, and black. When mica acquired the color and luster of the rising sun, it was regarded as fixed. *Vaikrānta* was white, red, yellow, and the blue of the down of a pigeon. *Sasyaka,* blue vitriol, had the color of the throat of the peacock. The colors of gems were also carefully observed: the diamond was white, like a conch, a water lily, or a crystal.[15]

The observations of the laboratory of alchemy and *tantra* became the symbols and attributes of the goddess. The goddess as energy incarnate, lustrous as the scarlet hibiscus, was made manifest in a flame issuing from the mouth of the gods. In *tantric* texts she was the source of all color as well as the form of no color, of that total darkness of the moonless night, *mahārātri.* Moonlight and sunbeam was she; she was the color of the two twilights. In her ascending manifestation she was Mahā Kālī, the inexorable power of time, black as *kājal* (collyrium). In her expanding tendency she was red. As Ṣoḍaśī, the sixteen-year-old goddess, she was the light of the infant sun; as Bhairavi, the light of a thousand rising suns; and as Chhinnamastā, the light of a million suns. As Tārā, she was dark blue, as Mātangī, black, as Dhūmāvatī, dark as the color of smoke, as Bagalāmukhī, yellow (see Appendix).

The body of the goddess was a geometric abstraction as well as color. The appearance of the circle, the double-spiral, the cross, the square, the triangle, the *svastika,* and the mystical diagram, constructed of an amalgam of mathematical figures, at the sites of the Indus Valley and in the cave art of India, established an ancient worship of the female divinity in the form of hieroglyphs and simple geometric forms. Associations of the sacred feminine principle with pictorial abstraction are so deeply embedded in the Indian unconscious that the anthropomorphic form of the goddess never replaces the diagram, but continues to coexist with it through the centuries. *Tantric* texts which codify archaic and accepted magical formulae describe the cosmic form of the ancient virgin mother. "The goddess of renowned form assumes in time of protection the form of a straight line | . In time of dissolution, she takes the form of a circle ● . Similarly for creation, she takes the brilliant appearance of a triangle ▽ ."[16] A secret language of hieroglyph and *maṇḍala* existed comprehensible only to the initiated. *Tantric* texts trace the origin of their pictorial presentation of the numinous form through *yantra* and *maṇḍala* to the *Atharva Veda.* The *Atharva Veda* was also the origin of the phallic doctrine of Kāma and Bhaga, the goddess in her sexual *yoni* form, and of the picture-writing that was integral to both worship and witchcraft practices. The symbol of Śakti and Kāma-Kalā, the goddess as erotic love, is described in a *tantric* text: "Two circles are the two breast nipples, one circle is the face, below them are three cave-like triangles; one who knows this as the enchanting form of Kāma-Kalā not only attains the enchanting form of the goddess, which is desired by all, but also becomes Kāma himself."[17]

The goddess was the seed of the universe in the form of a triangle ▽. The sign of Śiva was •|•, a ploughshare between two eggs. This was also the sign of Kāma as the god of phallic love. The sign is also described "as a rod between two dots, shining as a precious stone."[18]

The *bindu* or dot was male or female; it was the creative principle and the source of the world. The white dot was male, the red female. (The red dot is denoted by a black dot in this text.) The *bindus,* white and red, were written one above the other for facility of entrance of the white into the red ○/•. This was called *visarga* or emission.[19]

Along with the secret and the esoteric, a people's vocabulary of simple abstractions in the form of *yantras* and *maṇḍalas* had ancient origins. In a recent discovery at an upper paleolithic shrine in the Siddhi district of Madhya Pradesh, a group of archaeologists came upon a circular platform of sandstone. At the center of this platform was a fragment of a natural, ferruginous stone with triangular laminations, the color of which ranged from a light yellowish-red to a dark reddish-brown. Additional fragments of the stone were found lying around, and when the fragments were put together, the stone took a triangular form. It appears that the original stone had been placed at the center of the circular platform. The dating of these paleolithic finds is expected to be 10,000 to 8,000 BC. This find would certainly represent the earliest shrine to the mother goddess and is of utmost significance in determining the beginning of the worship of the goddess and the linking of her to geometric abstraction. The manifestations of the living presence of the goddess as austere abstraction continued at the most sacred Śakti *pīṭhas* throughout the country. At Kāmarūpa, in Assam, the goddess is worshiped in the form of a great *yoni*. At Bahuchara, the seat of the goddess of Gujarat, she is worshiped in the form of the *bālā tripurā yantra,* a triangle within which were enshrined the three circles of the goddess; at the shrine of Ambā, the virgin mother, she is worshiped in the form of *viso yantra,* a triangle enclosing the secret root letter of the goddess.

The most sacred of the diagrams was the *Śrī Yantra* (or *Śrī Chakra)*, the symbol of Śiva-Śakti in eternal union. It was conceived in the form of nine triangles, four presided over by Śiva pointing upwards, five presided over by the goddess Śakti pointing to the earth. The triangles overlapped one another forming a labyrinth of geometric pattern. At the heart of the triangles were the mysteries, the three circular *bindus,* the three dots which were the symbol of the goddess as Kāma-Kalā. Surrounding the nine triangles were two circles of lotus petals, one formed of eight and the other of sixteen petals. Enclosing the sacred diagram were the walls of the *maṇḍala,* with four gates facing the four cardinal directions.

The use of the geometric figure in witchcraft practices is perhaps as old as its use in worship. The *Atharva Veda* is filled with spells which suggest the practice of picture-writing in rites of sorcery to release or bind men or women. Kāma, the god of phallic love, is the presiding deity both in *tantric* rites of sorcery and in the witchcraft practices of the *Atharva Veda.*

In a *tantric* text "the picture of a woman to be captivated consisting of her face, throat and breast, navel and generative organs together with her peculiar ornaments and dress shall be drawn with yellow *rocana* in a secluded place. The picture of an elephant hook combined with the symbol of sacred knowledge and the name of the beloved is attached. The symbols of •|• Kāma are to be written on all the joints of the pictorial form."[20] Picture-writing, accompanied by spell-making, in the poetry of the local vernaculars, saturates the rural tradition. *Maṇḍalas* and *yantras* of protection are drawn, gateways opened, and guardians established against the entry of the malevolent. In a spell from Orissa, the ancient goddess Kāmākhyā, presiding deity of Kāmarūpa and guru of witchcraft, is invoked and the four gateways barred to keep out evil. The language is an Oriya dialect, the imagery is rich with Buddhist *tantric* symbols.

> Bajra Kilani, Bajra Devar
> Thunder bolt bar, thunder bolt door
> Four sides, four doors
> On the right is Dahan Chaṇḍī, on the left is Kshetrapal
> In the front is Narsimha behind are the eight Vaitals.
> *Mahā Mudrā* the great seal, the thunder door has fallen on my body
> If a myriad come do not allow them to enter
> By whose order?
> By the myriad orders of the virgin Kamakhyā.[21]

It had long been felt that *tantric* worship, with its extended use of the sensory instruments of heightened perception to seek extrasensory experience, its involvement with symbol and diagram, and its use of mercury and mica to evolve a body that was free from the processes of degeneration, originated at esoteric levels of *yoga,* breath control, and meditation. It was also felt that there was a later degeneration with mass application of *tantric* ritual from the rarified fields of *yoga* and mutation to witchcraft, astrology, and the physical rites of the *panchamakāras,* of meat and fish eating, wine drinking, ritual gestures, and intercourse. Rites were centered around the physical worship of woman, and the organs of sex in the woman's body which became the *ksetra,* the enclosed field of power, itself the instrument of magic and transformation. On investigation one finds, however, that the earliest texts dealing with *tantra* are associated with a people's ritual. In Orissa, *tantra* is known as *śavarī vidyā,* the wisdom of the Savara tribe; the early Buddhist *tantric* poetry of the northeastern river valleys, the *Charyā Padas,* written between the seventh and ninth centuries, is a poetry of the people. The main characters are the tribal gods Śavara and the Śavari. The imagery is of the village, the concern with *tantric yoga.* The Śavara cultivates the field; his female companion Nairomani uproots the undesirable shoots that choke the field.[22] In the *daṇḍa yātrās,* the mystery plays of rural Orissa, the leaf-clad Śavara and Śavari are *tantric* symbols of the male and female principles of Śakti and Śākta.[23] We shall see later that one of the earliest *tantras,* the *Kubjikā Tantra,* originated in the homes of potters. In the *vīra maheśvara tantra,* connected with the *liṅgāyata* sect, the ritual is associated with washermen.[24] The mysterious power inherent in numerals that enable them to express divine secrets, an area in which *tantric* doctrine was also deeply concerned, is revealed by potter priests of the *grāma devatās* of south India when drawing *muggus,* in the rites of exorcism and worship of malevolent female powers. These *muggus* are square diagrams in which the magician priest inscribed magical numbers as part of the ritual.

There were numerous *vratas,* which, in their use of magical *maṇḍalas, mantras* (incantations), and *mudrās* (ritual gestures) and in their active participation in the worship of generative principles, indicated the links of *tantra* with a people's ritual. In the *nikumbha pūjā* the participants besmear their bodies with mud and behave like the *piśāchas,* using lascivious words and suggestive gestures. In an autumnal festival, the *śabarotsava* (which survived till recently in Bengal) held in honor of the goddess Durgā, men and women wore leaves and flowers, danced wildly, sang obscene songs, and repeated the names of the organs of generation considered pleasing to the goddess.[25] Later, this was modified to suggest that the uttering of these words was only permitted to the initiates of the cult of Śakti.

The creation of form, the magical act that transformed inert clay into image, was the function of the woman and the craftsman. The woman operated in a magico-religious domain of *maṇḍala* and *vrata* ritual. She painted walls with diagrams, plastered walls with mica and with the auspicious marks of her palm; she molded image and icon. As the wife of the potter she painted the oculi and other archaic symbols onto the pot, and in areas where pottery is made even today without the use of the wheel, it is the woman who in Maharashtra molds the clay, or in Assam uses her hands and body as the wheel, circumambulating the clay, to give it shape.[26] The woman, however, played no part in the artisan traditions of the country. No women were members of the ancient craft guilds; there were no women goldsmiths, no carpenters, no carvers of intaglios. The producer and consumer relationship as it operated within the economic framework of the country was male-oriented.

The craftsman was the link between the monumental forms of the great tradition, the rural gods, and the tribal deities of the forests and the mountains. However diverse the forms and distorted the images, the roots of the creative process lay in this artisan tradition. It was from this tradition that the great temples were built and the sculpture of the *purāṇic* gods found expression; it was in the same tradition that the artifacts for the tribal peoples of this country, the grinding stone mills, the hero stones, and the memorial tablets to the dead were produced. It was the blacksmith, a lower-caste craftsman, who cast in the lost-wax process metal images of horses and riders and the icons of the goddess. A curious relationship developed between the tribal people and the artisans who served them. In Rajasthan, the craftsmen who provided the icons and objects to the Bhil tribe were known as the *kāmins,* or servants of the Bhils. These included carpenters, blacksmiths, stone masons, bards, basket-workers, and *jogis* or mendicants.

The early beginnings of this era saw the invention of a large number of tools (*yantras*). An interest in alchemy and *tantra* motivated many discoveries in metallurgy. *Yantras* (crucibles) were evolved for use in alchemy. There are descriptions of the different shapes of *yantras,* the most important of which, used in the fixation of mercury, was called *garbha yantra,* the womb instrument. Some *yantras* were shaped like a *brinjal*, some like a pot, some like a woman's generative organs.[27] Crucibles were made of black, white, red, and yellow earth, with earth from an anthill, or earth mixed with burnt husks of paddy or fibers of hemp charcoal and horse dung pounded in an iron mortar and combined with the rust of iron.

The flowering of the great *brahmanic* tradition sparked an awakening in the fields of poetry, music, the visual arts, and philosophy, enriching man's life and sensibilities. Man's concern with meditation and self-knowing had revealed vast dimensions of consciousness and had brought to art a comprehension of space and stillness, movement and passivity. This was to create within the great tradition splendid architecture, tremendous sculpture, great painting. As in all monumental art, it was vision, the direct seeing, listening, feeling, that projected the supreme image; later this was followed by complex theories of art, evolved to shape and make permanent the truths revealed to the artisan sage. Within this tradition, the artisan community with its *śrenīs* (guilds) took shape. Schools of hereditary craftsmen flourished under the patronage of the royal courts. Learning was through formulae in Sanskrit verse, diagrams, and sketches. The tradition was the alphabet, the training in the syntax of ornament and in the discipline of tool and material. Tradition was the great source to which the craftsman came for sustenance and contact with the sensibilities and aspirations of the community. Surcharged with ideological concept, rich in symbol and myth, elegant and sophisticated, the classical stream was responsible for the creation not only of great sculpture and architecture, but of objects of daily use that, in their concern for beauty of form and in their understanding of functional problems of needs, materials, and technology, have rarely been equaled. Artisan guilds emerged as patrons of the arts. There are records of silk weavers from Lāta (Gujarat) building a splendid temple to the sun at Manḍasaur and of ivory carvers from Bhilsa donating part of the railings and gateways of the great *stūpa* at Sanchi.

The son of the craftsman grew up in the atmosphere of the workshop. Exposed to the living tradition naturally, unconsciously, he grew familiar with the forms, the symbols, and the techniques of culture. Knowledge was communicated easily from father to son, from master to disciple. The craftsman was both designer and craftsman. The division between the fine arts and handicrafts had no validity. Every facet of life and creative expression was integrated and rooted in function.

The technological and economic life of village societies operated through the vernacular form of the artisan guilds. Habits, attitudes, the color of the skin, ethnic backgrounds, and technological proficiency determined caste and function. When the system was flexible, it continually absorbed new ethnic groups, people who fled after defeat in war, seeking shelter and anonymity in the countryside. It was with the crystallization of the caste structure and the ending of flexibility that the dynamic, perceptive approach to invention of form and tool ended.

A study of the structure of any of the northern village societies illuminates the extraordinary mixture of caste structure and the changing pattern of craft tradition. Around the agricultural life of the communities are the ancillary occupations, fulfilling the functional needs of the people: the potter, the tailor, the printer, the barber, the blacksmith, the goldsmith, the washerman. It is these same people who, in other contexts, became the image-makers, the carvers of icons and the magician-priests at the shrines of the goddess. At the festival of the *grāma devatās* of south India, the potter molds the image in clay, the carpenter carves the form of the goddess in wood, the washerman spreads the clothes before the shrine. In Gujarat, at the procession of the goddess Vardāyanī, or Vaduchimā, the palanquin which enthrones the mother, and in which she is carried, is without wheels. *Harijans* bring wood for the chariot, carpenters prepare the frame, barbers the canopy, gardeners bring the flowers, and the potters mold the clay lamps that light the procession. Muslims provide the cotton, the carders provide the cotton seeds, and the tailors provide the wicks for the oil lamps. The *Brahmins* cook the *khichri* which is distributed as holy food, and the *Rajputs* stand guard while the *Patidars* provide the garments of the goddess. Vardāyanī is mentioned in the *Skanda Purāṇa* as the goddess Vata Yakṣinī.[28]

The rural craft expression, the *deśī*, by its very nature demanded a total anonymity of name. It reflected the familiar unchanging forms of rural life, its simple needs, its links with archaic magic and ritual. New elements introduced into the rural environment were absorbed into the visual vocabulary and translated into the rural idiom. There has always been a plasticity latent in the craft situation as it operates in rural societies, a plasticity not only of soft materials, clay, wood, and the use of wax in the lost-wax process of casting metal objects, but also a plasticity of form free from the *brahmanic* imperatives of proportion and attributes. With this plasticity there has continued to be a spontaneity, a rapport between the community and the craftsman, and also poetic appreciation of the craftsman's skill. "As a carpenter carves wood, as a goldsmith prepares his ornaments, so she looked lovely."[29]

The craftsman played a pivotal role in village communities. A curious judgment of the Madras High Court toward the beginning of the nineteenth century, published by Oppert in his *Original Inhabitants of Bharat Varsha,* identified the flags that would be used in rituals by various south Indian artisan guilds. Many of the symbols listed have royal associations and give a clear indication of the ancestry of these craftsmen and of the importance enjoyed by them as the creators of the gods and of the functional objects of daily use. The mythical bird, the *garuḍa,* the tiger, the two white chowries, the white umbrella, the royal two-headed eagle, and an animal with a human face are some of these emblems. Five classes of artisans—the carpenters, the goldsmiths, the blacksmiths, the brass-smiths, and masons—regarded themselves as the original creators of form and called themselves *Brahmin kammalars.* They insisted on their right to enact the sacred rituals. In village societies, the craftsman was the officiating magician-priest at the shrine of the goddess. From the prehistoric period, the pot, as the vessel, has been the symbol of the mother. The place of the potter in the craft tradition has been unique. In a sense, as the most ancient maker of form, he symbolized the creative process inherent in the artisan tradition.

> In the corner by the plantain tree, who is there?
> In the corner by the plantain tree, is the potter.
> You in there, potter turn the wheel.
> My father and mother make for me.
> I will make them, my child, make them I will.
> But the breath of life I
> cannot give—but the breath of life I cannot give.[30]

The potter's special relationship to the earth and its uses linked him to the origins of agricultural magic. The discovery of a very early *tantra* manuscript of the sixth century, the *Kubjikā Tantra,* written in Gupta characters, associates the origins of *tantra* to the rituals of the potters. In this *tantra*, which reveals a sophisticated knowledge of chemistry, Śiva speaks of *pārada* (mercury) as his generative essence. "As it is used by the best devotees for the highest it is called *pārada.* Begotten of my limbs it is O Goddess equal to me. It is called *rasa* because it is the exudation of my body."[31] The seed of Śiva was mercury; the ovum of the goddess was mica; the union between the two transmuted base metals into gold and gave immortality to the human body.

The association of mica with the seed of the goddess enriches the symbology of the Indus Valley earthen pots, where mica is used in quantities to bind the local earth of the pots cast on the potter's wheel. To this day, mica is used in the earth with which the walls and grainbins of peasant dwellings in Cutch and Jaisalmere are plastered. Mica was also used to mold the sarcophagus, the urn that contained the dead in the ancient Nilgiri burial mounds.

In Andhra, the potter molds the form of the malevolent Śakti, in darkness, at the dead of night. He enters, alone, the inner apartment, the holy place where the form of the goddess is given shape. While the potter is making the sacred image, another image is drawn outside in the dust. Rituals are then enacted to propitiate the demonaic Śakti and induce her to enter the image. Once the rituals are over, the Śakti is buried, and a nail hammered into her body to bind her movements. Sometimes, the image is taken and abandoned at the boundaries of the village.[32]

The carpenter and the potter, as creators of the gods, enjoy magical functions. Among the Bhils of Gujarat, the *buā* (magician-priest) is the carver of the *pallias* (the wooden funerary pillars). The cycle of death and fertility is thus closely linked. The *buās* of today refuse to carve wood that is not of a freshly cut tree rich in sap. No dead wood is ever used to carve a funerary pillar. The image of Kanaka Durgāmmā, in Andhra, is carved by the village carpenter from the branch of a margosa tree. The freshly cut branch is not allowed to touch the ground. The carpenter, alone, at the dead of night, carves the image. It must be finished before dawn. The image, two feet tall, representing a woman with a sword, is placed in water, the ancient home of the goddess, and is kept there till the ceremonies commence. In the morning the village washerman takes the image out of the water and, after dressing and ornamenting it, takes it out in procession.

The Legends of Integration

Hidden in the obscure spirals of the rural unconscious are memories of vast migrations and wars of prehistory. The most potent of these remembrances are of the battles between the fair-skinned invaders, the nomadic herdsmen who worshiped the male sun divinities, and the dark, earth-ploughing, autochthonous people, worshipers of the Great Mother. Powerful memories survive of conflicts between the people of the fields and furrows and the primitive dwellers in the forests and mountains. These memories are invoked and released through subtle nuances of myth, image, and song. The myths that reveal the process of transformation and integration of matriarchal and patriarchal societies, of the mingling of gods and goddesses, are recorded in the *purāṇic* texts, while the memories of the people of the soil, "the Dravidization of the tribal folk of middle India, which preceded in many ways the Aryanization of historical times,"[1] are sung by the hornblowers, the Gond bards, and the minstrels attached to the female divinities, the sacred mothers of rural India.

Two viewpoints emerge, the *brahmanic* and the autochthonous, recounting power given and taken, conquest and absorption, destruction and reemergence. Perhaps the most poignant of these legends and the best remembered are stories of the *purāṇic* goddess, Durgā Kātyāyanī, and the demon, Mahiṣāsura; the archaic legend in the Karnataka of Durgamava and Dayamava; the legend of Pedammā-Mariammā of the deep south, and the autochthonous myth of Reṇukā-Elammā, half-Aryan, half-outcaste.

THE LEGEND OF DURGĀ

Mahiṣa was the son of Rambha, an *asura* (tribesman), and Mahiṣī, the goddess Gaurī in her form as a female buffalo. The *asura* chief, skilled in magical prowess, was invincible and threatened the *brahmanic* gods. Having failed to vanquish the tribal hero, the *devas* invoked the goddess for assistance.

To resounding incantations and *mantras,* the goddess appeared as a mountain of light, the color of gold, with the brilliance of a thousand suns. Her eyes were like the *nīlotpala* flower, the blue lily; her hair was black as night; her high, round, prominent breasts proclaimed her feminine divinity. To her, each god contributed his fiery energy and his weapons. Śiva gave his trident; Viṣṇu, his disc; Varuṇa, his conch; Agni, a dart; Yama, an iron rod; Vāyu, a bow; Sūrya, arrows; Kubera, a mace; Indra, a thunderbolt; Brahmā, a rosary and waterpot; Kāla, a sword; Viśvakarmā, an axe; Himavān, a lion. Thus armed, mighty with the power and essence of all the gods, Durgā Kātyāyanī went to her home on the Vindhya mountains, where she was worshiped by the tribes of the Śavaras and the Pulindas. The *asura* Mahiṣa, the conquering demon king, hearing of the intoxicating beauty of the fair lady of the mountain, sent a messenger to her claiming her for his own, for was he not lord of the three worlds? The goddess smiled and replied that she could only wed the hero who defeated her in battle. The arrogant *asura* accepted the challenge of battle and at first sent his *asura* army to war with the slender maiden. Kātyāyanī lifted her bow and arrow and her sword and, mounted on the *śarabha,*[2] a mythical animal, half-elephant and half-tiger, she defeated the *asura* hosts. Seeing the slain, she seized a *vīṇā* and a *ḍamaru* and, laughing with joy, played music. Then Mahiṣāsura advanced, assuming by his magic the form of a deep-black, maddened buffalo, now bellowing, now running, now stamping the ground with his hoofs. A cataclysmic battle commenced. The mountains were rent asunder, the oceans trembled, and the clouds scattered in the sky. In vain the goddess used her god-given weapons, but the buffalo hero escaped her. At last, filled with engulfing anger, she flung aside her weapons, dismounted, and with her bare hands sprang on the back of Mahiṣa; with her tender, fragrant foot she smote his head. The *asura,* immune to the weapons of all the gods, fell senseless at the touch of the goddess's feet. And she, poised in the serene knowledge of her all-consuming power, took her sword and cut off the head of Mahiṣa. Then, making the gesture that dispels fear with her hand, the goddess appeared smiling, unblemished unto the full moon. Seeing her victorious, the male gods of the *Purāṇas* hailed her:

> Whatever gentle forms of thine,
> And whatever of thy terrible forms wander in the three
> worlds,
> By these forms protect us and the Earth.[3]

The gods proclaim her eminence—then, having taken to herself the energy of the *purāṇic* gods, she destroys Mahiṣa and places the buffalo horns of divinity on her own head. But the legend does not end there. Undergoing weird transformation, the buffalo-headed demon, killed and trampled underfoot in ritual conflict, reappears in Maharashtra as Mhatobā, an incarnation of Śiva, and is united in marriage to his loved one Jogubāī-Yogeśvarī Durgā.[4] Terracotta shrines of Mhatobā, shaped in the form of a dolmen soul house, are found in Maharashtra. The image and worship of Mahiṣāsuramardini, the goddess, exists in juxtaposition with the shrines of Mhatobā and his wedded goddess.

In Himachal Pradesh, one of the most powerful of the *gramā devatās* is Mahāsu, a god of mystery, for no one has been able to describe his image. The shrine of the god is in an inner cave of darkness, where only the priest can enter. There is no light and no torches are permitted. In this cave of the legendary labyrinth, the cave of darkness, the origin of the half-man, half-animal deity Mahāsu, a corrupt form of Mahiṣāsura, is to be sought. Mahāsu, in the Himalayas, has also close associations with the *nāgas*. At times he is identified with Śiva:

> Thou art the God of all Gods and wondrous is thy glory thy
> light is like that of the moon and thou art full of
> water like the ocean,
> Thou art Mahāsu, the creator and destroyer of the three
> worlds.[5]

The buffalo image and the power of the animal are portrayed in a Harappan culture seal, where the dark, massive, male, horned animal shatters the environment, an explosive symbol of unharnessed energy, riotous and even demoniac.[6] In village shrines the delineation of the Mahiṣāsuramardini image is the first icon to replace the aniconic stone.

The Karnataka version of the goddess and the destruction of the buffalo king has possibly more archaic elements than the *purāṇic* story of Durgā, although here, too, the fusion of *brahmanic* myth and indigenous magic and fantasy are apparent.

The Legend of Dayamava and Durgamava

Dayamava and Durgamava were sisters, daughters of a learned *Brāhmaṇa.* A sweeper of the *Holaya* or *Mahar* caste fell in love with Dayamava and, in the guise of a *Brāhmaṇa,* seduced her. Dayamava, not knowing that her seducer was a *Holaya,* married him, and had several children by him. One day Mātaṅgi, the *Holaya's* mother, came to dinner. While eating sweet cakes, Mātaṅgī said to her son that they tasted like roasted buffalo tongue. Dayamava was filled with horror. Recognizing that her husband was a *Holaya,* not a *Brāhmaṇa,* she set fire to Mātaṅgī's house, killed all the children she had had by the *Holaya,* and tried to kill her *Holaya* husband. He fled and hid in the form of a buffalo. Dayamava found him and killed her husband, the buffalo.

The temples of Durgamava and Dayamava are small buildings of brick and mud. Except in some old shrines, the images of the goddesses with twelve hands are generally made of wood. The six right hands hold respectively a *chakra* (discus), a *triśūla* (trident), a drawn sword, a spear, a dagger, and a long knife; the six left hands respectively hold a *śankha* (conch shell), a snake, a crooked dagger, a scabbard, a short knife, and a vessel to hold either blood or red *kum kum* powder. The images are made out of several pieces of wood. The two images are always set side by side, Durgamava painted green, Dayamava painted red. The *badigas* (carpenters) are the hereditary ministrants (*pujāris*) of these goddesses. Once every third or fourth year, in the month of May, a special festival is held in honor of Dayamava, called the *Dayamavan jātrā* ("Dayamava's fair"). Though Durgamava's name is not mentioned during the fair, the image of Durgamava is carried side by side with that of Dayamava, and is treated with equal respect.

The car on which the goddesses ride is ornamented with colored clothes, flags, plantain trees, fruit, flowers, and mango leaves, and generally one or two carved naked human figures to keep off the evil eye.

At the close of every fair of Dayamava, a fine male buffalo is sacrificed. Turmeric and red powder are rubbed on the brow of the living animal, *neem* leaves are tied to his neck, and sandalwood paste and flowers are laid on him. He is set free and called *paṭṭaḍakoṇa* ("holy buffalo"). Men and women of all castes bathe, dress in fine clothes, and stand before the temple of the two sisters. The village painter awakens the goddesses by painting in the eyes. The *desai* hands the *pātil* two gold *mangalasūtras,* which the *pātil* ties round Dayamava's and Durgamava's neck. The *deshpande* hands the *kulkarni* two gold nose ornaments, called *mugtis,* one of which he puts on Dayamava's nose and the other on Durgamava's nose. After this, the carpenter *pujāris* decorate the images with flowers, rich garments, and ornaments, burn incense before them, and bring them out of the temple. As soon as the goddesses are brought out, a man of the *Madigar* (tanner) caste called the *ranigia,* who represents the brother of Dayamava's husband, comes forward and raises his right hand, in which he holds a stick with a bell and a handkerchief tied to it. He stands in front of the goddess and shouts the names of her private parts before her; he continues to shout until the car is drawn out of the village boundaries and the goddesses are placed on the raised seat built for them. Several coconuts are broken and two sheep killed in front of the goddesses.

In the evening, women of the *Asadi* caste, a subdivision of the *Madigars* or *Mangs,* dress in fantastic clothes and dance before the goddesses, singing their praises and recounting their great deeds. The *Asadi* men beat drums and play music behind the women, while the *ranigia* continues to shout filthy words, chiefly the names of the goddesses' private parts. In front of the shed, an area of about ten feet long by ten feet broad is plastered with cow dung and ornamented with figures drawn with different colored powders. The *paṭṭaḍakoṇa* (holy buffalo), supposed to represent Dayamava's *mahar* husband, is brought to the decorated ground. The head of the buffalo is cut and taken to the hut called Mātaṅgī's cottage.

The next day the goddesses are taken in procession to a spot outside the village. Another plot of ground of about two feet square is spread with cow dung and decorated with diagrams in colored powders. A lamb is set free on the square. A member of the *Holayas* called *poturāju* (buffalo king), stripped naked with a few *neem* leaves round his loins, comes running like a tiger, pounces upon the lamb and carries it away towards the village boundary. Some of the *Holayas, Madigars,* and others pretend to run after him, to catch and kill him. When the buffalo king has killed the lamb, the goddesses are taken in procession to the village boundary. As soon as the goddesses are taken out of the shed, the grass hut representing Mātaṅgī's cottage is burned to ashes and, on the spot where the hut stood, the head of the slaughtered buffalo is buried. When the goddesses reach the village boundary, they are placed on a raised seat and flowers, turmeric, and red powder are rubbed on them. A curtain is drawn before the goddess to hide the dead body of Dayamava's buffalo husband. The carpenter ministrants stand inside the curtain, break the glass bangles on the goddesses' wrists, strip them naked, take the red powder off their brows, pull off their heads, hands, and legs, and put them into two baskets. Then, mourning the death of the divine ones, they carry the baskets to the goddesses' temple and lay them in the idol room for three days. The doors of the temple are locked from outside. On the third evening the *pujārīs* enter the temple door and put together the bodies of the goddesses, dress them in new clothes, mark their brows with red powder, put fresh bangles on their wrists, adorn them with flowers and ornaments, and surround them with lighted lamps. Prayers are then offered to the goddesses asking that the village be free from cholera and smallpox, for Durgamava is believed to preside over and cause cholera, while Dayamava is the presiding deity of smallpox.[7] The villagers also pray for many children and plentiful harvests. All night long *Asadi* women dance and sing, and *Asadi* men beat big drums and play pipes. The *ranigia* and the *poturāju* join the *Asadis* in the dancing and singing. This is called the golden play. The same night a new buffalo is brought and worshiped. Turmeric and red powder are rubbed on his forehead, *neem* leaves are tied round his neck, and he is set free and proclaimed as the holy buffalo of the goddess Dayamava. If this buffalo dies before the next fair, a successor is at once chosen.

The Legend of Pedammā-Mariammā

"Before the existence of hills or trees or fields or plants there was only water. In the midst of this existed the great world light." Pedammā-Mariammā was born of this cosmic light meditating on itself. The moment she was born she grew to womanhood, and the desire for man arose within her. As she wandered in a garden near an anthill, a jasmine bough bent over her, and the lady plucked a flower and said, "This will be my love." The virgin goddess took the jasmine flower and placed it within a lotus blossom which floated on the surface of the water. Then, with the magic powers held within her, the goddess transformed herself into a bird and settled upon the lotus, brooding over the jasmine flower. The sacred bird became pregnant of the flower and laid three eggs within the lotus. From one egg was born the heavens, the sun and the moon, the stars, and the all encircling sea. From the black speck within the egg was born Śiva, Viṣṇu, and Brahmā. From the second egg were born the *rākṣasas* and demons; the third egg was addled.

The goddess nurtured the three gods, and, when they were twelve years old, she taught them the *om mantra* and built for them three cities. As she looked on the radiant young gods, she lusted after them. Adorning herself with jewels and fragrant flower garlands and dressed in shining garments, she went to Brahmā and asked him to satisfy her passion. He replied, "You are my mother, how can I!" and shut his ears and his eyes. The goddess said, "That is not so. I am not your mother, but only your grandmother. Do what I ask." Brahmā refused and sent her to Viṣṇu, who gave the same reply. Then the goddess, filled with a mighty anger, went to Śiva. Seeing her rage, Śiva said, "So be it, but first you must grant me a boon." The goddess readily agreed, and Śiva asked for the third eye of the goddess, the jewel that rested on her forehead. The lady handed over the jewel, the third eye, to Śiva, and suddenly her youth and incandescence vanished, and with it all desire disappeared. The centuries were upon her, and in an instant she was an old woman.

Desire having disappeared with her youth, the ancient ancestress then decided to fight the demons. She asked the new gods to remain and guard her lands, the waters and the vegetation, and to send her jasmine flowers every day while she herself went and began to kill the demons. But as she slew them, their blood fell on the earth, and millions of new demons sprang to life. She then assumed her divine form and put out her tongue, which extended and covered the earth. As she killed the demons, she licked the falling blood with her tongue before it could touch the earth. But a drop of blood had fallen unnoticed. From this was born Dundubhi, the buffalo demon. He fled from the wrath of the goddess and took refuge in the garden guarded by Brahmā, Viṣṇu, and Śiva. When the gods found the buffalo demon destroying their garden, they questioned him, and a battle ensued between the gods and the buffalo, dark as a thundercloud.

The buffalo breathed on them, and they, with their cloud chariots, were carried away in the storm. He stamped with his foot, and the earth trembled so that their chariots were shaken to pieces. In terror the gods rushed to the goddess to seek her aid. She armed herself with a weapon in each of her seven hands and searched for the monster. She found him and hit him with all her weapons, but it had no effect. Then she asked the buffalo to attack her, but he said, "How can I attack a woman?" and breathed on her and she too was carried away by his breath. She fled in terror and Dundubhi pursued her. From her sweat she created an anthill with three horns, and the goddess turned herself into an ichneumon and rushed into the anthill. Dundubhi snorted and stamped and destroyed the anthill, but it sprang back into shape. Meanwhile, the goddess descended into the bowels of the earth, reached the land of the serpents, and found the *siddhas,* masters of magic and *mantras.* With an army of ninety million *siddhas* and chanting incantations, the ancient one marched up to the upper world. The thunderous river of the magical sounds reached Dundubhi, and he dropped dead. The goddess with her army reached the outer world and saw the dead buffalo demon. The victorious *siddhas* rejoiced. They cut off the head of the buffalo and laid it before the goddess. They set an oil lamp on the head of the buffalo demon, placed one of its forelegs in its mouth, and chanted *mantras* in praise of the ancient goddess.

At the festival of the goddess, an earthen image of the goddess is made. This is dressed and adorned with jewels and put in a small booth made by the people of the washer caste. Food and arrack are placed in front of this booth, and the history of the goddess is told by the *Asadi* bards. The *Malas* bring forward the buffalo which is sacrificed; the *Madigas* cut up the carcass. The *Malas* take the buffalo head and put it in front of the image, with a lighted lamp on the head of the sacrificial animal. After the ceremonies are over, the image is taken to the boundary of the village and thrown away.[8]

THE LEGEND OF REṆUKĀ

Reṇukā, the chaste wife of the *Brahmin* sage Jamadagni, saw Chitraratha, the wondrously beautiful *gandharva,* reflected in the waters of the river Kaveri. Passion arose in her at the sight of the radiant singing *gandharva,* and her chastity was corroded so that the magical powers born of her chastity disappeared—powers that enabled her to mold vessels out of sand within which the waters of the sacred river were contained. Jamadagni, meditating in the forest, grew aware of the violation of the chastity of his wife, and he was filled with a *yogī's* anger. Calling his sons, he demanded of them filial obedience and commanded them to kill their mother. Four sons refused, but the youngest, Paraśurāma, the fierce one, took up his axe and turned on his mother. She fled and took refuge among the outcaste *madigas.* Paraśurāma pursued Reṇukā and, finding her among the outcastes, he struck off her head and killed the people who had given her shelter. Then, taking his mother's head, he returned to his father. Jamadagni, well pleased with his son, asked him to ask for a boon, and Paraśurāma asked for the life of his mother. Jamadagni, his anger pacified, agreed and gave his son the *mantra* (a magic incantation) to revive his mother. Paraśurāma returned to the dwellings of the outcastes, but in his agony failed to identify the body of his mother and placed the head of Reṇukā on the body of a *pariah* woman. Once the act was accomplished and once the *mantra* was recited, the body was revived and came to life.

But was she the Aryan lady Reṇukā or the *pariah* outcaste woman? The riddle was solved by a brilliant Brahmanic interpretation. The composite female form of the half-*Brahmin,* half-outcaste was named Elammā, the *grāma devatā,* the primeval Śakti of the South. She was to be worshiped throughout the country south of the Vindhya mountains by the *pariah* and the outsiders. The main stone image of the mother, before whose shrine blood sacrifice was to be offered, was buried in the earth, with only the Brahmanic head visible, and it was this head that was worshiped.[9]

To expiate his sin of matricide, Paraśurāma wandered the earth, till, in Kerala, he found and worshiped the image of his mother in her form as Ambikā-Elammā. It is in her shrine that he found final refuge. Images of Paraśurāma, along with the violent sage, Jamadagni, are enshrined in the temples to Reṇukā-Elammā.[10] These temples of Reṇukā are built at a distance from the village. They are overshadowed by a margosa tree. Inside the temple is a stone image of Elammā with three eyes, and near it there is a small metal image made of five metals. The metal image of the *grāma devatā* holds in one hand a noose, in the other the skull of Brahmā. This skull is said to hold all the blood of man and beast sacrificed throughout the world, and yet the cup never overflows.

The Balnenivandlu, the bards of the goddess, play upon instruments and recite the wondrous tale of the sacred one. A buffalo is sacrificed at the festival of Reṇukā-Elammā, while the sacred square, the *muggu,* is drawn with colored powder before her shrine.

The *Veda* of the Rural Tradition

The *Atharva Veda,* compiled by singing sages several centuries after the *ṛgvedic* hymns, contains very archaic elements and is possibly the earliest record of the beliefs, the imagery, the rituals and worship of the autochthonous peoples of India as they met and transformed the conquering Aryan consciousness.

The *Atharva Veda* is named after Atharvan, a fire-churning priest of great antiquity who, during fire sacrifice, revealed the paths and established ways of communication between men and the gods. Through his magic powers the sage also discovered the means of overcoming the malevolent and the hostile.

The Atharvan hymns are concerned with incantations and magical spells. These spells, and the manifold rituals that made them operative, impregnated the popular beliefs of this country, providing the potent verbal imagery, the aural texture of archaic man's sensibilities.

In the Atharvan hymns the cosmic landscape of the arrogant young Aryan wanderers has shrunk. The *ṛgvedic* hymns were resonant with praises to the sky, to the sun, to thunder; the bard of the Atharvan hymns has descended from the high places; he sings in the valleys, from within the limiting contours of settled agricultural communities. The focus has now shifted from the sky to the earth, drawing the perceptive life forces into the inward and downward spiral of the Earth Mother.

> The Earth on whom waters flow day and night with never ceasing motion—The Earth that is brown black and red in color—A vast abode.[1]

A sense of mysterious sacredness and of wonder, a recognition of the earth as the life-giving, tranquil, fragrant mother pervades the Atharvan hymns.

Out of this earth-directed gaze arises ancient man's primordial fear of the dangers inherent in the use of the plough to lacerate the breast of the Earth Mother and his need to propitiate and allay her pain by prayer and sacrifice. This echoes in the words of the Atharvan sage, "What of these I dig out, let that quickly grow over, let me not hit thy vitals or thy heart."[2]

A new obsessional concern with fertility and a quickened awareness of "the heroic power of forest trees," of the thousand-fold energy of plants as growing things, and of energy-transforming sap are evident in the songs. The talismanic power of plants and trees to protect and to destroy, their usage as energy-transmuting amulets in magical rites, are understood and established. Plants are recognized as having an independent sacred presence, shining like light, and as being rescuers of the simple, slayers of the demoniac. Plants are widely used as weapons against witchcraft, and to destroy sorcerers and hags. The distinction between the functions of the magician spellbinder and the witch is also of much interest and percolates through the whole fabric of the rural tradition. The magician-priest is the channel of communication through which cosmic forces flow. It is only through the magician (*bhopa* or *gunia*) that man can contact the invisible. The witch frustrates the cosmic principles; her spells thwart the laws of nature. The Baigas, ancient people who live in the heart of India, recount a myth that blood flowed from the body of the old, naked ancestor Naṅgā Baiga: from his left side black blood emerged, from his right, red blood. Whosoever drank the black blood became a witch; the drinker of the red blood became a magician. When Naṅgā Baiga died, part of the magical essences of his body were eaten by witches. The battle between the magicians and witches permeates the tradition.[3]

The animal- and bird-faced mothers, the *auṣadhis*, and their primordial link with vegetation and healing was already part of the Atharvan consciousness. "The sheep-headed goddess Avi sits enveloped with might—by her forms these trees are green, green garlanded."[4] There is a luminous awareness in it of the use of plants for inducing visions by quickening of the visual nerve. The Atharvan seer invokes the deified plant with a thousand eyes, to "make manifest the form of things, hide not their essences from sight." Filled with the fluid that rises in the plant at night when the moon is dark, the holder of the amulet "sees in front, sees behind, sees far away—sees the sky, the firmament and the earth."[5]

The imagery of some of the Atharvan hymns has a wild, piercing beauty; the perceptions are filled with delight. Spells to exorcise jaundice invoke the potency of color: "With the color of the red bull, we enclose thee, in order to lengthen life." The yellow of jaundice is conjured away into birds: "In the parrots, in the *ropaṇaka*, we put thy yellowness, likewise in the *haridrā* we deposit thy yellowness."[6]

The piercing cry for protection against the known and unknowable and a demand for the auspicious echoes through the Atharvan hymns with the same devastating intensity as is encountered today in distant village societies: protection from magic, protection from witches and sorcerers, from the devastation of nature, from disease and death, protection from the lurking images in the subconscious, the devourers who on the night of the new moon rise to destroy. There is, in these hymns, a recurrent propitiation of these dark forces, the drawing of them into the auspicious transforming circle of sun-directed energy.

From across the rivers, from the autochthonous people dwelling in the walled cities of the Indus Valley, from the people who dwelt in forest and cave came the energy-transforming rites, the earth-claiming and life-binding secrets that guarded the mysteries.[7] An ambivalent attitude of fearful attraction to, and equally fearful withdrawal from, the dark and mysterious peoples pervades the *Atharva Veda*. The *gandharvas*, the *yakṣas*, the *apsarās,* and the *piśāchas* were unfamiliar beings, mighty magicians with intimate knowledge of plant chemistry and its uses in healing, in destroying, and in granting extended godlike vision. The outsiders also had a knowledge of the power of plants in rites of alchemy and metamorphosis. They could transform themselves into trees, into streams, into birds and animals. "The Āsurī woman conquered in battle took shape as a forest tree providing through her body the healing sap for curing dread disease."[8]

Kāma as desire, the first-born, who existed before the gods,[9] appears as the presiding deity in several hymns. He is recognized in his dual role as the creator and the god of lust and phallic love. The myth of Kāma's destruction by the leaping fire of Śiva's third eye is not yet known. Kāma is invoked not as Anaṅga, the bodiless god, but as he who has a lovely and auspicious form.[10] Kāma appears in several savage love rites of magic and witchcraft: "Want thou the body of me? Want thou the eyes? Want thou the thighs? Let the eyes, the hair of thee, lusting after me, dry up with love."[11]

The *Kauśiku Sūtra*, written several centuries after the *Atharva Veda*, places the hymns in their ritual setting. The spells of the Atharvan hymns were gathered and their corresponding ritual practices recorded. There are a large number of rites and magical acts, the *strīkarmāṇi*, that pertain to women. They are prescribed to obtain a husband, to become fecund, to destroy a rival, to protect the embryo, to capture a truant woman. There are charms for increasing sexual vigor. There are rites for procuring rain and for correcting faults in vision. The making of picture and effigy to do evil and to protect are integral to many of the rituals. Later many of these magical rites were translated into thousands of *vrata* practices and cults. These were the keys to mysteries and energy, held and kept secret by women.

The *āsurī kalpa*, a witchcraft practice built on Atharvan foundations, contains important rites used in connection with the *āsurī* plant, rites to destroy the hated one, to cast a love spell, to fix like a post. The text indicates that the *āsurī* plant was regarded as a form of the goddess Durgā. To propitiate the goddess, rites were enjoined for the preparation of a *kuṇḍa* (fire-pot) into which the fire oblations were made. This *kuṇḍa* took the form of a triangle, a *yantra,* symbolic of the goddess as the *yoni*. An oblation of *ghee* (clarified butter) and brown sugar was offered to the *kuṇḍa*. The person performing the rites put on garlands of red, sweet-smelling oleander, wore red garments and ornaments made of red sandalwood and lay on the ground facing the south. The fundamental *mantra*, called the whisper spell, was then uttered to invoke the *āsurī* woman: "*Om*, reverence Rudra, *om*, O pungent one, thou of the pungent leaf, blessed, *āsurī* reddish one, thou of the red garment, O daughter of Atharvan, nonterrific one, nonterrific wonder-worker (so-and-so), smite, smite, burn, burn, cook, cook, crush, crush, so long burn, so long cook until you have brought (him) into my power, *Svāhā*." This was followed by the limb-touching ceremony and a meditation on Durgā. Then commenced the oblations. The seeds of the *āsurī* plant were ground and an image made to symbolize the person against whom the magic was directed. A fire was kindled and the image was cut into pieces and offered to the fire. This practice accompanied by the *mantra* was enacted one hundred and eight times during six days. On the seventh day the *mantra* became operative and the victim succumbed. The *Kalpa* ends by saying, "He is neither divorced of power nor destitute of children, in whose house the divine *āsurī* is."[12]

With the emergence of potent spell and ritual, in the Atharvan hymns, the need for a sacred object to support these two became imperative. The *mantra*, the *maṇḍala*, and the *mudrā* are in a sense incipient in the *Atharva Veda*. They together form the energy-charged base against which and from which the numinous forms emerge. *Mantra* is spell and incantation that uses abstract sound, repetitive alliteration, antiphonal singing, nonsense words, and wild savage poetry to create the sensitized energy-transforming and energy-releasing field. *Mudrā* is an energy-generating gesture, action, or ritual, keyed to the source of energy as manifest in the sun and earth, tree and animal. *Maṇḍala* is the fixation of the ritual gesture and the creation of the enclosed sacred space that holds the surcharged energy and power.

Supporting and sustaining the magic, the new, intimate knowledge of the Earth Mother, the growing, penetrating insight into *mantra, mudrā,* and *maṇḍala*, there appears in the Atharvan hymns a cosmic concern with spirit and the clarity of sight that makes manifest the form of things. With this there is a growing awareness of breath as weapon of sight and of mind, of incantation and of penance.

Out of this fusion of magic and vision, there emerged in the Atharvan hymns symbols of profound mystery, symbols that were to fill and refresh the subconscious of the peoples of this country for many thousands of years. The faces of the pervading goddess and the many elements that went to build her later composite form are nascent in the Atharvan hymns.

The *apsarās* appear as the forerunners of the *yoginīs* and the *ḍākinīs*, the beauteous deities of vegetation and destiny, of death and wealth that permeate popular lore and art. Born of the fragrant earth, with their home in the waters, the *apsarās* bear the names of sweet-smelling herbs and exude the fragrance of the lotus. They dance and sing and play on musical instruments. They are eternal virgins. Their mysterious association with the waters and with trees is recognized and so is their power to destroy the minds of men with their incandescent beauty. In a later text they are referred to as the wives of Kāma, the god of love, "rendering him mad that is mad." They are also referred to as the wives of the *gandharvas*.

There are hymns in the *Atharva Veda*, the *Mātṛ Nāmāni*, which are the obeisance to the Mothers, in which the *apsarās* are included. The female principle as the personification of formidable malignant forces "mighty, vast in size, penetrating all points of space" had already taken deep root. The principle is invoked as *Nirṛti*, who is of the golden hair and Arāti, who comes as a naked girl, haunting people in their sleep.[13] There are poignant forebodings of female forces that destroy embryos and cast magic spells. The old witch that peeps from behind the tree trunk is an image charged with formidable potency.

The female principle is also recognized as a pervading cosmic force. As the radiant and auspicious Viraj, she is identified with the earth and with sound. She is also identified with a forty-syllable meter which has miraculous powers. At birth all fear her, for the thought arises that "she will become this all." She enters the sacrificial and household fires, the villages, and the plants. She ascends, she transforms, she permeates, she fills. Then recreating within her body the mystery of birth and death, portending the sacrifices of man and beast to propitiate and make fruitful the earth, she arises, she stands, she strides four-fold in the atmosphere and comes to the trees, to the fathers, to the gods, and to men. They each kill her in turn, and she in turn arises, springing back into existence, for she is *prakṛti*, the indestructible energy principle, the womb of transformation, that is born, permeates, sustains, and dies in the mysterious circle, the *Śrī Chakra*, which is her symbol and her source. She is also the earth, filled with fertility and abundant fruit. They that have killed her call to her to come and live with them, each seeing the numinous principle in her image. Each draws from her body, which is the cauldron of life and death, of energy-transforming resources. The iron-smelting *asuras* receive the life-essence from her in a vessel of metal, men in an earthen pot, the *gandharvas* in a leaf cup of the blue lotus, the serpents in a poison gourd.[14]

Another profound symbol to emerge from the Atharvan songs is the wandering *yogī*, the star-marked mendicant and magician, the *vrātya*, with his lord, Eka Vrātya, who is also Mahādeva. A hymn evokes the image of the *yogī* who stands erect with the immobility of stone, with indrawn breath, with arms and hands stretched to the sides and with eyes fixed in meditative trance. This is a posture that had already found expression and form in the seals of the Indus Valley, the living manifestation of which must have been familiar to ancient seers. The Atharvan singer describes the *vrātya*: "He stood a year erect." He asks, "Vrātya, why standest thou?" In reply, the *Vrātya* calls for an *āsana*, a sacral seat. He ascends and sits wide-lapped, explosive with power this *mudrā* appears in the Indus Valley seals and is one that fertilizes the Indian tradition. The "thus knowing" *vrātya* arises and moves about, encompassing all directions.[15]

Later texts describe the *vrātyas* as wandering magicians who wore black garments marked with mystical signs. In their hands they held a rod and a bow, with a magical amulet tied around their necks. The *vrātya* magician-*yogī* traveled through the country on a cart drawn by a horse. He was accompanied by a bard and a prostitute. During the *Mahāvrata*, the solstice festival held to awaken the earth after the harvesting, the *vrātya* drew *maṇḍalas* on the cart which served as his altar, and performed secret rites and chanted incantations, while the bard and the prostitute performed ritual intercourse to fertilize the earth.

The Ritual Art of the (Indus Valley) Harappan Civilization

The walled cities of the Indus Valley stretched from Mohenjo-Daro in Sindh, to Ropar in the Punjab, Lothal in Gujarat, to the cities that lay at the mouth of the Narmada River. Their culture reveals the earliest visual expressions of the autochthonous peoples of India. The archaic art of these river cities bursts on the Indian landscape, revealing an ancient and mature vocabulary of images and symbols, visual representations of the Atharvan spells, forms that have concretized primordial mysteries. A living ritual and technology that telescopes five thousand years is manifest, linking rites and symbols with the contemporary art and ritual of villages and tribes. This gives to the rural arts of today a time-free perspective, within which the past and present coalesce in a great convolving continuity.

A vast number of amulets, seals, miniature carvings in clay, faience, metal, and semi-precious stones have been discovered at Indus Valley sites. The talismanic nature of these objects is unquestionable. We have seen in the *Atharva Veda* the extent to which amulets and their use in ritual had penetrated and encompassed the life of the people.

Before the establishment of settled agricultural societies, and a relatively protected existence that made possible the emergence of temple and icon, the amulet, "charged with life breath and heroism," operated as the holder of power and divinity. When worn on the body, the energy-generating rituals carved on the seal became operative. The amulet became a portable shrine, drawing the wearer of the amulet into a field of protection, giving him the magical powers that lay in the inscribed incantations.

The impact of a city confined within walls is visible in this art of seals and amulets. Though the seal pictographs are confined to small spaces and monumental forms have been reduced to miniatures, the feeling for mass and volume survives. The perceptive energy revealed in the pictographs, the precision and control of the line, the awareness and capacity to suggest volume and form, and the spaces created reveal the hands of skilled and sensitive sculptors. The detailing is masterly; it is the art of the goldsmith. Spatial tensions are created in these pictographs by the concentration of objects within a clearly specified, enclosed area. This use of space, this concentration of object and meaning, and the energy created thereby, is visible in most tribal and village shrines throughout India. It is also found in the amulets worn by primitive man through the centuries.

Mastery of material and technique had given the craftsman of the Indus Valley the power to create images and, through the images, to reveal a story. A narrative art is evident in the pictographs and seals of the Indus Valley. The undeciphered script appears as a visual statement within the enclosed space. The script is used pictorially: fish found in rivers, birds, the waterman, leaves, and inverted receptacles appear as symbols. At times the script is placed above the image, at times it divides the areas of narration and forms pictorial barriers. At all times the script is visually related to the pictograph.

A knowledge of geometry and the sacred nature of abstract form that was later to develop into *maṇḍala* and *aripan* is visible. These appear in amulet and seal, in the form of the circle, the *Śrī Chakra,* the *aṣṭadala,* the eight-pointed diagram, the double-spiral, the *svastikā,* and the Greek cross. Numerous seals depict twin breasts as symbols of the female principle.[1]

With the seals and amulets we enter the grim inner world of the Indus Valley dweller. Like the hymns of the *Atharva Veda,* this is a world of dark mysteries, of god and demon, in which the sun and the moon have no place and never appear. It is an earth-directed vision in which the *neem* and *peepal* trees form the heights of man's perceptions and horizons. A landscape of primeval forest and of wild and savage animals that move in splendor across the open space is depicted. The numinous form as image and icon is not readily recognizable among the artifacts of the Indus Valley. Rites and rituals that anticipate the later forms of the goddess are distinguishable, the symbols already charged with a sacral presence. These recurrent symbols nourish the Indian unconscious, the source of the classical as well as the "little tradition" of field and forest. In later centuries these symbols were translated in the hand of the artisan into cult images and icons. The *yogī* with indrawn breath, sitting cross-legged in meditation, surrounded by animals and by serpents; the female numinous form dwelling in the *neem* tree in mysterious dialogue with the tiger; the composite form of man and animal; the standing figure, the form within the tree trunk or the *lingam,* strong, young, immortal, and ancient—these are timeless symbols that were later to find powerful expression.

A square seal from Mohenjo-Daro,[2] a six-pronged star, enclosing an empty space, expresses the terror and fluid mystery of creation. The head of a unicorn thrusts itself out of the emptiness, virile, arched, and alive. The enclosed space is the womb, the vessel of energy, from which life becomes manifest. The spaces created by the arms of the six-limbed form are fluid, suggesting the expanding and contracting of a live organism. The resemblance to a starfish and to sea forms is marked. The seal is a *maṇḍala* of supreme magic, a paradigm that reveals the circular rhythm of birth and dissolution and the awesome secrets of transformation. The movement of the Eka-Śriṅgī, the mythical unicorn, is against the sun; the head points backwards. The spaces around the arms of the circular form are crowded by geometric diagrams and mystical signs.

In another seal from Mohenjo-Daro, the Eka-Śriṅgī, the unicorn head, and the amorphous five-pronged star have completed the cycle, the magic of transformation. Six animal heads, taut with the energy of new birth, have replaced the fluid arms of the earlier receptacle. From the sea forms have been born the animals of the land. The heads of the animals are swept backwards by the release of powerful energies in a movement against the sun. The animals depicted are male, the Eka-Śriṅgī, the first-born from the chaos of space, then the bull, the antlered stag, the tiger, and two animals whose heads are broken and cannot be identified. The arched necks of the animals are deeply grooved with marks of a continuous spiral. The empty space of the earlier *maṇḍala* has contracted, having expelled the forms dormant within it. A serrated band, coiled like a serpent, looking like the transverse section of a seashell, holds the heads of the animals in an inner spiral and it is from this tightly coiled circle that the centripetal forces of birth, life, and movement operate. The spaces around the animal heads are clear and uncluttered. The circular form of the *maṇḍala* and the movement of the animals against the sun link these ancient amulets to magical rites, the *Yātudhāna,* aimed to control and direct the laws of nature.[3]

Marshall and Mackay take the first seal of the unicorn to be a sun symbol. The obvious connections of this to the second seal of the animal heads have remained hitherto unnoticed.

The deep grooves on the arms and bodies of some of the human figures and on the necks of animals etched on Harappan seals are suggestive of the coiling of wax on clay core images, to be found in the lost-wax process of casting metal, practiced by primitive *ghassias* (blacksmiths). In tribal Bastar, where the lost-wax process of casting is still extant, potters mold the clay horses that are offered at forest shrines by coiling clay strips around the necks and bodies of the animals, creating an identical visual effect to that found in the ritual seals of the Indus Valley.

A study of tribal cultures and iconography may throw some interesting light on the Harappan seals. The complex rhythm of life, death, and sacrifice is epitomized in a seal portending the ancient worship of the Earth Mother: "She who dwells in darkness whom darkness does not know, whose body is darkness." From her womb a plant springs, straight and lithe, with its five leaves upright and auspicious. The earth is the great *yoni.* The woman's body in the Indus Valley seal is the earthbound root, the fecundating source. The arms of the inverted figure are stretched to touch the knees as in the *yogāsanas* (*yoga* postures). The rampant tigers, guardians of initiation, protect the mysteries and the immense magic of creation. The tigers are separated from the Earth Mother by the Indus Valley script, a *mantra* or *dhāriṇī* of protection.

On the reverse of the seal is a figure who sits with streaming hair and arms upraised, while a figure holding a knife and a cup approaches.[4] Is this the moment of death, of human sacrifice to propitiate the Earth Mother? Significantly the identical script appears on both sides of the seal, connecting the two rituals of death and birth. Blood sacrifice and dismemberment to propitiate the Earth Goddess and to ensure fertility is ancient magic, prevalent in primitive societies. Blood fecundates the earth and through a magical process of alchemy transforms it into rain and food. "At first god offered man as victim. When he was offered up the sacrificial essence went out of him and entered into the horse. The horse was offered up and the essence entered the ox." In turn the ox, the sheep, and the goat are offered, and the potent essence leaves them. When the goat is offered, the essence enters the earth. "They searched the earth by digging and they found the essence in rice and barley."[5]

Among the Khonds of Orissa, in the Marriah sacrifices to Tari Pennu, the Earth Mother, pieces of the human victim were spread over the fields to ensure a rich harvest. It was only then that the golden turmeric was planted. Human sacrifice appears to have existed among the Oraons, where the goddess is named Anna Kaurī. In Kalahandi, in Orissa, a lamb was substituted for a human victim, and pieces of the animal were distributed and buried in the fields.

The Baigas, a tribe in central India, who consider themselves the first-born of the earth, are magicians with powerful fertility spells. An ancient Baiga myth recounts the descent of Annadai, she of the essence of seed, from the abode of the gods to the earth, for the enjoyment of men.

Now as she stood there on the earth,
leaves sprouted from her,
like the leaves of a wheat field.[6]

Seeing her, the Baigas came running, they caught her and shook her, and the grain fell on the earth. Then they began to sow her in their *bewar,* and the people sang, "Let the drums sound for joy. Let there be no hunger or thirst anywhere." The *kathā* unfolds. Thakur Dev, the Baiga *kṣetrapāla,* guardian of fields and boundaries, demands human sacrifice.

> Then Annadai grew strong and fat in that Baiga's field. When she was ripe, twelve men had to be brought to cut her down. They worked for eight nights and nine days, and when the work was done, the goat and the pig were killed. A little was offered to Dhartī Mātā (the Mother Earth) and the rest was cooked and eaten. Then when all was over, they started to carry the grain to the house. But Thakur Dev was angry because they had forgotten to give him any offering, and he brought all the chaff back on to the threshing floor and said, "I will not remove it till you sacrifice to me." The Baiga said that he would give his first-born child if Thakur Dev would remove it. Then Thakur Dev called for Pawan Deserī, and he blew all the chaff away. The Baiga brought his son and made him sit in the midst of the threshing-floor, by the pillar, and Thakur Dev came in with his bow and arrow and shot the child. The boy died there in the place where he was sitting. When the villagers came and saw the boy dead, they all began to weep. They carried his body to the jungle and burnt it on a pile of wood.[7]

Sacrifices to the earth were performed at the main solstice rites to awaken the Earth Mother, the *mahāvrata,* in autumn after the rains and in the spring after the harvest. In time, human and animal sacrifices to the goddess were replaced by offerings of metal and clay images in the ancient rites of fertility. Archaic memories of human and animal sacrifices to the earth also appear during *navarātra,* the nine nights of the bright half of the moon that are sacred to the goddess. During *navarātra,* women plant corn in baskets or pots, symbolic of the body of the goddess. The corn sprouts arkness, and the pale golden shoots are worshiped for nine nights and then consigned to the waters. These rituals are found in peasant, tribal, and urban societies. Among the tribes of central India, the corn seed is sown by the daughters of the headman, in sandy soil mixed with a quantity of turmeric. When the blades sprout and unfold, they are pale yellow. In autumn, the sprouted corn is taken up by the roots and carried in baskets to the open meeting place of the village. A *karma* tree is worshiped and the sprouted blades distributed among young unmarried boys and girls.

The best known seal of the Harappan culture is the famed buffalo-horned figure identified as the earliest representation of Śiva Mahādeva, in his form as Paśupati, lord of the animals.[8] A hymn to the thousand-eyed Rudra in *Atharva Veda* assigns to him the forest animals, the wild beasts, the birds, and the cattle.[9] The figure in the Harappan seal is ithyphallic, sitting cross-legged and wide-armed in the *yogic padmāsana.* The image has been described as having three faces, but a microscopic examination fails to reveal this. On the face of the seated figure is a mask, covering and projecting sideways, reminiscent of *kathākalī* masks. On the head rests a pair of wide buffalo horns, between which projects a vertical shaft, previously identified as sprouting corn or matted hair. The body and arms of the figure, as well as the mask that covers the face, are marked with bands, a treatment which creates a taut, continuous spiral—suggesting the coiled dynamism of contained energy and also providing an enclosing breastplate of protection. The still body of the *yogī* establishes the expanding field of luminous listening. A process of osmosis permits the world of plant and animal to enter and flows through the silent form. The arms of the image, pointing towards the earth, the *yogic* nature of the wide-lapped stance and the curving horns transmit power and establish equilibrium. Natural enemies, wild and virile animals, the buffalo, the leaping tiger, the rhinoceros, and the elephant surround the seated figure, their bodies transfixed by the powerful magnetic forces that emanate from the figure, seated in supreme equipoise. The undeciphered script is arranged horizontally over the headdress, crowding space and suggesting the denseness of forest. Is this Eka Vrātya, familiar from the *Atharva Veda,* seated wide-lapped on his sacral seat, who by his inbreathings and outbreathings created the universe?

In another seal, the horned figure appears seated on the stool of divinity, guarded by two serpents with flaring hoods.[10] A comparison of the headdress of the horned *yogī* with tribesmen of central India, the bison-horned Maria of Bastar, reveals astonishing similarities. Both have identically balanced buffalo horns between which projects an elaborate peacock feather ornament. In the wood carvings of the Gonds of Bastar, dancers with drums are depicted wearing the horns of divinity with the peacock feather. In other wood carvings, the horns are placed alone to suggest the sacred presence. Buffalo-headed theriomorphic menhir figures made of wood are also erected by the Gonds of Mandla.

To primitive man, the wearing of buffalo horns establishes the sanctity of ritual. The power that vests in the ancient gods is invoked by the officiating magician-priest, who, potent with energy, in trance and dream, establishes the invisible kernel of power. This spirit or god rarely takes shape or form. It is the magician-priest, vested with ancient authority, who stands between man and the dark, terrifying forces of nature. Is it not likely, then, that the horned and masked figures of the Indus Valley are the ancient magician-priests, the channels of communication, rather than the numinous form itself? The absence of temple and shrine, the absence of icons in bronze and clay of this horned personality is significant and would support the view that these images represent the magician-priest possessed with divine powers.

In a seal from Mohenjo-Daro, a man stands erect, his arms outstretched, holding up two rampant tigers.[11] At Jambūdvīpa in Panchmari there is a cave painting depicting a similar subject. Here the hero stands erect, taut with power and majesty; out of his body emerge, on either side, two leaping tigers. The rampant tails of the tigers are held tautly by the magician-priest.[12] Are these also representatives of ancient magicians, who, like the Baiga priest, have special intimacy with and control over tigers, who have the power to summon them from the forest, to catch them by the ear and whisper to them their secrets, and the capacity to transform themselves into tigers at will?

The magician-priests of primitive man, the *gunias* and the *bhopas,* draw their authority from great antiquity. They claim power over the potency of bridegrooms, the malevolence of witches, and the ferocity of tigers. Their magic is derived from the original guru-preceptor Naṅgā Baiga, whom the Baigas name the first magician. A myth recounts Naṅgā Baiga's pact with the tigers, by virtue of which only he could bind their mouths. As the *baiga* (magician-priest) drives iron nails into trees to guard the boundaries of the village from the influx of the terrible man-eater, he calls on his ancestor Naṅgā Baiga. To do this the *gunia* makes two images, one of *pāpa* (sin), the other of *vanaspati,* the plant, the symbol of the Earth Goddess. He then calls on all the tigers by name. "The white *sheet-bāgh,* the horned *singh-bāgh, lataria-bāgh,* the hyena, *jalaria-bāgh,* the cattle-eating *dhor-bāgh, kowachi-bāgh,* the leopard, *bundia-*

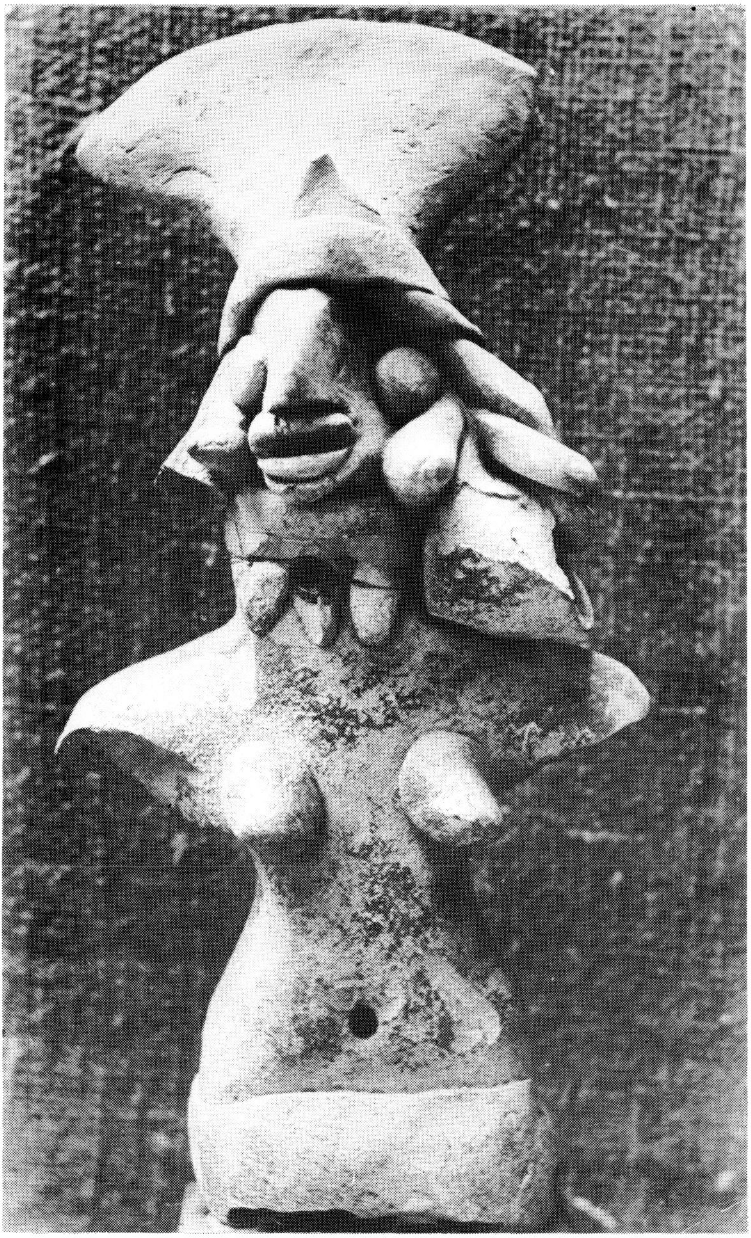

1

1. The sacred female with elaborate headdress, prominent eyes, and thick lips. The breasts are separately molded and attached to the body; the navel is deep. Terracotta, Harappa, 3rd millennium BC.

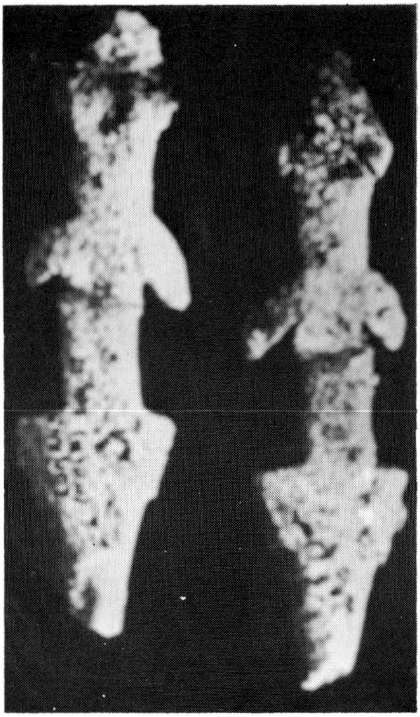

2

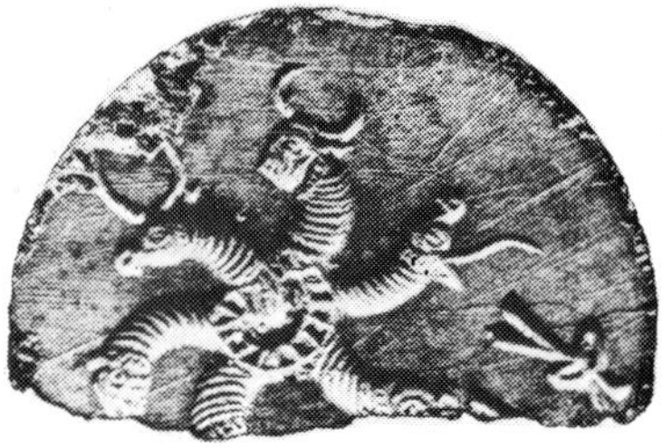

3

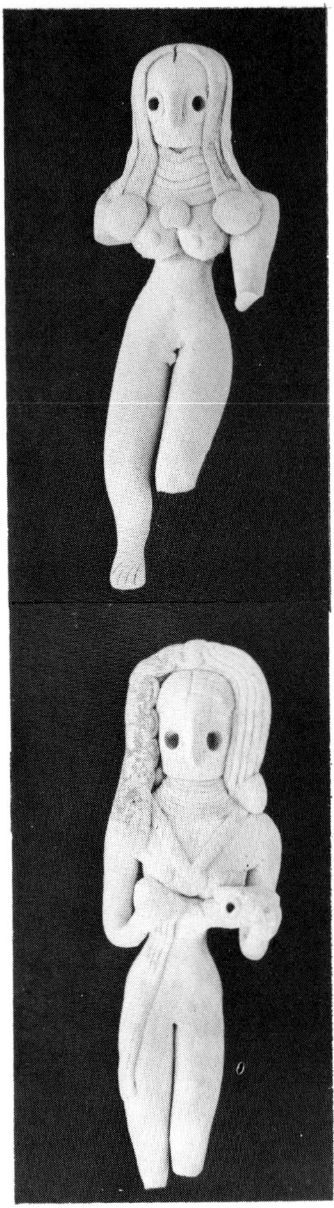

4

2. Mother Goddess from Bellan. Uttar Pradesh, bone, 18,000–17,000 BC. Courtesy: Archaeological Survey of India.

3. Six animal heads emerge from the waters of creation. The animals depicted are the Eka Sringi (the unicorn), the bull, the antlered stag, and the tiger. The remaining two heads of the animals are broken. Seal, Mohenjo-Daro, 3rd millennium BC.

4. (a) Terracotta figurines of the Earth Goddess, Mehrgarh, Baluchistan VII, 2700 BC. (b) Terracotta figurines of Mother Goddess holding a baby. Mehrgarh, Baluchistan VII, 2700 BC. Courtesy: Mission Archéologique de l' Indus, Musée Guimet, Paris.

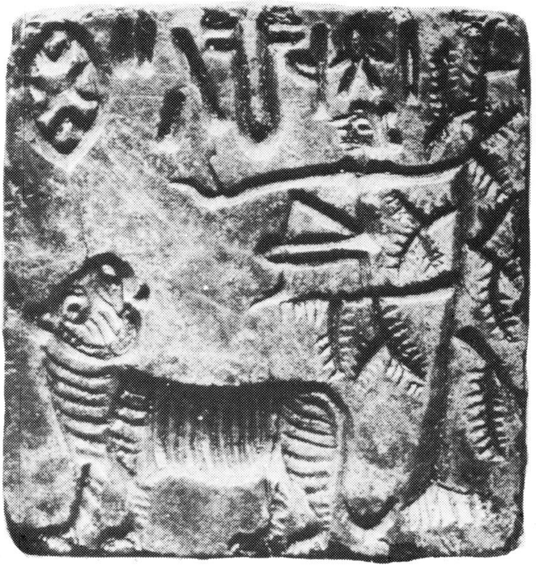

5

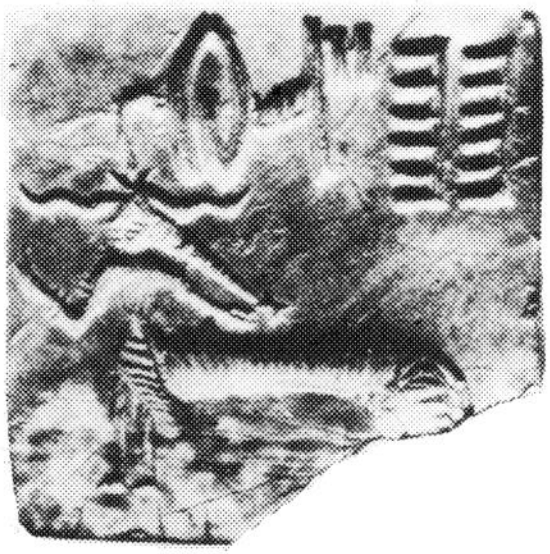

7

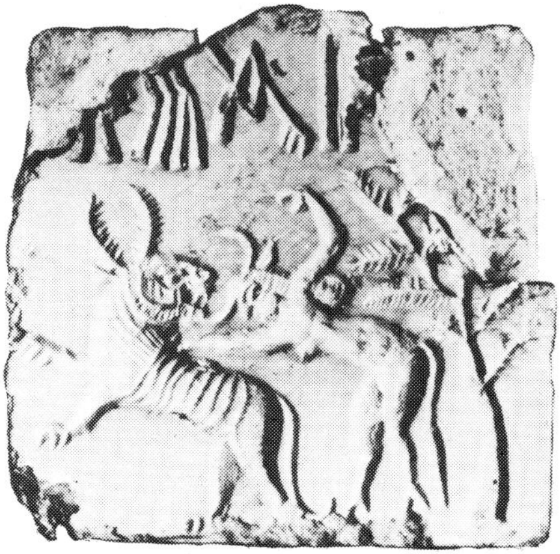

6

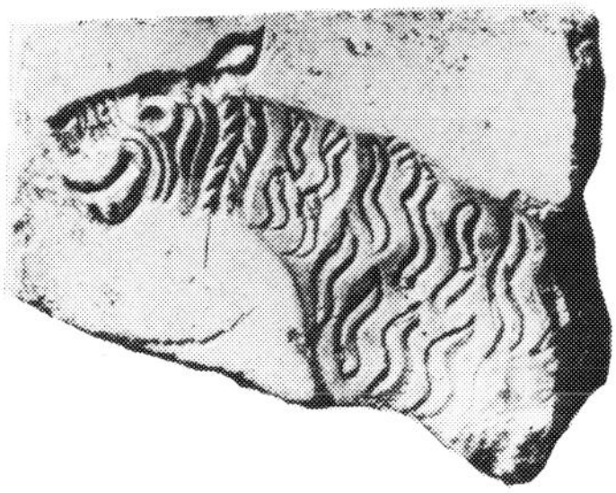

8

5. The mysterious woman, her body a tendril of the *sami* tree, summons the tiger. The first of the seals of transformation. Mohenjo-Daro, 3rd millennium BC. Courtesy: National Museum, New Delhi.

6. The *sami* tree, the half-bovine, half-woman, wearing the horns of divinity and the leaf-formed tiger with horns formed of the leaves of the *sami* tree, at the moment of metamorphosis. Seal, Mohenjo-Daro, 3rd millennium BC. Courtesy: National Museum, New Delhi.

7. The woman and the tiger united. Seal, Mohenjo-Daro, 3rd millennium BC. Courtesy: National Museum, New Delhi.

8. The tiger. Seal, Mohenjo-Daro, 3rd millennium BC. Courtesy: National Museum, New Delhi.

9. Stark headless abstraction of the blind Earth Mother. Terracotta, Bhilwalli, Madhya Pradesh, Chalcolithic period, c. 1500 BC. Courtesy: Deccan College, Poona.

10. Sanjhi relief of the dread Mother molded in clay relief on village walls in rituals to fertility, at the time of sowing of seed and harvesting of crop. The schematization of the forms to three triangles gives to the Sanjhi images a taut sacrality. The bodies of the divinities formed of clay jewelry, are virgin, the breasts tender; the faces are gaunt, emaciated death masks. Unbaked clay, Haryana, 20th century.

11. An abstract form of the Earth Mother. Terracotta, 2nd century AD. Courtesy: Victoria and Albert Museum, London.

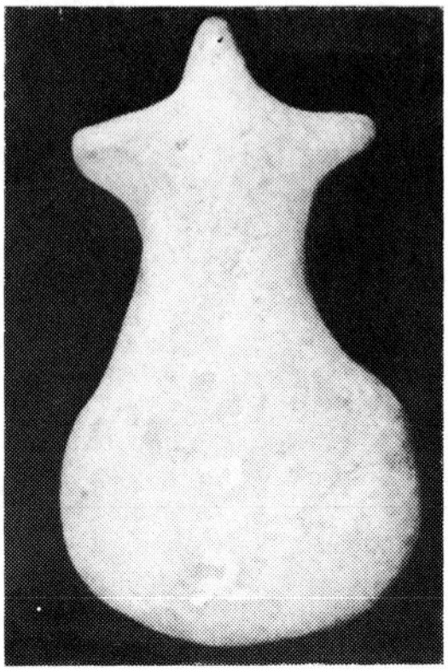

9

10

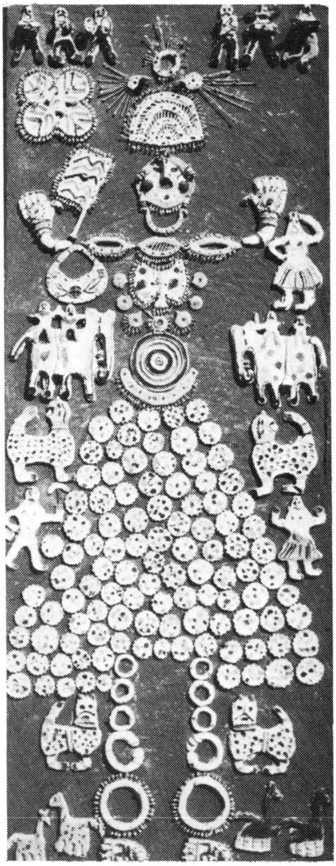

11

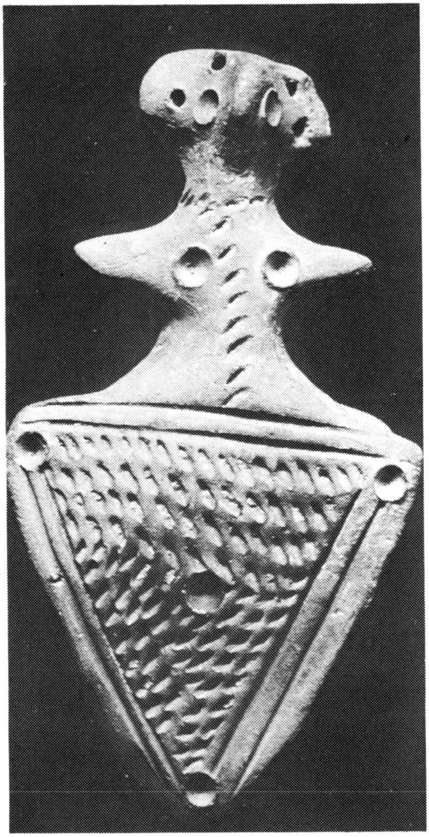

12

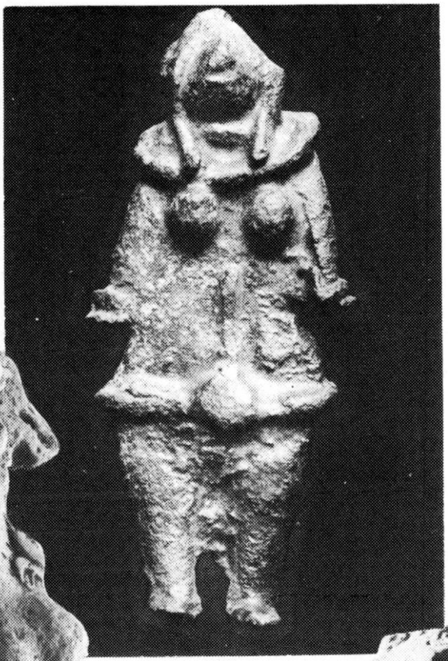

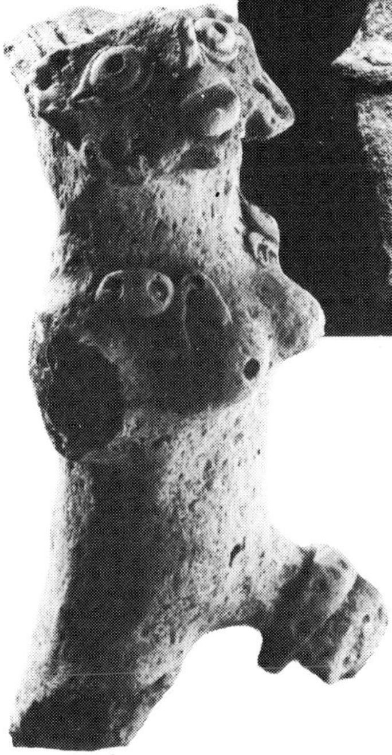

13

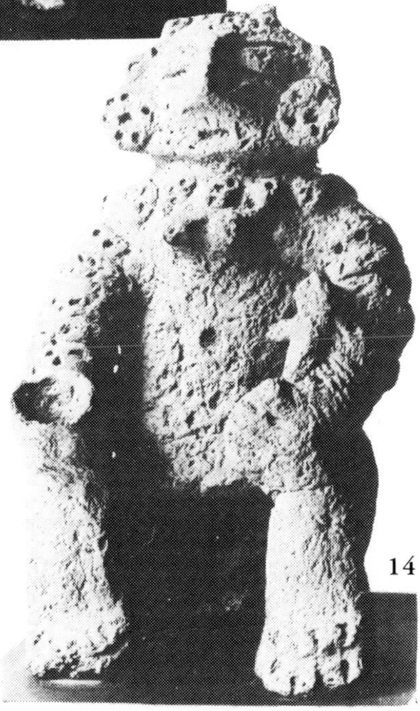

14

12. Image of the Mother. Bronze, late iron period (1st century BC), Adichannalur. Courtesy: Madras Museum, Tamil Nadu.

13. The Earth Mother, her face a grim contortion of terror, of agony, and the foreknowledge of death. Farakka, West Bengal, Archaeological Survey of India (Eastern Circle), Calcutta, 2nd century AD.

14. *Grāma devatā,* the village Mother holding a cup and a baby in her two hands, seated on a stool. The body is squat, the face broad and massive, the breasts immature. The toes point backwards as in all rural terracottas connected with rites of death and fertility. Terracotta, Ganges valley, 2nd century.

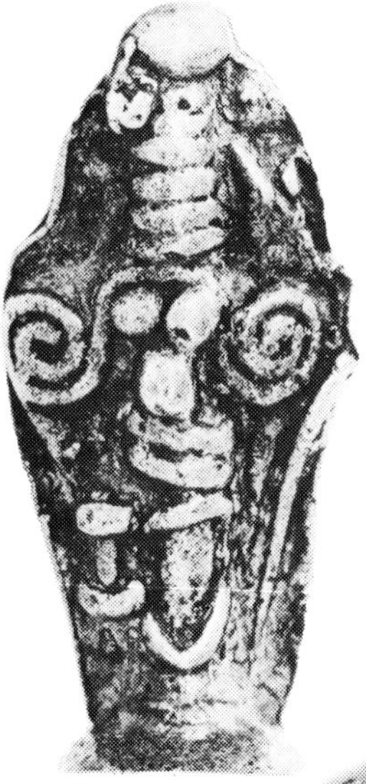

15

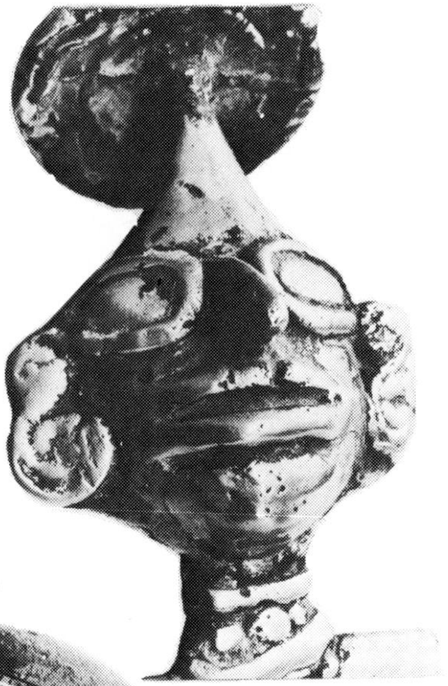

16

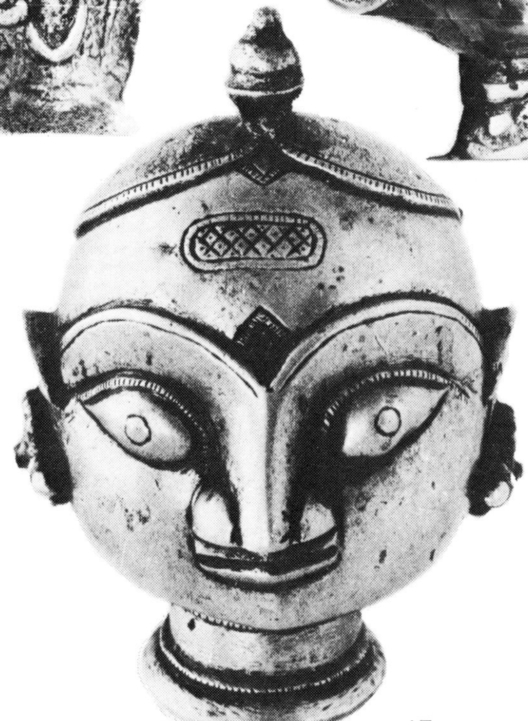

17

15. Bird-headed Mother. Her arms are withes of coiled metal; she wears a girdle, and her breasts are tender (ht. 6 cm). Bronze, Himachal Pradesh, 7th–8th century.

16. The Earth Mother. The face is massive, the eyes all-consuming, the lips prominent. Bronze, Himachal Pradesh, 9th century.

17. The mask of Gauri placed over nine plants that form the body of the goddess. Brass, Maharashtra, 19th century.

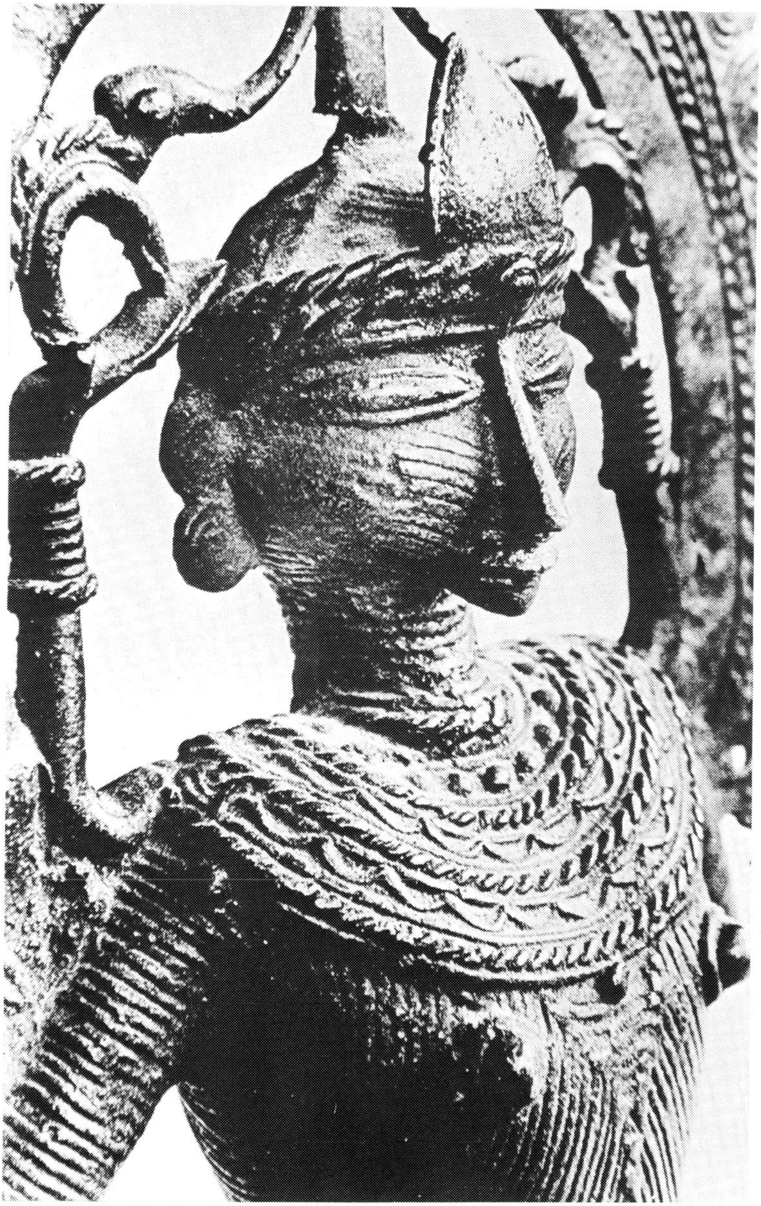

18

18. Gajalaksmi. Cast in the lost-wax process by the *ghassias* of Kantillo, Orissa, metal withes encircle the body of the goddess. The face with its pointed nose and chin and its firmly cast eyes indicate the hand of a great master of metal casting (ht. 18 cm). Bronze, Orissa, 17th century.

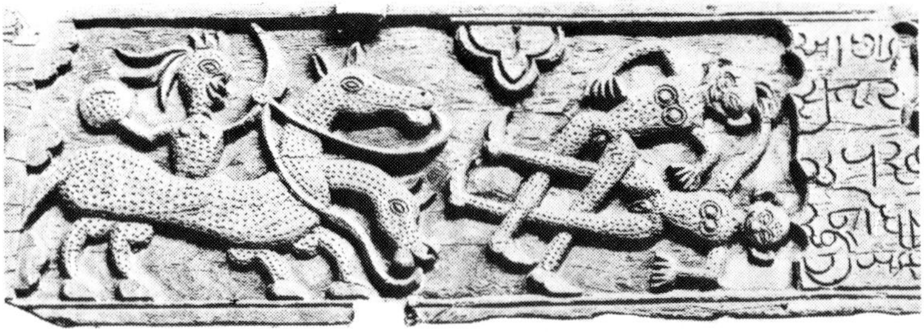

19

19. A warrior with sword and shield rides a mythical two-headed horse, while two maidens lie intertwined. The geometric form of the interlocking legs of the girls is of interest. Bhil wood carving, Gujarat, date unknown.

20. The nude image of the virgin *grāma devatā,* having tender breasts and a prominent *yoni,* is cast in the lost-wax process of metal casting with magnificent precision and command of technique. She holds the cup and the knife of the Grāma Devatā in her two hands (ht. 6.5 cm). Chanda, Maharashtra, 5th–6th century.

21. A slim shaft of metal, the *grāma devatā* holding the cup has the archaic face and body of the Indus Valley bronze figurine. (ht. 6 cm) Maharashtra, 5th–6th century.

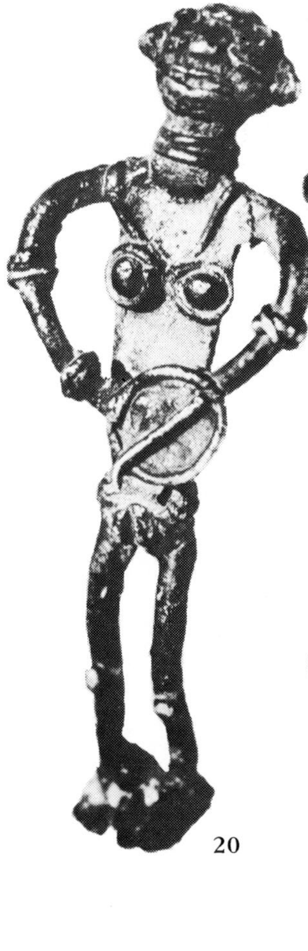

20

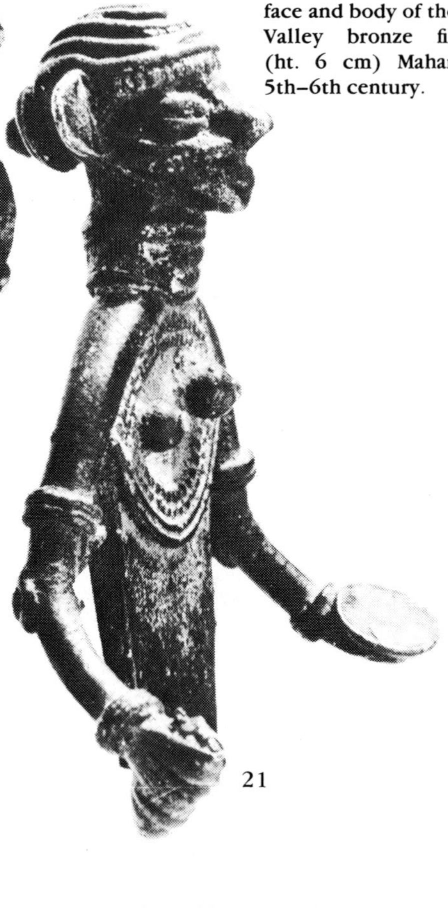

21

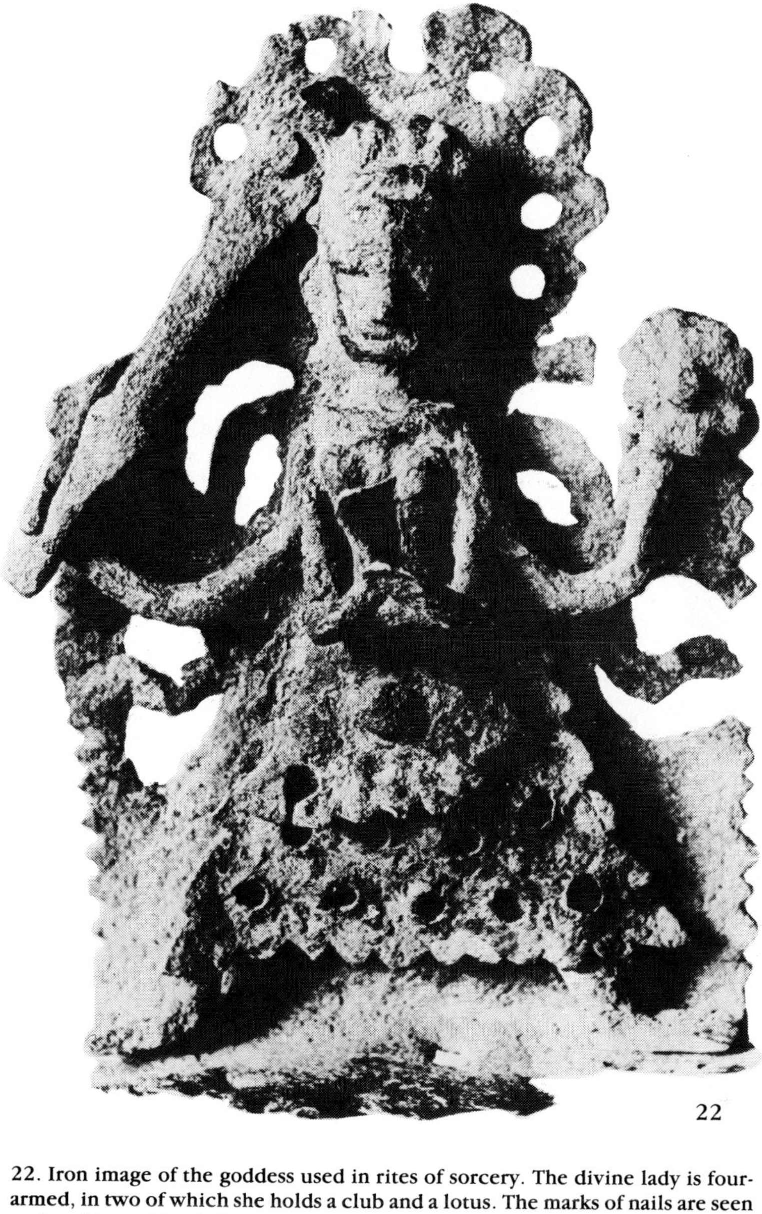

22

22. Iron image of the goddess used in rites of sorcery. The divine lady is four-armed, in two of which she holds a club and a lotus. The marks of nails are seen on her skirt and her halo. A nail is hammered into her waist. Iron, Himachal Pradesh, 11th century.

23. The boar-headed Mother sits majestically, with a baby on her thigh. Bronze, 5th century AD. Courtesy: Allahabad Museum.

24. Mhālsā, the malevolent divinity, the consort of Khandobā, appears in swift movement. Her body creates a focus of surcharged energy; plants cluster around her body; and her hands are tender leaves. A dog accompanies the leaf-formed Mother. Silver amulet, Maharashtra, 17th century.

25. Vārāhī, the boar-headed goddess holding plants in her two hands. Silver amulet, 17th century.

26. The goddess, her body formed of leaves, riding a tiger. The long-armed gesture of the sacred body is reminiscent of the Harappan seal (see illus. 5). Silver amulet, Nasik, 17th century.

27. The *sapt apsarā,* the seven water maidens worshiped at times of drought. The eighth figure is male and represents Skanda. The bodies of the virgins are formed of a single leaf and plants spring from their heads. Silver amulet (ht. 2 cm), Maharashtra, 18th century.

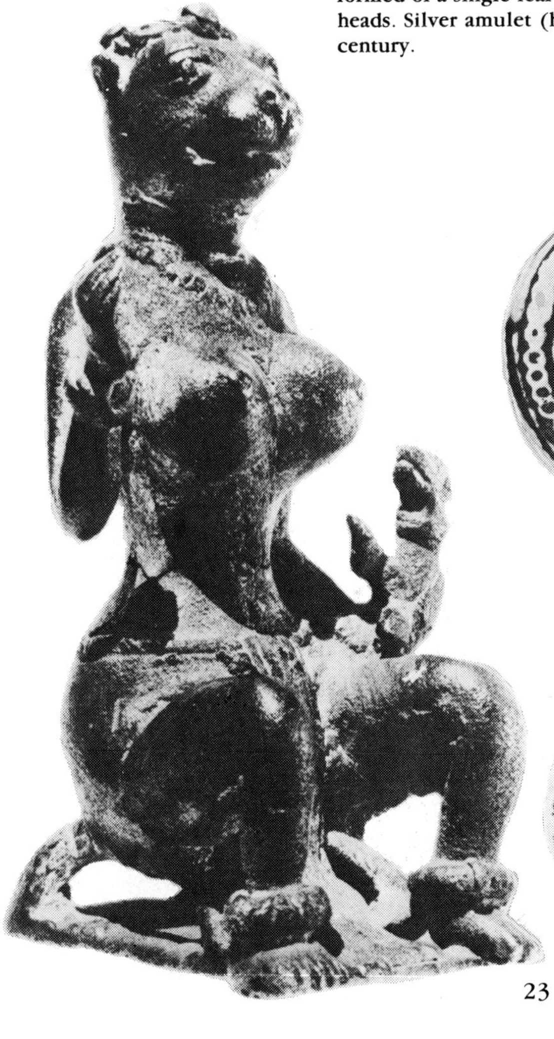

23

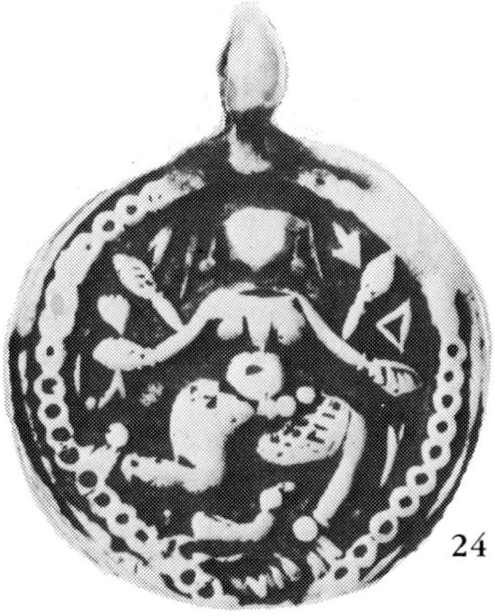

24

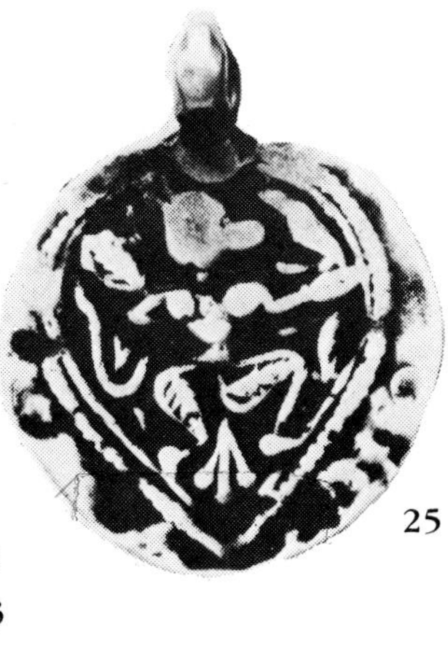

25

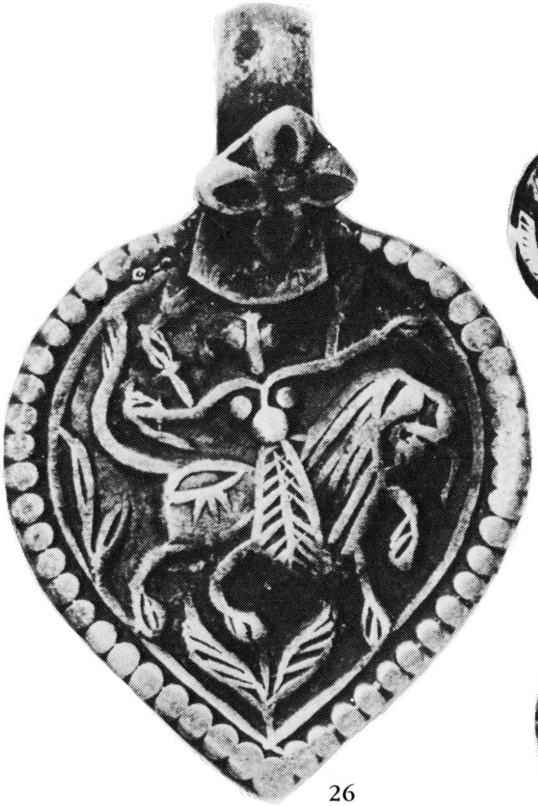

26

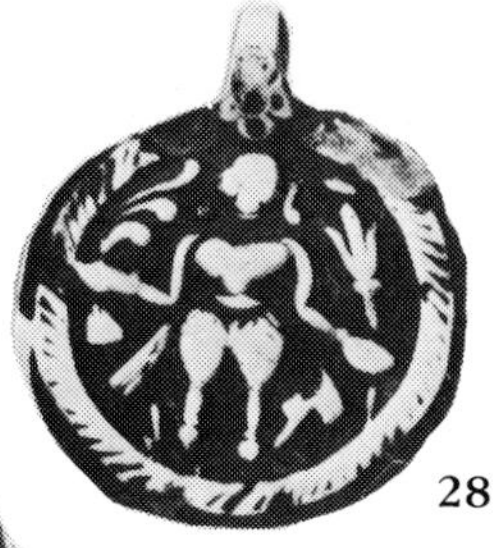

28

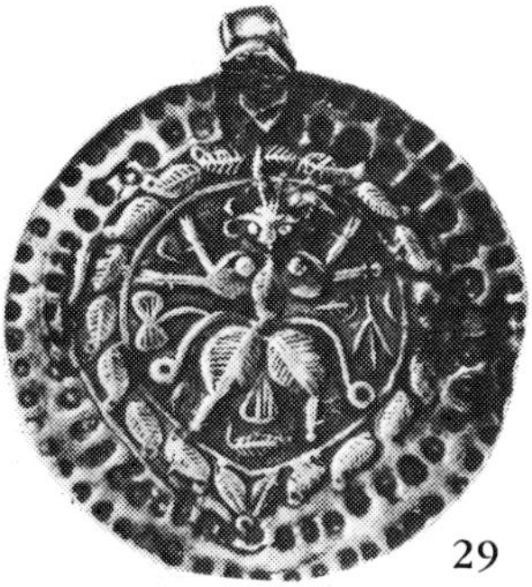

29

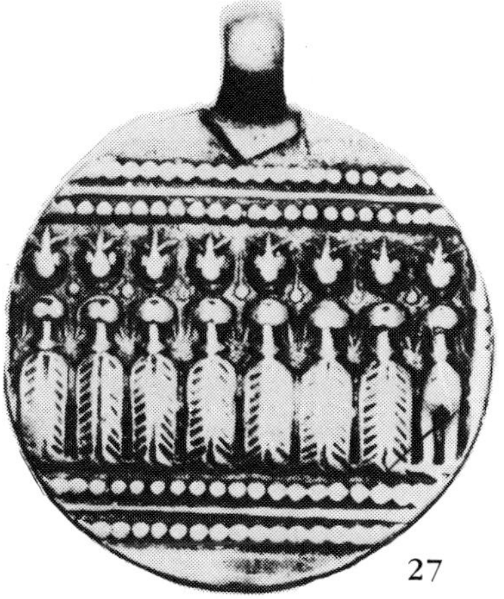

27

28. Kansari, the corn goddess, holding sheafs of grain in her hands. Silver amulet, Maharashtra, 17th century.

29. A circular punch-marked amulet with an archaic image of Mhālsā. She is born of living plants, two leaves form her thighs; one leaf is her torso. Tendrils and buds sprout from her body and form her slender legs and four arms. The face is primeval, the eyes ablaze with exploding energy. A leaf-formed dog rests at her feet. An aureole of leaf-formed animals encircle the Sakti, she who is the elemental energy inherent in plants, animals, and growing things. Silver amulet. Maharashtra, 15th century.

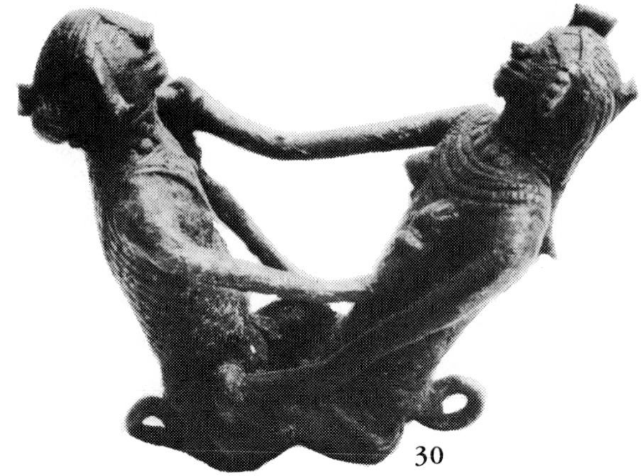

30

31

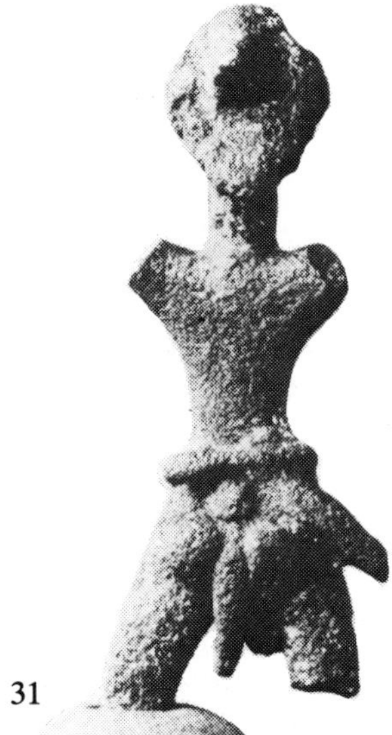

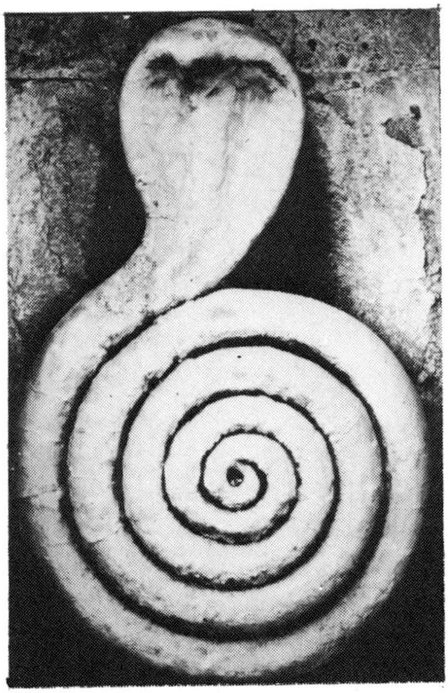

31

32

30. Male and female figurines in union. Cast in the *cire perdue* process by the *ghassias* of the Kuttia Konds of Orissa, date unknown. Courtesy: Craft Museum, New Delhi.

31. Squat, eyeless image of the *kṣetra devatā* with pendulant phallus. The arms are broken, a knife is thrust into the waistband. The torso and legs are molded to project massive strength. There is a thrust upwards. The stance is virile, heroic—the concept of the *vīra* is taking shape. Bronze (ht. 3.8 cm), Kausambi, 3rd century BC. Courtesy: Prince of Wales Museum, Bombay.

32. Gūgā Pīr in his form as a coiled cobra. *Nātha jogī* shrine from Tryambaka, Maharashtra. Stone, 15th century.

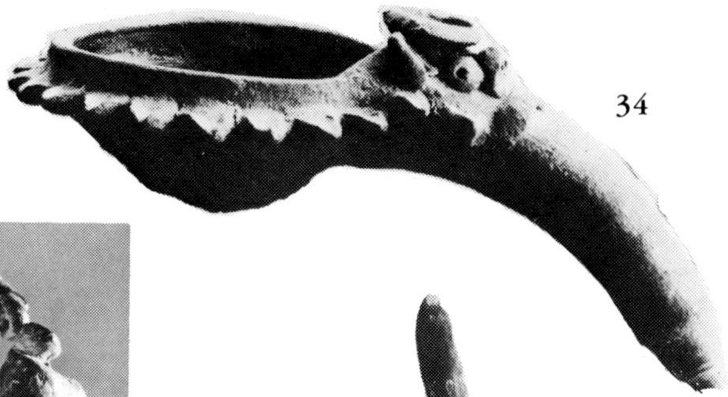

34

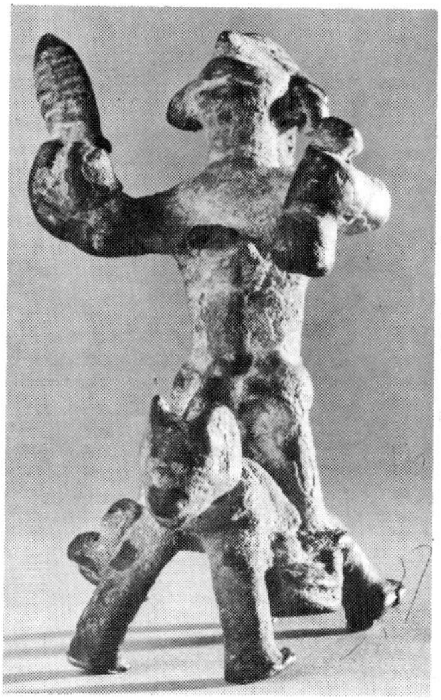

33

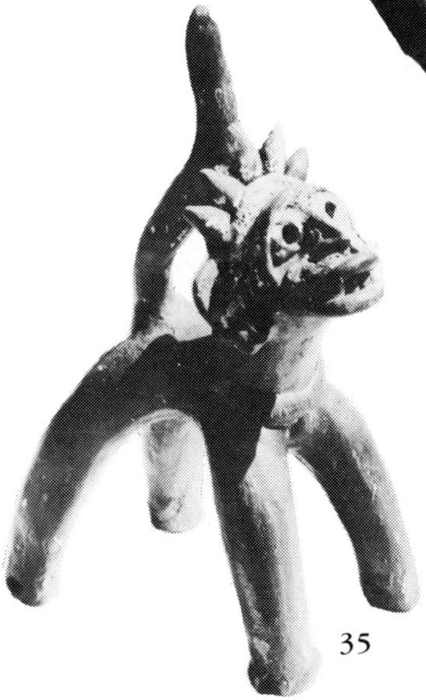

35

33. Kṣetrapāla holding the stick of fertility and riding a galloping ram. Bronze, Maharashtra, 3rd century AD.

34. Oil lamp used in ritual worship by the Muria Gonds of Bastar. Terracotta, Narainpur, Bastar, Madhya Pradesh, 20th century.

35. Hanumān, with prominent eyes and thick lips. Terracotta, Sonepur, Orissa, 20th century.

36. Roof tiles with hand-molded images of male and female monkeys. Terracotta, Potter Shri Manbodh Rana Sambalpur, Orissa, 20th century.

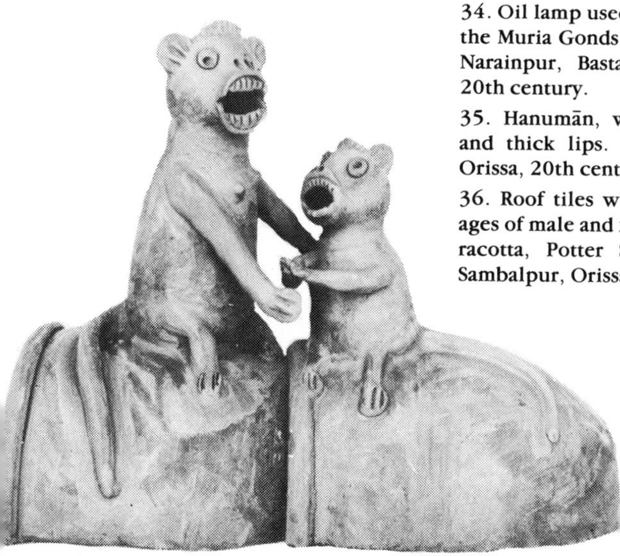

36

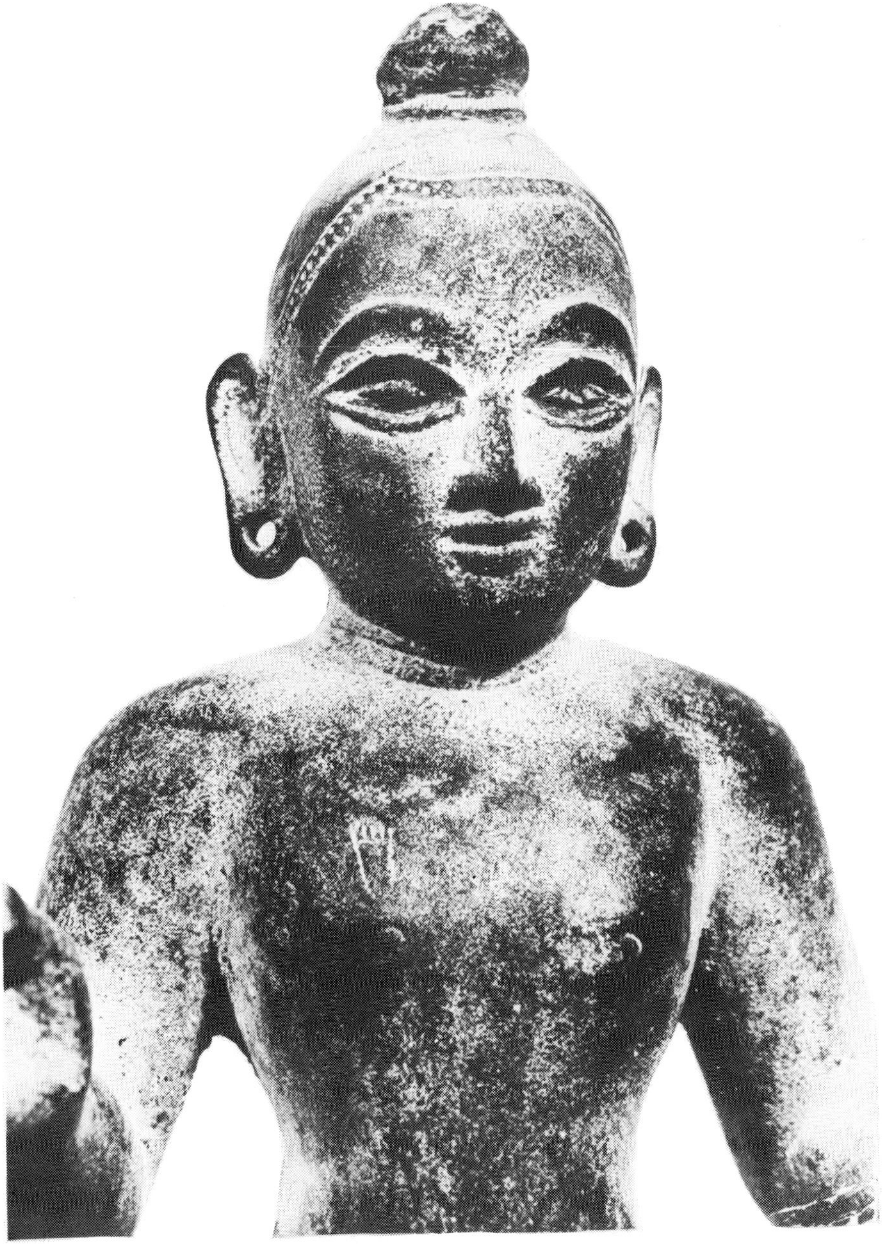

37. Kṛṣṇa, Brass, Bengal, 18th century.

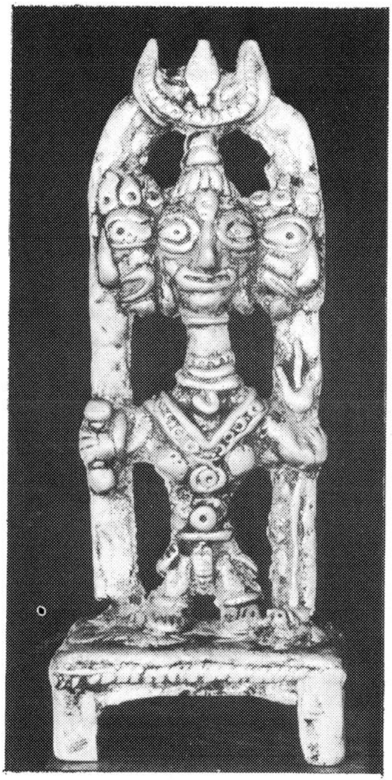

38

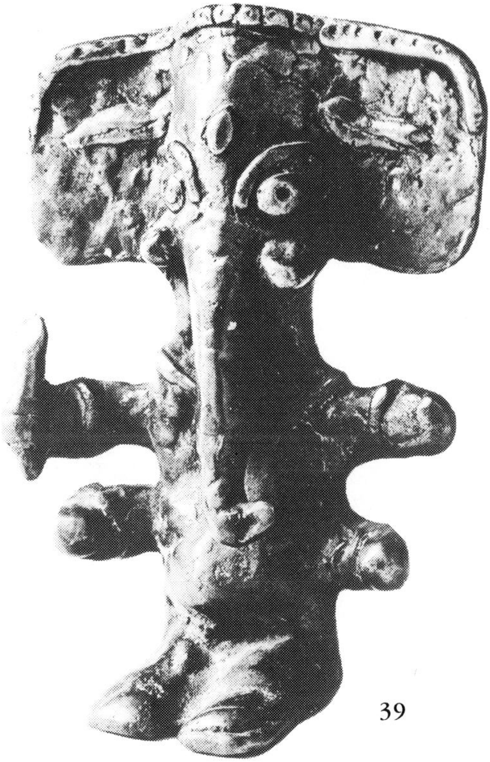

39

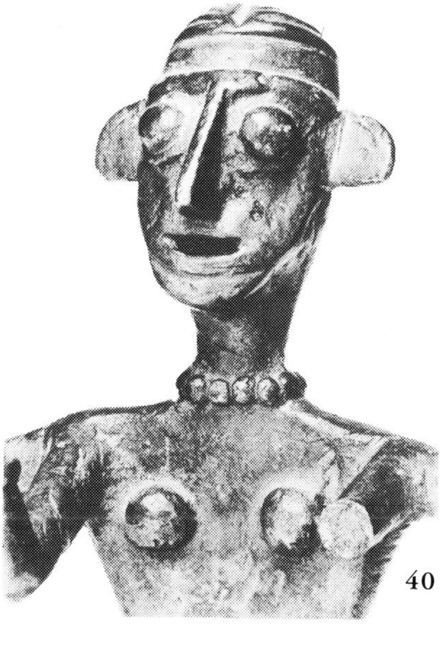

40

38. Śiva, the grim-faced, three-headed lord of the autochthones, with squat body, foreshortened legs, and two stiff arms that hold a trident and a *damaru*. The moon, resembling bison horns, rests on the head of the forest god. Metal alloy, Himachal Pradesh, 10th century.

39. Gaṇeśa cast as a male vertical shaft, in a pure alloy and hand hammered into shape. The eyes are coils of metal, the trunk accentuates the vertical line of the body. Himachal Pradesh, 10th century.

40. Kālī, black as the night of darkness, cast as a thin shaft of metal. The breasts are virgin. The face is lean and gaunt, open-mouthed, the eyes reflect the passionless gaze of she who is the Mother, the devourer, and protector (ht. 5 cm). Himachal Pradesh. 12th–13th century.

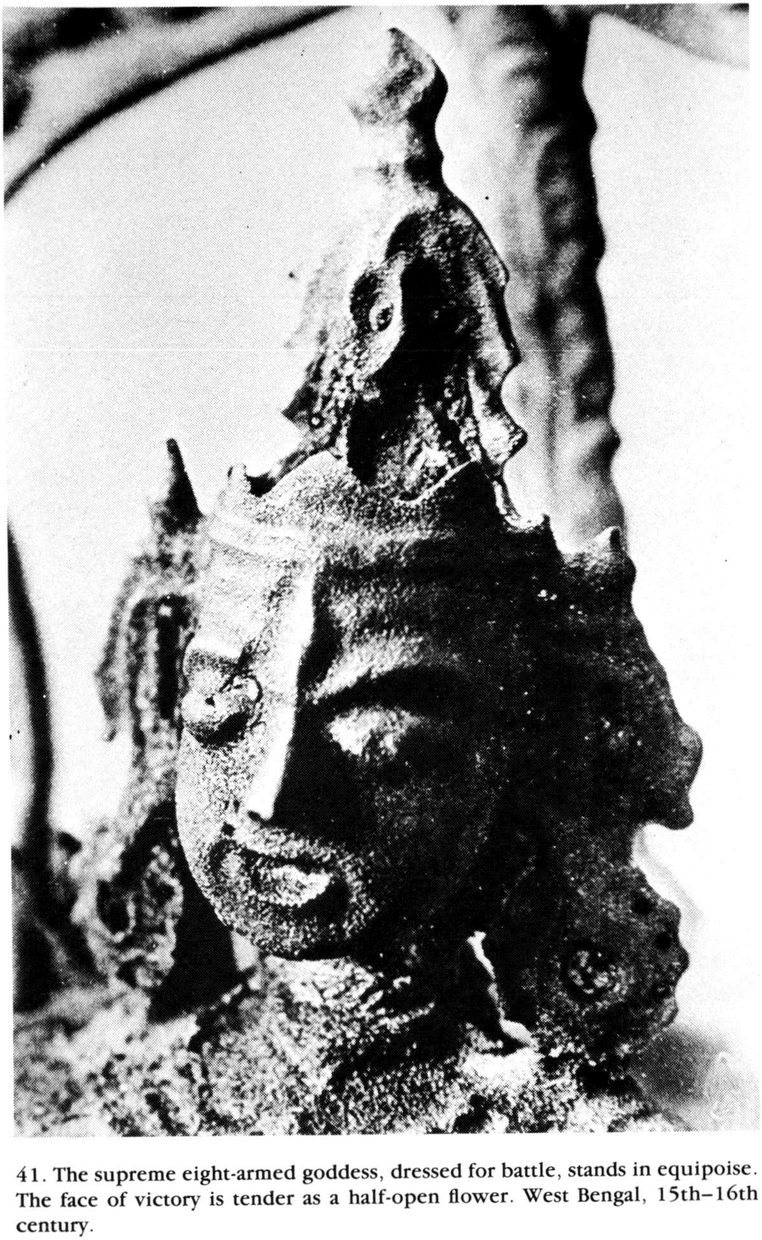

41. The supreme eight-armed goddess, dressed for battle, stands in equipoise. The face of victory is tender as a half-open flower. West Bengal, 15th–16th century.

bāgh, gul-bāgh, the small *dorcha-bāgh,* the tiny doglike *bhusur-bāgh, bandhia-bāgh,* the tailless *buchi-bāgh,* the small-eared *tajia-bāgh,* the magic wooden *khunta-bāgh,* the *tendua-bāgh,* the panther, *chītā-bāgh* and *son-chitti-bāgh.*" A man in the audience is filled with the spirit of the *bāgh* and devours the image of sin. The *baiga* then drives a nail into four trees to guard the four quarters of the village and invokes the image of *vanaspati* as Dhartī Mātā, the Earth Goddess, informing her that henceforth Naṅgā Baiga has fixed the boundaries of the village and made it safe from tigers.[13] The antiquity of these rites is manifest in an identical spell, an Atharvan charm, to bind the mouths of tigers. "The jaw, O tiger! that thou shuttest together, thou shalt not open up; that which thou openest up, thou shalt not shut together."[14]

The intimate relationship of primitive man to the earth, to plants and animals, and their use as catalysts for initiating the secret mysteries of metamorphosis, is evident in many of the rituals revealed on the Indus Valley seals. The magician-priests of the Indus Valley must have had access to the secrets of a highly developed plant chemistry and alchemy. The ritual scenes project a fluid movement and a free changeability of form and identity between plant, animal, and human. A ritual scene that repeats itself in endless variations on the seals of Mohenjo-Daro and Harappa is that of the spirit of the tree in mysterious dialogue with the tiger. One example shows the spirit, an *apsarā,* sitting erect, her body held in perfect *yogic* equipoise, on the branch of a *neem* or *śamī* tree. The long, linear body of the tree-spirit has no separate volume or substance; it is part of the tree and its branches. The arm of the tree-woman is stretched, moving out from the trunk of the tree. It has the appearance of a fragile tendril. The finger beckons; the script that projects from the tree-top suggests extended foliage. The tiger stands below the tree, motionless, in a still moment of listening. His head is turned to face the figure within the tree, to catch the sound of the rustling leaf.[15]

In a continuing dialogue with the tiger, the lady on the tree appears on another seal; the tiger, grown to the size of the tree, listens. Two people are shown tearing out a tree by its roots. They are bent backwards like bows by their exertion. From between the uprooted trees, from the lacerated earth, springs a figure, the spirit of the earth, young, naked, and lithe. The arms are outstretched, the hands of the two people on either side forbidding such destruction. On the back of the seal is a *maṇḍala,* a square with eight projections, or petals, in the form of triangles protecting the gateways to the sacred spaces.[16] Is this the *aṣṭadala,* the earliest form of the eight-petaled lotus? After this diagram is the Indus Valley script, a standing figure enclosed within two vertical lines and a kneeling figure holding a U-shaped object, worshipping a *neem* or *śamī* tree.

In the next seal the tree-woman has separated from the tree. The tree, in rhythm with the body of the woman, bends to release her. The tree-woman has undergone transformation and metamorphosis. The linear bodiless form has given place to a rounded woman's body. The virgin breasts are clearly visible. She is now half-woman, half-buffalo. Her head is crowned with horns, she has buffalo hoofs and a tail. The body of the buffalo-woman bends forward, one arm stretched to touch and claim the tiger. The other arm is curved and upraised. The great tiger of a thousand-fold energy has sprung into movement. A magical figure of powerful potency, he wears two widespread horns, but they are formed of sprays of *neem* leaves. His chest is leaf-shaped and so are his paws. "Tiger-like is the amulet made of herbs, a savior, a protector against hostile schemes."[17] The forelegs of the tiger are raised. The expression has changed, the listening has given way to action. The leaf-formed tiger roars, filling the rustling forest with sound. The tree, the buffalo-lady, and the tiger have established contact. They move in rhythm in that still moment of magic. The movement of mutation has commenced.

In the last seal of the series, the tiger and the woman have become one.[18] The tree-buffalo-woman retains her horns. She stands erect with a long pigtail, her arms stretched sideways, her waist curved indicating flesh and substance. From the spine, at an angle to the standing figure, springs the tiger marked with stripes. The massive body of the tiger has now assumed the fragile, linear elegance of the lady on the tree. It is the lady who lifts her head and rides the tiger. The tree has disappeared. Its place on the seal has been taken by a mysterious diagram. The mutation is complete.

The importance and power of this series of seals and the mysterious relationship of the lady to the tiger is revealed in a continuing tradition at Kalibangan, where the horned lady, the tree, and the tiger appear on a seal of almost identical composition and in another seal where the tiger and the lady have merged into a composite form.[19]

Nāgārjuna, the Buddhist sage and a master of alchemy, whose works were translated into Chinese by Kumārjīva in the third to fourth centuries, reveals in his *Rasaratnākara* the process through which he gained access to the secrets of alchemy. For twelve years, he worshipped the *yakṣī,* the mysterious female spirit, who dwelt in the *aśvattha* tree. When the goddess appeared and asked Nāgārjuna to ask for a boon, he asked for the secret of the fixation of mercury, the touchstone that transmuted and freed the mind and body from the ravages of time and decay. Nāgārjuna also affirms an ancient knowledge of alchemy, wherein plants were used in rituals of transformation.[20]

A ritual scene from the Indus Valley possibly illuminates the ancient rites and worship of the alchemist.[21] A resplendent *yakṣī,* wearing the sacral buffalo horns of magic, with a swinging pigtail, stands erect with arms stretched to the side, within the *aśvattha,* or *peepal* tree. The trunk of the tree is shaped like the *garbha yantra,* the womb vessel, wherein the ultimate secrets of alchemy were revealed. The leaves of the *aśvattha* tree are auspicious and uprising. At the base of the tree on the ground around the trunk a circle is drawn, the *Śrī Chakra,* the mark and altar of the goddess. To one side is another *maṇḍala,* also symbolic of the female divinity, a square, a *chatuṣkoṇa* (quadrangle) enclosing a cross. A kneeling figure, the magician-priest, the disciple of alchemy, also wearing buffalo horns, faces the tree divinity, in an attitude of worship. Before him are what appear to be ritual offerings. They may even form the sacred fire on which the magical chemical changes were manifest. Behind the figure is a towering goat with a human face and a garland around his neck. The magnified size of the animal reflects its importance. A fish, forming part of the script, is sharply defined and is placed above the human goat. The size of the fish is out of proportion to the rest of the script and within the fish is a dot, the *bindu.* The fish is a recurrent female symbol in the Indian aphrodisiacal tradition and was later identified with *bhaga* as the sexual, the female, divinity; the *bindu,* the dot within the fish, is the *yoni,* the eye of love, the mark of the goddess, a symbol of the female generative organ, the doorway to the secret places, to the mysteries of creation. The position of the fish and its downward thrust towards the goat, a symbol of the potent male, establishes the sexual nature of the imagery and links the rituals portrayed to rites of union, birth, and transformation. Below the main scene, standing erect in a straight line, are seven figures with faces in profile, with swinging pigtails and strange conical caps with streamers floating from them. These are the seven virgins of rural symbology, the vegetal and water nymphs found throughout India, the *sat sahelīā* of the northern river valleys, the *sapt kannigais,* the seven virgins of Tamil Nadu, the *sat asarā,* the seven *apsarās* of Maharashtra—seven forms fusing into a composite image, held within a single field, the water divinities invoked at times of drought, protectors of tank and water dam, the essences that make the earth fertile.

The quality of listening and of silence, in which sounds of vast forests are contained, is the clue to the woman and the tiger seals of transformation. The form of the tree, the long-armed gesture of the woman, the posture of the tiger, and the stillness of the wild and fierce animals of the forest imparts a fluidity, a dimension that dissolves barriers and prepares the ground for metamorphosis. The magical nature of plants and their capacity to initiate the spiral of transformation is suggested in the horns of the tiger, which are formed of sprouting leaves, and in the tendrils and leaf patterns that form his body. "He who wears this *parna* (leaf) amulet becomes a tiger, becomes a lion, becomes a bull."[22]

There is a Chenchu tale of a woman who turned herself into a tiger to prove that she was an adept at the secret rites of metamorphosis. While a tiger, she killed and ate her own baby. When the *mantra* to turn her back into a human form was recited and ashes sprinkled, she remained half woman and half tiger, the eating of human flesh having destroyed the potency of the spell. Is the half-woman, half-tiger of the Indus Valley seal an image of such an ancient belief? Are the vast numbers of theriomorphic images of composite forms of man and animal the expressions of magical acts of metamorphosis? The half-animal, half-human monsters, terrifying images of the unconscious, are deeply embedded in primitive man's mind.

Composite animals are motifs familiar to the student of Indian art: the *kinnara,* half-human, half-horse, the *gaja siṁha,* half-elephant, half-lion, and the *gaja mīna,* half-fish, half-elephant. Coomaraswamy, in his *Medieval Sinhalese Art,* mentions a Tamil form of *sarpa mūrti,* which has a lion's face, a human trunk, four hands, a lion's body, two forelegs, and six hindlegs. In *kathi* embroideries from Gujarat and Saurashtra, composite animals with legendary names are often embroidered along with the illustrations of mythical animals: the *gaja siṁha,* half-lion half-elephant, the *sāvaj,* the tiger with a human face, the *kesarī siṁha,* the *sonā no hans,* the golden swan with the head and beak of the royal swan and the body of a spotted deer.[23] In Orissa, a mythical animal, the *nabakuñjara,* is an auspicious symbol frequently carved in wood and cast in metal. The head is of Kṛṣṇa or a peacock; the forelegs have the form of human hands; the body is a strange, distorted amalgam of the bull, the camel, and the tiger.

Separated by five thousand years, an amulet worn by primitive people who dwell on the banks of the Narmada River depicts a woman riding a tiger. The body of the tiger and the skirt that covers the body of the goddess are leaf-formed. Plants sprout around the luminous, uprising presence. The arms of the lady are outstretched in the all-including sacred gesture of the goddess. The arms are tendrils, sprouting and extending from the trunk of the body. The fragile nature of the tiger-lady, the interchangeability of plant, animal, and human, and the outstretched arms embracing the cosmos affirm the mighty roots of the visual tradition. In Indian myth it is always the lady who rides the tiger. An archaic symbol of great power, it personifies the goddess in her primitive, magical form, before she is absorbed into Brahmanic theology and abandons the tiger for the lion. The symbol of the two beasts illuminates the nature of she who mounts their bodies. On the tiger the lady is potent with magic and mystery. On the lion the goddess is the benign protectress.

The tiger is not known to the singers of the *ṛgvedic* hymns; the lion does not appear on the Indus Valley seals. Among forest shrines of the Bhils of Gujarat, there is a wooden *palia,* a pillar in the shape of a two-armed woman riding a tiger. Clay offerings of horse, bull, and tiger are made to her. Her image suggests the *purāṇic* goddess Ambā or Durgā. The Bhils refer to her as Hurā Purā, the old ancestress. The lady astride the tiger appears also in several tribal metal icons from Mandla in Madhya Pradesh. In the *Matsya Purāṇa* there is a legend wherein Brahmā, pleased with the *tapasyā* of Pārvatī, grants her a boon. She asks that the tiger be chief of her *gaṇas* as Vyāghrapāda.

There is in Tamil Nadu a legend that Subramaniam, the son of Śiva and the forest mothers, loved an aboriginal virgin, Valli. To win her love he turned himself into a *vengai. Vengai* is the Tamil word for tiger; it is also the name of the *neem* tree in its male aspect before it flowers.[24] The association of both the male *neem* tree, as well as the tiger, with Subramaniam is of great interest. Are the Indus Valley virgin, tiger, and *neem* tree illustrations of an ancient legend, memories of which survive in the Subramaniam story? In ancient magic, the tiger is the guru of initiation. In the great birth seal, he guards the mysteries. In the Indus Valley pictographs, the tiger is never visualized as violent; he never kills. His role is protective. He is in communion with the energy sources of nature. The horned tiger is familiar in *baiga* myth. When the *baiga gunia* calls on all the tigers of the world by name, the "horned *bāgh*" is one of them. The tiger is a phallic symbol of the wildness and grandeur of the virile, heroic male. The *Atharva Veda* refers to the tiger as the first of all creatures. In Nepal, Bhairava is worshiped in the image of a tiger, and in the painting of the Maithil women of Bihar, the tiger mask covers Śiva's loins.

The Oral Tradition

The epic poems *Rāmāyaṇa* and *Mahābhārata*, *purāṇic* stories and legends that sustained the Kṛṣṇa myth, as well as tribal legends traveled by word of mouth through the vast lands of India. In valleys, on mountain tops, in deserts and dense forests, the myths and stories arrived, richly ornamented with the living imagery of tree, bird, and flower. Legends that permeated the landscape with a vocabulary of picture and symbol, using song, dance, mime, drama, picture, icon, and all other creative media known to man, gave to the participating listeners and viewers a multiple exposure to ancient myth and symbol. Legends established and recreated the myth, giving it contemporaneity, touching heart, eye, and ear, reaching the tribal man, the woman in village societies, reaching the lowly, the outsider.

The bardic tradition is an ancient one. The Vedic bards were Atharvan and Aṅgirasa, Bhṛgu and Agastya, Vaśiṣṭha and Vālmīki. Hymns were composed by singing priests, in which heroes and gods were magnified to dramatic proportions. The dread bardic curse, the *traga*, that gave to the Chāraṇa bards immunity from attack and freedom to travel the countryside, originated in the Vedic age. The Vedic bards attached to the courts were known as *kathā vāchakas* and *sūtas*. These were both the court minstrels and also the official chroniclers and guardians of royal genealogies.

Bards were known in early Tamil Sangam literature. The *koothars* were actor-singers who performed in balletlike compositions; the *panars* were associated with harlots. *Parunnars* were bards attached to the king and *viralyars* were female bards attached to the queen. The bardic tradition survives in Kerala in the *chakiar koothu* songs and dances performed in the countryside by Chakiar singers who claim descent from the *sūtas*, the ancient storytellers of the *Mahābhārata*.[1] These songs, mimes, and dances center around the worship of the goddess Bhagavatī. In the *Kudiyattam*, the Sanskrit drama enacted at the temples of Kerala, Sanskrit mixes with Prākrit and Malayalam in the story that unfolds through dance, gesture, and song in front of the worshipers who gather in the temple courtyard. The singers who recite the stories claim an unbroken tradition of two thousand years.[2]

The oral tradition was not confined to the Vedic seers. The non-Aryan *vrātya* priests of non-Vedic fertility cults mentioned in the *Atharva Veda* were the forerunners of the *jogī*, the *fakīr*, and the wandering mendicant. The image of the homeless, wandering holy men, dressed in earth colors of red and yellow ochre, with amulets and *rudrākṣa* beads around their necks, rhinoceros-horn earrings in their ears, ashes on their arms and foreheads, unkempt hair tied in a top knot, singing praises of god, behaving like madmen, dancing, roaring like a bull, making the noises called *huḍukkāra*, "*huḍu huḍu*," is to dwellers of village India an archetypal image of profound terror, potency, and poesy. The word *jogī* is derived from the Sanskrit *yogin* (magician or juggler), and the image of the itinerant mendicant encompasses many nuances of mood and meaning. To the *jogī* nothing is forbidden. By donning this robe he symbolically renounces the earth and its fruit and frees himself from society and its moralities. The *jogī* is he who is alone, he who meditates and seeks god. He is the magician-sorcerer, the *rasasiddha*, the master of alchemy, and the practitioner of the forbidding *tantric* ritual. He is the astrologer, the palmist, and the juggler; he is the poet, the faithless lover, the seducer of mind and heart. He is also the symbol of awakened man. When the *jogī* carries the fiddle, the *sāraṅgī*, or the *eka tārā*, he is a bard singing of the history of the race, of heroes and battles, singing songs created for oral transmission, charged with the intensity of perception that is the gift of the wanderer. The songs of the wandering religious men are vernacular vessels that contain the wisdom of the race, keyed to the mind and heart of the village listener. The *jogī* sings of *śūnya*, the void of the enlightened one, of *alakha*, the formless, of *tantra, yoga,* and *bhakti*. The image of the *jogī* as the magician-sorcerer, the practitioner of fierce rites, is a wild and fearful image explosive with power and conceived in terms of the sublime, the insane, and the irrational.

The Kāpālikas, among the fiercest of the non-Vedic Śaivas, claim: "The might of our religion is such that I control Hari-Hara, the greatest and most ancient of the gods; I stop the course of the planets in the heavens; I submerge the earth in water, with its mountains and cities; and I again drink up the waters in a moment."[3]

Of these non-Vedic Śaivas, the most important to art and literature were the *nātha jogīs*. The founder of this order was Gorakhanātha, a mysterious hero figure, a magician, a *rasasiddha*, and the founder of *haṭha yoga*. It is from the original *haṭha yoga* treatise of Gorakhanātha that the *yogic* images of the lotus and the *chakras*, with their individual colors, sounds, and numbers, also have their origin as abstract visualizations of *yogic* phenomena. From Gorakhanātha also originates the imagery of the *kuṇḍalinī*, the dormant energy of *yoga*, asleep, coiled like a serpent at the base of the spine, as does the terminology of the *yoni*, the female generative organ, the "eye of love."[4]

Legend associates the early life of Gorakhanātha with Buddhism, though his active life was that of a Śaivite. He and his followers were the main bridges that carried Buddhist *tantra* into the ritual and rites of Śaivite *tantra* of Bengal, Orissa, and Uttar Pradesh. Gorakhanātha was later deified as one of the incarnations of Śiva and was worshipped in icons wherein he is depicted accompanied by a dog. Numerous legends connect him with the spiritual and romantic figures of the northern river valleys, Gūgā Pīr, Rājā Rasalu, and Pūran Bhagat—heroes who at times of crisis become *jogīs* and disciples of the great *guru*. Gorakhanā tha is the mysterious stranger, the magician who appears in the legends at critical moments to revive the dead, to give the magic fruit that ensures the birth of sons, to cure the stricken from snakebite, to bring rain to a drought-weary soil, to comfort the hero and convert him to the cult of the *nātha jogī*.

Gorakhanātha's advent transforms the material world of the story into a realm of mystery and fantasy. The chief of Gorakhanātha's disciples was Gūgā, a Rajput, who later became a Muslim and a *jogī*. He acquired great powers over serpents, and in the legends associated with his name he goes to the forest and plays on the flute, while serpents gather and dance around the man of music and of god. Gūgā was deified and is worshiped as a serpent with an upraised hood. His images, made in clay and painted orange, green, and yellow, are made by the potters of Molella village in Udaipur and installed all over Punjab, Rajasthan, Uttar Pradesh, and Gujarat.

The *jogīs* of Gorakhanātha's sect included Hindus, Sikhs, Muslims, and women. The *nātha jogīs* were recognizable by their necklaces of white stone from Hinglaj in Baluchistan, by their bracelets, which had an image of the *lingam* with the *nandi* and the trident, and their split ears, in which they wore rhinoceros earrings. They cured disease, exorcized evil spirits, and practiced black magic. As the importance of the sect grew, great centers were established in western India. Total secrecy was enjoined around the *nātha jogī's* rites and practices—but the need for *maṇḍala*, icon, and painted image permeated their doctrines, and the monasteries became repositories of art and literature concerned with *tantra*, astrology, palmistry, and magical ritual. An ancient alchemic text, the *Rasaratna-sammuchchaya*, enjoins the building of monasteries, where the secrets of matter and the psyche were investigated. These laboratories were well-ventilated places with walls adorned with paintings of the gods.[5]

The *nātha jogīs* were great bards, and the many legends of Hīra Ranjha, Puran Bhagat, and Raja Rasalu were carried by them from village to village. Music, song, dance, religion, and magic intermixed with the appearance of the *jogī*. The legends, sung with the aid of a *sārangī*, were filled with ogres, giants, saints, *fakirs*, witches, and beautiful women. Magical acts and metamorphosis were natural phenomena in the atmosphere of fantasy generated by their appearance. Serpents, birds, mythical animals, and plants participated in the unfolding of the story. The parrot often was the main character, the friend of the hero, guiding him in his misfortunes.

In Orissa, the *nātha jogīs* carried the compassionate truths of the enlightened one into the Śaivite doctrine. For centuries the *nātha jogī* moved through the countryside begging alms and singing ballads and *bhajans* to the sound of a one-stringed *kindra*. The *Sisu Veda* was one of the earliest collections of their songs:

> Like the crane that does not disturb the water
> Keep thou thy mind and breath calm
> only when thou makest the crane and the fish
> the same undifferentiated
> shall thy body understand life.[6]

In the *aripans* and *osas*, the rural *maṇḍala* paintings of Bihar and Orissa, the silent spaces of these teachings find expression. The cosmic waters, the fish, the lotus, and the crane are frequent symbols. The circle of the *aripan* has a radiant completeness that expresses the mystery and innocence of the emptiness within the full.

The Bāuls of Bengal are singing and dancing beggars. They appear as god-possessed madmen who wander on the primitive village tracks carrying their *eka tārā*, their *gopī yantra*, their *duggī*, a kettle-drum, and living under trees with no belongings save a patchwork quilt. The songs of the Bāuls contain luminous truths reflecting a simple abandonment. Their songs are sung in the peasant vernacular, voicing the peasants' refusal to express life, love, and religious ecstasy except through the physical, sought in "the temple of your limbs." The demand for the passionate flowering of the senses permeates the songs.

> Release
> the sensation
> of tastes in your tongue,
> open the door of feeling
> lust and love
> and the erotic acts
> are housed in a single place.[7]

The songs are lush with imagery of the Bengal countryside, the roaring rivers, the wild torrential rain, the healing green of sprouting rice fields. A background of memories of Buddhist and Śaivite *tantra,* the *shahajiā* cult, ancient rituals of the *vratas*, and Sufi mysticism enriches the texture and gives direction to the simple inquiries of the Bāul poet. In the Bāul songs and in the tales of the *nātha jogīs*, the distinction between Hindus and Muslims grows dim. Hindus worship the Muslim *pīrs*, and Muslims, the Hindu gods Hanumān and Bhairava.

The bardic tradition was from the earliest times closely associated with the worship of the goddess. In the various Śakti *pīṭhas*, where the goddess was enshrined, the poet-priests chanted the *Chaṇḍīpātha* or *Saptaśatī*, the verses that extolled the praises of the goddess and recounted her splendid victories over Mahiṣa, Chaṇḍa, Muṇḍa, and Raktabīja. The association of the bardic singer and the goddess assumed many forms. In Saurashtra, the daughters of the Chāraṇas, the bards of the Rajput kings, were themselves installed as primeval goddesses. A legend of Bahucharajī, one of the famous Śakti *pīṭhas* of Gujarat, associates the origin of the goddess with a Chāraṇa girl, the daughter of Bapal of the Maru Chāraṇa clan, from the village Ojala, in Marwar.

Bahuchara and her two sisters were attacked by Bapaiya, a Koli plunderer at Shakatpur. To save themselves from rape and abduction, the sisters killed themselves. Bahuchara cut off her breasts with the sword carried by Chāraṇa women and pronounced the dread *traga* on the Koli bandit, cursed him, and prophesied that he would become impotent. Bapaiya begged forgiveness, and the dying Chāraṇa girl, realizing that the *traga* once having been called forth could not be recalled, advised Bapaiya to install her as a goddess and worship her image. Bahuchara also promised that any eunuch who would stay at her shrine, dressed as a woman, and worship her would attain salvation.

The shrine of the goddess Bahuchara has no icon; Bahuchara is worshiped through the symbol of the *bālā tripurā yantra*, the simplest form of the *yantra*, a triangle with the mark of the goddess at the heart, originally made of crystal but now of silver. The *yantra* of the goddess is a geometric design drawn to certain measurements containing letters and numerical digits on metal plates. It is a mathematical abstraction, a sound form made meaningful to the initiate. The *yantras* of the goddess at Bahuchara and Ambikā, another important Śakti *pīṭha* in Gujarat, are clothed in magnificent garments, the changing colors of which reflect the changing seasons. Ambikā, or Aṃbā, is a young woman in the morning, a middle-aged woman in the afternoon, and an old woman in the evening. The draped form of the goddess establishes her presence, but the form is empty and at the heart is the sacred diagram, the linear abstraction potent with power. The *yantra* of the goddess is rarely revealed to the worshiper. With the changing seasons, the colors of garments of the goddess change; so do her *vāhanas*, the animals on which she rides to victory. At the shrine of Bahuchara, eunuchs dressed as women dance and sing. Many minstrels attached to the shrine wander from village to village as singing beggars. The eunuch Bahurūpiās, singers, and dancers "dress one day as a god, one day as a *ṛsi*, one day as a milkmaid."[8]

The Bangaras are a sect of the Chāraṇa bard community, wanderers of the forest who, because of their traditional immunity from attack, have added trade to their original occupation of singing and storytelling. For centuries they have traveled from court to court seeking patronage and trade. They are protected from attack by the sacred custom of

Chaṇḍi—they kill themselves, then curse their assailants with the dread fate of being haunted by their ghosts. The Bangaras have been the fertilizers of tribal society. Penetrating dense forest and traversing mountains, their caravans brought the artifacts and the produce of the city to interior tribal villages, along with customs and rituals, gods and legends, language, morality, and songs and dances.

In the south, the bards attached to the shrine of the female *grāma devatās* were also the astrologers, the exorcizers of evil spirits. The legends relating to the goddess remain alive only in the memories of these bardic priests. The songs contain very archaic elements, details of which have never been recorded. The *malas* were the storytellers and priests, at the curious worship of Angalammā. The poet-priest, dressed as a woman, mounts the cart and accompanies the sacrificial animals being taken to the shrine of the goddess.[9]

The tribal kings of middle India also had an ancient bardic tradition. The Gond kings, who ruled kingdoms up to the seventeenth century at Mandla, Deogarh, and Betul, had attached to the courts the Pradhans, the official genealogists and musicians of the tribe, the priests and diviners, who, in time, absorbed Hindu legends and even Hindu morality into their epics and ballads. They recounted the ancient stories of the Gond hero-kings and warriors.

The Pradhan of today worships the god Bara Pen, present in his musical instrument, the *bana*. "As his sacred books to a Brahmin, as his scales to a Baniā, as his plough to a peasant, so is the *bana* to the Pradhan." The *bana* of the Pradhans is a simple fiddle, richly decorated with bells, peacock feathers, and balls of colored wool. The Pradhan singers describe it with ecstasy. They say that the wood used for the *bana* is from Kochi Kochar, the magic forest where gods and fairies live. The *bana* is made in the shape of the tortoise. The bamboo used is part of the maiden Basmolin Kanaiya, the beautiful girl who lives in the bamboo clump. The leather is from the skin of the Surabhi cow. The hair used to string the bow is from the tail of the great mythical horse, Hansrāj. The bow is the fiddle's bridegroom. "As when a man rides his love there is sweet music, so when the bow climbs on the *bana*, our ears are filled with beauty."[10]

The primitive attitude to the mystery of the changing face of the woman is revealed in a remarkable statement made by a Pradhan minstrel. "In the course of a single day, a woman appears in many different forms."

> When she comes out of the house early in the morning with an empty pot on her head, she is a sight of ill omen. In this form her name is Khaparadhāri, an evil spirit carrying a broken bit of earthenware.
>
> Within a few minutes, when the woman returns with a pot full of water, she becomes Mātā Kalsahin, the best and most auspicious of goddesses. The Pradhan who sees her then, is ready to worship her. He throws a coin into the pot and goes on his tour with a singing heart full of hope.
>
> The woman then reaches the house and begins to sweep the kitchen. Now she is the goddess Bahiri-Batoran, who removes cholera from the village, but when she comes out to sweep the courtyard and the lane in front of her house, she sinks into a common sweeper-woman. In a moment, however, she changes again, for by going into the cow-shed, she becomes Mātā Lakṣmī, the goddess of wealth and good fortune.
>
> Now it is time to serve the family with food and again her nature changes. She becomes Mātā Anna-Kuarī, the goddess of grain.
>
> In the evening she has to light the lamps in the house and now she becomes Mātā Diā-Motin, the goddess who shines like a pearl. This done, she feeds her child and gen-

tly fans him to sleep. As she does this she becomes Mātā Chawar-Motin.

And then last of all she appears at night as the insatiate lover who must be satisfied. Now she is the goddess who swallows her man just as Laṅkā-Dāhin swallowed Laṅkā in the flames.[11]

The *Apabhraṁśa* and the *Deśī*

By the tenth century, the city culture of northern India had been firmly established. Pāṭalīputra, Kāśi, Prayāga, and Ujjain were flourishing cities. Caste flexibility was at an end, and the castes were clearly defined. The Greeks, the Huns, and the Gujar invaders had been absorbed; the processes of integration of the Aryan and indigenous streams had been established. It was a period of comparative peace and security.

With the *Manu Smṛti* and the *Dharma Śāstras,* the germ of male supremacy inherent in the Aryan creed had established itself and had evolved the religious and moral norms and the legal and social institutions through which to operate. Women in pre-epic India had enjoyed a very free existence. With the new doctrine, Vedic learning was closed to women and the subordinate position of women in caste society was made absolute. In the post-Vedic epic, the *Mahābhārata,* Pāṇḍu tells Kuntī, "Women formerly went about freely, enjoying as best liked by them. They did not adhere to their husbands faithfully and yet they were not regarded as sinful, for that was the sanctioned usage of the time."[1]

Refusing to accept the rigid disciplines of Brahmanic authority, a people's culture of *tantra* and *vrata* had taken root in the countryside. A powerful, flexible, ancient, and secret undercurrent made operative through women, magicians, alchemists, and wonder-workers had emerged. The main *devatā* of these observances were the goddess and Kāma, the ancient yet ever-young Gandharva, lord of love and procreation.

Significant changes were taking place in the worship of Kāma. Among the most ancient of the *vratas* were those associated with Kāma. The god was worshiped through painted icon and image, with mango blossoms, perfumes, and sandalwood paste. With the spread of Buddhism and Jainism, and their obsession with the annihilation of desire, Kāma became identified with Māra, the magician-tempter of the supreme hero, the Buddha, and the arrows of Māra with the mango blossoms, the serpent-shafts of Kāma. The word *kāma,* meaning "phallic desire," became synonymous with the dark forces. The legend of the destruction of the god of lust by the *yogic* fire of Śiva's third eye symbolizes the physical disappearance of the face and limbs of the presiding deity of erotic love from temple and household shrine. Kāma became Anaṅga, the bodiless one, only remembered in the secret *vrata* rituals of women and in the saturnalian spring festival, the *holikā,* sacred to Kāma. The image and presence of Kāma, "the one, immortal, and indestructible,"[2] however, could not be annihilated; his fragrant face, his lotus eyes, his sensuous limbs, and his inextinguishable fires fused with the new emergent deities. The numerous *vratas* that centered around the worship of Sūrya, Śiva, and Kṛṣṇa reveal the subtlety with which the transformation was accomplished.

As the first-born, the lord and generator of life, Kāma became one with Sūrya. In the *Kāmada Vidhi Vrata,* the sun, as Kāma, was worshiped by women with *karavīra* flowers and red sandalwood paste. In the *Kāma Vrata,* women worshiped the sun as Pradyumna, the son of Kṛṣṇa.[3]

As god of phallic love and creation, Kāma merged with Śiva as Śmara, the destroyer of mind and body, and with Rudra and Hara. In the vocabulary of *tantric* ritual, Śiva and Kāma gained a common symbol, the ploughshare between two eggs •|• and became the presiding deity of numerous magical rites surrounding the phallic mysteries.[4] In the *Anaṅga Trayodasi Vrata,* Kāma as Anaṅga, the bodiless one, was identified with Śiva, as Sambhu and Śmara, and worshiped with colored flowers. In the same *vrata,* a picture of Kāma Śiva was painted on cloth and worshiped for a year under twelve different names, one for each month of worship.[5]

With the later *vratas* and the emergence of Kṛṣṇa, the ravishing god of romantic love, passion, and ecstasy, Kāma fused with Kṛṣṇa. The classical myths identified Pradyumna, the son of Kṛṣṇa, with Kāma, but in the development and acceptance of the divinities, Pradyumna faded away and it was Kṛṣṇa, the cloud-dark lover, the blue-black thunderbolt of desire, who inherited the limbs, the eyes, and the enchantment of Kāma. The *gandharva* lord came to be regarded as Kāma himself. Kṛṣṇa and Kāma had become one. The arrows of Kāma were transformed into the piercing sound of Kṛṣṇa's flute.

Holikā or *Holī,* the main festival sacred to Kāma that heralds the advent of spring, was and still is celebrated on the full moon of *phālguna.* It is a festival in which men and women, the young and the old, enjoy utmost freedom of behavior. Colored water and perfumed powder are thrown on friends and strangers alike, and obscene songs are sung with erotic language and gesture. A great bonfire is lit, and Kāma is burned to the sound of *mantras,* singing, and dancing.

On the next day Kāma, the god of love, is worshiped. A beautiful woman applies cool sandalwood paste to the image of Kāma to extinguish the fires. She then eats mango blossoms mixed with sandalwood paste, a delicacy sacred to Kāma. In later centuries the Kṛṣṇa-Rādhā madness took over the *holī* festival. Kṛṣṇa's name permeated the songs, dances, and ribaldry. Every woman was Rādhā, every man, Kṛṣṇa: "*Savariyā lāl tose khelun horī re*" ("O thou dark one, with thee I shall play *holī*"). Songs in the liquid language of Braja, saturated with the *raṅga-rāga-rasa* of Kṛṣṇa-Rādhā, were heard in deserts, on mountain tops, and around the village well. In West Bengal, the festival of *holī,* sacred to Kāma, was transformed into the *dolāyatra,* in which freshly-made clay images of Kṛṣṇa were worshiped and placed on a swing. Men and women swung the image, danced and sang in praise of Kṛṣṇa, and offered to the icons of the divinity *damana* leaves, the plant in which the bodiless god was made manifest. In Gujarat, at the *holī* festival, virgins mold images of Gaurī out of the ashes of the *holī* fire. In Orissa, the ashes are swept away at the site of the fire, where married girls make drawings with powdered rice. In Indore, Madhya Pradesh, nude, ithyphallic human icons are molded of clay, and the god of fertility is worshiped as Nāthurām.[6] Among the Bhils of central India, the Bhil god, Kāmaparvan, is married to the goddess Kājal on the *akhātrij (akṣaya tṛtīyā)* day, long before the sowing of grain. They make two wooden images to symbolize Kāma and his consort. After the rains the icons are thrown into a stream. In Karnataka, *holī* is celebrated as Mojin Kāma (playing Kāma). The images of Kāma, the god of love, and Rati, his spouse, are installed and worshiped, accompanied by the singing of bawdy songs and dancing.

Kāma as Hari Kṛṣṇa also became the presiding deity of courtesans in numerous *vratas* centered around erotic love. In the *Anangadāna Vrata*[7] the image of Hari as Kāma was worshiped. The woman performing the *vrata* of love had to give her body on a Sunday to a Brahmin who, when accepting her, repeated a *mantra* from the *Kāmastuti* of the *Atharva Veda,* whereby he was absolved of the sins of accepting the love and body of the lady of love:

> Whose gift was this
> And given to whom?
> Kāma to Kāma gave the gift
> Kāma is giver, Kāma is receiver
> Kāma passed into the sea
> Through Kāma do I take thee to myself
> O Kāma, this is thine.[8]

A vernacular language had developed in villages in the early part of this century. A growing rural population had formulated a young, alive, and urgent language that could contain and communicate the texture of rural sensibilities. The absorption of the classical, its quickening in contact with the complex rural subconsciousness and aesthetic, and its transformation and projection was the process that established the *Apabhraṁśa*, the *deśī,* the vernacular, that was to express itself through literature, art, music, and epic performance.

One of the earliest vernacular texts was a group of Buddhist *Charyā* songs that were written towards the seventh or eighth century by Śavara tribal poets, who were reputed to have been great adepts at both Buddhist and Śaivite *tantric* ritual. *Śavara Pāda,* profound with poesy, describes a *sahaja sundari savri* and her mad, god-intoxicated Śavara husband. The young cloud-dark, wildly beautiful forest girl, adorned with flowers, the brilliant feathers of a peacock, and *vajra*-shaped earrings, tense with desire, roams alone restlessly in the forest highlands, while her husband, the mad Śavara, spends his nights in dalliance with Dari Nairomani, the courtesan and the mystic Śakti of *yogic* insight.[9]

In another song, *Guṇḍarī Pāda,* the singing *tantric* master cries, "I embrace the *yoginī*. O *yoginī,* I shall not live a moment without thee. I shall kiss thy lips and drink thy lotus juice."[10] The imagery is erotic and physical; the eyes and ears are filled with sensuous delight; passion and love intoxicate the poet and the lover.

Kṛṣṇa is hardly mentioned in the *Kathā Sarita Sāgara,* a compilation of ancient stories, recorded in the tenth century. In this ocean of story, the Kṛṣṇa legend leaves no mark. The name Rādhā has not yet assumed any significance. The *Bhāgavata Purāṇa,* also recorded in the tenth century, does not mention Rādhā or Kṛṣṇa. The legends do not appear to have impregnated the life and thoughts of rural people. The Rādhā-Kṛṣṇa consciousness had not yet been born. Another two hundred years were to lapse before Jayadeva's *Gīta Govinda* exploded over India, transforming and quickening the Kṛṣṇa legend, bringing to the psycho-erotic consciousness of the people of India a new *rasa,* an ecstasy, born of Rādhā's passion.

What happened? How did Hindu society with its rigid moral codes, evolved from the *Artha Śāstra* and *Manu Smṛti,* permit Rādhā, with her free erotic passion and abandon, to be deified? How did the liquid sounds of Rādhā take their place with austere Sītā in the mouths of the peoples of the Ganges valley? This wanton Rādhā—dressed in wild yellow, the color of falling *amaltāsa* blossoms, who had abandoned husband and family to seek her dark-skinned lover, who sought him in forest and riverbank with a hundred nuances of erotic mood, danced with him in the moonlight in forest glades—how was her image of wanton love made the central theme of art and worship? How did Kṛṣṇa, the non-Aryan tribal hero, the young phallic god of life, become the prime deity, breaking barriers of caste, creed, language, and society?

Between the eleventh and the thirteenth centuries, cataclysmic events were to shatter the settled culture patterns of society in the cities of north India. Invasions infiltrated deep along the northern river valleys. Mohammed Ghorī and his generals penetrated to the interior of Bengal in the twelfth century. Iltumish laid waste the ancient city of Ujjain in the beginning of the thirteenth century. The impact of these invasions on the cultural life of north India was cataclysmic. The invaders sought political power, but they also attacked in depth the Hindu consciousness. Cities fell in the path of the invader; temples and icons were shattered; centers of learning and the arts were devastated. The sounds of the Sanskrit chants grew dim. Confronted by this total onslaught, deprived of the patronage of royal courts and religious endowments, faced with insecurity and destruction, traditional cultural life withdrew to interior rural societies, far from the invading armies. Saints, poets, painters, craftsmen, and musicians fled, seeking sanctuary and anonymity in forests, across rivers and mountains, to Mithila, Bankura, Saraikhela, Bhramaur, to the Maikal hills, and other oases where the hand of the invader did not reach.

In seeking sanctuary, an ancient and sophisticated tradition, classical in vision and direction, found itself exposed to a robust landscape, to forest tribes, the Baigas, the Gonds, the Śavaras, the Bhils, and to the pastoral nomads, the Ahīrs. Poets who had sung of royal heroes and beautiful women, of entangled relationships and romantic and sophisticated love, found themselves confronted with a free and passionate man-woman relationship, where the girl was innocent yet full of abandon, where she sang and danced and participated actively in erotic play, where there was a naked, laughing, joyous acceptance of the art of love.

O creator honour to Thee who didst create the folds
of the dress where lovers meet.[11]

And again,

The *kachnāra* tree blossoms by mother Narmadā
O girl, if you love me let me sleep with you.[12]

And yet again,

The girl whose beauty captures the mind
stands beneath the tree.
Her hair is all about her shoulders
She glances down the forest path to see who comes
Her long hair is all scattered on the ground
I am going to pick the flowers
At sunset her hair is all scattered on the ground
And I am going to pick the flowers
At bed time her hair is scattered on the ground
I have picked a lovely flower.[13]

Language was the first to reflect the new ethos. The tribal *nandan vana,* the forest of delight, the *madhuban,* the forest of honey, the cloud-dark Yamunā waters, the peacock feather in the *chelik*'s hair, the *dādariā,* the love songs of the forest, the *virahā,* the song of the Ahīr wanderer, flowed into classical Sanskrit poetry, releasing it from the confines of ornament, sophistication, and city morality. The tribal Kāma songs, the staccato sound of drumbeats, the sound of cows returning to the village in the twilight, the cry of the parrot and the *koel* entered the verses; vowels and consonants became alive, transforming the *chhanda,* the metric rhythm.

To create the Kṛṣṇa image, the lost face and limbs of Kāma, the fragrant *gandharva* lord, are fused with the dark, long-limbed *banbāsī* (*ban,* forest; *bāsī,* dweller) youth, the Ahīr, the Gond, the Baiga, the Śavara, with peacock feathers in his hair, his limbs alive to dance and song, his identity with the forest, with birds, trees, and animals, and his wild passion and his fierce love. A Baiga *dādariā* song evokes the erotic energy of Kṛṣṇa, the pastoral god.

He comes from the house as lightning flickers in the sky
His hair is tied in a knot on one side
He stands shining in the court
What is he doing standing in the court?
What is the boy doing? He is shining like the lightning.
He is standing on tip-toe playing on the flute,
He leaps in the air as he beats on his drum.
Come, let us go and listen to his flute.[14]

When Jayadeva wrote the *Gīta Govinda,* a Sanskrit love poem on the erotic play of Rādhā and Kṛṣṇa in the twelfth century he broke away from the classical interpretation of love, for this Rādhā he created was not the faithful, passive heroine of classical literature, who is wooed and shyly surrenders. Rādhā is the *nāyikā* expressing her passion through many moods. She is the woman newly awakened to love, the virgin, the desolate one, saturated with love's melody. She actively seeks her lover and lies with him in abandon in forest glades or on river banks. She is passionate and unashamed.

A surge of erotic energy impregnates the *aṣṭapadī* of the *Gīta Govinda.* The *padāvalīs,* the musical interludes, sung in various *rāgas* create the changing moods of Rādhā. The *Rāga Vasanta* narrates the love play of Rādhā and Kṛṣṇa. In the *Rāga Bhairavī,* Rādhā rebukes Kṛṣṇa for his faithlessness. The *Rāga Karnāṭaka* is tuned to Rādhā's misery.

There is an integration of sound, color, mood and meaning, rhyming and alliteration. A repetition of tonal words vibrant with color is used to give life and energy to the verses. There is an acute observation of nature, of mango groves and jasmine glades, of breezes heavy with perfume, of peacocks, clouds, and flowering trees. These erotic symbols, poignant with association, are impregnated with tense perceptive energy and made eloquent by the superb quality of the melody.

The *Gīta Govinda* traveled to Kerala, Kangra, Assam, Orissa, Gujarat, Rajasthan, Mithila, and Mathura in song, painting, and rural opera. In Kerala, Jayadeva's *aṣṭapadī* became the inspiration for the theater forms of *Kṛṣṇa aṭṭam,* the *aṣṭapadī aṭṭam,* and the *aṭṭa kathā.* The fierce, terrifying, indigenous art forms of Kerala merged with the tempo and mood of Jayadeva's verses, projecting the Kṛṣṇa theme through mime and dance. The masked actors of *kāthākāli* perform at the time of *Kṛṣṇa jayanti* at the Guruvāyur temple. These masked figures, often of Kṛṣṇa and Rādhā, reappear in woodcarvings, in masks and temple clothes of Kerala village temples, and, traveling to Tamil Nadu and Andhra Pradesh, appear on the temple cloth of Kalahasti and Nagappattinam.

A stream of vernacular poetry followed Jayadeva, based on the loves of Rādhā and Kṛṣṇa in Braj Bolī, Maithilī, Bhojpurī and Avadhī, Avahatta and Deśī Bhāṣā. It was a poetry tuned to the moods of love, evolving symbol, theme, and situation in melodious language and emotions that impregnated the consciousness of the people of India. Vidyāpati further delineated the moods of erotic love, in the *Padāvalī* written in Mithila, Bihar, in the fourteenth century. Rādhā is the central theme of the songs, the symbol of all women, delicate, tender, shy, wanton, and abandoned in surrender.

The songs of Vidyāpati continued to be sung through the centuries in every Maithil home and are one of the major sources of themes for the contemporary lyrical paintings that appear on the mud walls of the Brahmin and Kāyastha Kulīna houses of Mithila.

By the fourteenth century an important integration of Hindu and Muslim culture took place at the village level. Mullā Dāūd (AD 1370) wrote the *Chandāyana* in Avadhī, a poem that was to be the beginning of the tradition that produced the *Rāma Charita Mānasa* of Tulsīdasa, the vernacular version of Valmiki's *Rāmāyaṇa.* A folk version of the *Chandāyana,* the *Chanaini,* was sung by Ahīrs and became the source of the Laur Chandā legend.[15]

It was two religious saints, Chaitanya from Bengal and Vallabhācharya from Andhra, who in the sixteenth century took up the Kṛṣṇa legend and added to the erotic *bhakti* the dimension of ecstatic worship. Chaitanya brought Rādhā-Kṛṣṇa to all the people of Bengal, through frenzied group songs and dance, in his *Līlā Sankīrtans.* Vallabhācharya also did much to spread and extend the Rādhā-Kṛṣṇa legend. He came to the Braj Bhūmi and to Mathura and taught the *puṣṭī* cult of *bhoga, līlā,* and *sevā;* Kṛṣṇa was the beloved and his devotees, both men and women, were the *gopīs.* The rituals of the *puṣṭimārga* included *kīrtans,* community singing of the loves of Rādhā-Kṛṣṇa in Braj Bhāṣā, the *rāsa līlās,* the ritual dances of Braja, and the *sevā,* the ritual bathing and clothing of the icon of Kṛṣṇa. Kṛṣṇa, clothed in rich garments of colors that changed with the seasons and decked with jewelry of precious stones and intricate ornaments of jasmine and lotus, participated in the festivals, was placed on a swing, was put to sleep and offered delicate foods. Around this worship, a number of crafts—painting, paper cutting, jewelry, toy making, and embroidery—developed.

In the sixteenth century, with the Aṣṭachhāpa poets and the blind bard Sūradasa, a new erotic poetry came into being, rich with landscape, creating its own language, a juxtaposition of musical vowels and consonants, a vernacular of vivid word pictures. It established the *Rasavṛtti* of Rādhā-Kṛṣṇa that projected through *dohā,* painted picture and embroidery, through song, dance, and rural opera, the tautness of the cloud-dark Kṛṣṇa, as the *naṭa, nāṭya, rasika, kavara.* A geometry of angles and triangles had replaced the *lāsya,* the curved line of the creeper, in all creative expressions. This was to bring into language and painting the *tat kāra* of the *kathak* dancer, the staccato *bols* of the *pakhāwaj.* It was to generate pulsations of erotic energy that, in time, freed the woman psychologically and emotionally from the old classical canvas, and filled the eyes and hearts of people with rapture.

This love poetry of Braja Bhūmi, rendered in narration, mime, song, dance, and painted scroll, was taken by communities of Chāranas, Dadhis, and Rasadhārīs of Mathura to the vast countryside, where, in the light of oil lamps, in front of temples or at village *akhārās,* under flowering mango and *gul mohur,* the story of Kṛṣṇa was enacted, the passionate retelling of the legend, making it alive and contemporary.

The age of the monumental tradition of architecture and sculpture was over. The vernacular art of the *dohā,* the *nātya* and the *chitra* had taken its place. The robust and bawdy Ahīr legends, the *Mrgāvatī,* the *Dholā Mārū,* the *Laur Chandā,* the recitations and performances of Tulsīdasa's *Rāma Charita Mānasa,* in village and city, the recounting of the Kṛṣṇa story, created a new narrative visual art full of movement.

A transient tradition of the spoken word and song was in the process of being recorded through the written word and illustration. The *bols* of the singers, the sound of bells and stamping feet, the beat of the *pakhāwaj* established the geometry and the structure; the taut confrontations of the antiphonal *sawāl-jawāb,* the dialogue of the *bhavaī* and *dādariā* created the spatial tensions. *Chitra* (painting) was born of the frozen stances of dance, epic performance, and song. Pictures appeared on festive occasions on cloth, on pots, on paper, on the clay walls of village huts, but the mood was impermanent; the *chitra* was whitewashed over, disappearing, but continuing to dwell in the eyes and hands of women and in the perceptive storehouses of tradition.

Kṛṣṇa appears in early paintings, Ahīr-bodied, with slim shoulders but heavy haunches, and with prominent, silver lotus eyes. He is cloud-dark *abhinavajaldhara,* the color of thunder clouds heavy with rain.

This was *deśī* art, concerned with present existence, with an event, a *līlā,* where the gods exist in human form, where great battles rage, where demons lurk in forest darkness and with changing mood, where men and women embrace, the flute is heard, birds fly, the tiger roars, clouds are filled with thunder, the landscape is fluid with changing seasons.

The Paintings of Settled Village Societies

Painting and ritual in the settled villages of rural India have for centuries followed the rhythm of two cosmic movements: the sun and its two solstices, and the waxing and waning of the moon.

The northern, ascending journey of the sun, its movement into the constellation of *Makara,* the crocodile, Capricorn, was the period of *uttarāyana,* a period when the virgin earth awakened to a new cycle of fertility and the sun, dispensing light, destroyed the terrors of darkness and the unknown. It was months of longer days and shorter nights. It was the time for the *bhūmi pūjās* and the *bhitti sobhās,* the worship and adornment of the earth and walls of the home; it was the period for the harvesting of sun-ripened corn and yellow mustard flowers, for lean-haunched village women to adorn their blue-black bodies with new garments of scarlet, yellow, or parrot green. The sun creating the color, the earth creating the space, the movement of desire creating the intention—and paintings appear wherever space is available on the walls and floors of village huts, on ceilings, pots, cloth, paper, on the palms of hands. The forests of lotus, the *kamalabana,* the overflowing water pots, the *pūrṇa kumbhas,* the auspicious diagrams, the *ālepans* (*ālpanas*), the circles of fertility, the *khobar,* the delineations of the *purāṇic* gods, these are all paintings that are auspicious, protective, and life-giving.

The sun in its southern journey into the constellation of *Karka,* the tortoise, Cancer, was the period of *dakṣiṇāyana,* the *mahāvrata.* It was a period of longer nights and shorter days. This was the period of the *chāturmāsa,* the four months when the earth lay dormant and the gods slept. It was the time for the *srāddhas,* the rituals to the dead ancestors, the time for the goddess to be in her descending tendency, the time for the worship of the primeval, black mothers, Kālī and Chāmuṇḍā, with offerings of blood sacrifice and hibiscus and oleander, for the worship of Bhairava and Hanumān, for the recitation of spells and the practice of magic and witchcraft, and for the propitiation of the spirits of mountains, trees, and forests.

The waxing and waning of the moon was also integral to the mood and direction of the visual arts of rural India. The bright half of the moon, the *śūkla pakṣa,* was in honor of the gods. The dark moonless night, the *Kṛṣṇa pakṣa,* was a time for the rites to the ancestors.

Paintings emerge to propitiate the dark forces. Geometric diagrams drawn in white, black, and somber red, the *yantras,* the *maṇḍalas,* the *srāddha* pictorial writings, the secret *muggus,* the magical diagrams of south India serve to appease and drive away evil. Pure and intense energy-charged colors seen by the silent eye of meditation in the darkness and space within explode on paper in the *maṇḍala* and *yantra* drawings. Each color represents a sound form that is audible to the inner ear. Forms, concentrated circles, lapping and overlapping squares, lotuses, angles, and triangles emerge, creating visual illusions, expanding and contracting, ascending and descending, projecting in their eternal movement the complex labyrinths, the sounds and spaces of the cosmos and of human consciousness. These are the tools used as supports for meditation of energy and the inner spaces, the *pītha,* or abiding places of the goddess. The *bindu* appears, the vermilion dot, the sacred circle of the goddess, stripped of form, burnt away by her awesome energy. The *yantras* of the goddess, the triangle, the square, the hexagon, the circle, and the spiral are manifest along with the six-pointed star formed of two triangles made one, Śivas and Gaurī, in eternal union. Expanses of red *sindūra* on iconic stones are placed on the roadside and in the village *devasthānas, chakras,* as diagrams of the planets, astrological charts, paintings of the cosmos held within the human form along with paintings of Bhairon (Bhairava). Hanumān and Kālī appear at the shrines of the non-Vedic Śaivas, the Kaulas, the Nātha Jogīs.

The drawing of *maṇḍalas* with its use of sexual imagery, the invocation of Śiva in a *kumbha* or water pot, the use of *kuṇḍas* or *yantras* as sacrificial vessels shaped like the womb or the generative organs, wherein the fire offerings were made, were enjoined as part of the rituals connected with the Dīkṣā, the secret initiation rites of the non-Vedic Śaiva *jogīs,* alchemists, and tantric adepts. Little is known of their *mantras, maṇḍalas,* and *mudrās* of initiation, but the appearance in recent years of a vast number of magnificent diagrams and paintings connected with secret rites, with magic, and with the stark worship of the generative organs and with sexual processes, is significant. The subject of many of the paintings is *lingam* and *yoni* worship. The imagery is phallic but the treatment of the paintings has little to do with the exploration and excitation of the erotic; these paintings are explosive diagrams of the generative principles, and the mood is immensely grave.

The magical use of *mantra, maṇḍala,* and *mudrā* as spell, image, and gesture continues to have mysterious power in rural and urban societies. Spells and ritual diagrams exist for the fertility of crops, potency of bridegrooms, destruction of witches, and protection from tigers. Urgency is given to the magical act by the use in the *mantra* of the name of the magician spirit invoked, and in the recital of the events which are sought to be brought about. Many of the couplets are colored with vivid visual imagery. A tribal Baiga *mantra* starts: "I bind the glow-worm of a virgin."[1] In a love spell from Bihar, the great enchantress Nonā of Kāmrūpa is invoked. The ancient *yoginī* in Bihar folklore is known as the Jogan, Lonā or Nonā Chamārin. "The flower plays, the flower laughs, he who smells the fragrance of the flower will come to me, come to me swiftly. If he does not come, may he die, his liver cut to pieces. Dohāī, I seek refuge in the *Yogana Yoginī,* Dohāī, I seek refuge in Kāmrūpa, the Kāmākhyā, the eye of love, she who sustains the Universe."[2]

Bhitti Chitras and the Paintings of Mithila

The adornment of walls of homes with earth plaster, mirrors, seeds, reliefs in clay, paintings of the *purāṇic* gods and ornamental forms of birds, serpents, flowers, and geometric diagrams is common in areas in India, where the clay walls of village huts provide a suitable canvas for such decoration. These paintings and ornamentation are the work of women. They appear in the more prosperous village dwellings, in the *devasthāna* or the *gosāinghar* where the *gṛha devatās* and the *kula devatās,* the household and clan gods, are installed in the *khobarghar*. The *khobarghar* is an inner room made auspicious with fresh plaster and painted icons of gods and goddesses adorned with the flowering bamboo and the lotus *maṇḍalas* of fertility, *mantras* of protection, fragrances, and flowers. In this room, the bride and bridegroom spend their first married days and nights together; it is in this room that babies are born. This is the radiant, auspicious heart of the hut.

The delight in color, the overwhelming concern with fecundity, and a live participation in the loves and wild adventures of the gods is visible in these paintings, with which whenever possible the villager surrounds himself: the walls of the hut, the street, the shop, and the marketplace become the picture gallery, the canvas on which the records of the race and the exploits of gods and heroes are maintained. The paintings, however, are transitory and anonymous. They appear on walls, fade, are whitewashed over and reappear with the cyclic movement of the seasons and the related rituals.

In desert dwellings, in Cutch and Jaisalmer, where the eye of the artist is not nourished with lush images of growing things, ornamentation is brought about by use of earth plaster, mica, and mirrors. Broken bangles, seeds, and beads are used to give texture to the wall surfaces. Broken fragments of mirrors are used on the walls, as in mirror embroidery, in which the designs of parrots and peacocks, stylized human figures, and geometric circles and squares are molded in clay and the mirrors inserted into the body of the design. In more prosperous dwellings, miniature paintings framed in glass are inserted into the mica-surfaced wall, as focal points of color and story.

The use of glass as ornament is not limited to walls. Chests, platforms, and grainbins are all clay-molded and ornamented with mirrors. In India, the use of glass as ornament has extensive decorative application. It is used on cloth, on wood, on clay, on silver, and on gold. Unlike in the West, where glass has mainly been used for the percolation of light, in stained-glass windows, in India glass is used to reflect back the light and the image, reflecting and shattering the image. Thousands of fragments of mirrors used on walls within a confined area create a unique visual experience of unending, fragmented images. This form of decoration is used in palaces; it is also used in village huts.

A factor that has obscured the understanding of the rural arts is the general belief that these arts are the product of illiterate people, of worshipers of trees and aniconic stones, people without access to India's wealth of myth, legend, and symbol. This is far from correct. We have already observed that sanctuaries of religion, art, and literature had sprung into existence in villages from the earliest times, when the religious teachers, poets, painters, musicians, and epic performers sought refuge in the countryside. These sanctuaries made possible the survival of archaic myth and history. The cataclysmic drought that devastated Bihar several years ago gave me an opportunity to study in depth the visual traditions of some of these communities and to tap the resources and energies that lie unexplored in their racial subconscious.

Mithila, the ancient Videha, the birthplace of Jānakī or Sītā of the *Rāmāyaṇa,* is an area in the district of Darbhanga in Bihar. It lies in the Terai, the foothills that divide India from Nepal. The rivers Gaṅgā, Gaṇḍakī, and Kosī separate it from southern Bihar and the vast plains of central India. The association of Mithila with epic myth and legend link it to the earliest memories of this land. For centuries it has retained its isolation. The art expressions of its people have a total impact and freshness. Nurtured on the lyrics of Vidyāpati, who sang his supremely sensuous poetry in the fourteenth century, songs of the loves of Kṛṣṇa and Rādhā and of the energy-charged worship of Śakti as Bhagavatī-Gaurī, Mithila has an ancient history of rich cross-fertilization. It was in Mithila over three thousand years ago that the Vedic onthrust was contained. Sanskrit learning flourished through the centuries, along with a vital stream of vernacular expression in literature, painting, and theater. The Karnataka dynasties that ruled Mithila from the twelfth to the fourteenth century brought royal patronage and security to the arts of the region.[1] Surprisingly, the exposure to the cultural mores of south Indian rites and rituals left little mark on the rites and rituals of the Maithils. Later, under the Oinvāra rulers, the ancient *saṁskāra* rites and rituals that governed the life of the householder were even more rigidly enforced.[2]

Mithila was also one of the earliest areas where the impact of nomadic tribes led to the release of streams of vernacular poetry. It was in AD 1324 that Harisimha Deva of the Karnataka dynasty, one of the great patrons of the Mithila arts, introduced a mixed Sanskrit vernacular operatic form known in Mithila as *kīrtanīya nāṭaka.* "This unique style of drama became a vehicle of the Bhagwad creed."[3] There is also mention in the *Varṇa Ratnākara,* a Maithili text of the fourteenth century, of *Lorika,* an Ahīr legend, being performed as a dance.

It was W. G. Archer, with his perceptive curiosity, who first drew attention to the mural paintings of the Brahmin and Kāyastha village communities of Mithila.[4]

I had visited Mithila in the mid-fifties, but the village walls were blank and printed lithographs and calendars hung in the *gosāinghars.* The bleak dust of poverty had sapped the will and the energy needed to ornament the home. Traces of old paintings were sometimes to be found, fragments that bore testimony to an inherited knowledge of color, form, and iconography. I had spoken to some of the fair, lean-faced women. The frugality and austerity of their lives was projected through their hands and their noble, ancient faces. The seeming drying-up of the stream had left me anguished. The Bihar drought of 1968 accentuated the problem of finding light labor schemes for the women of the area and encouraged me to start a project to provide these women with handmade paper on which they could paint.

The technique of painting and drawing on paper was familiar to the women of this region. Paper paintings were traditionally used as *aide-mêmoires,* to teach the growing daughter the basic vocabulary of *alaṅkāra,* the ornamental forms and symbols unique to each family group and caste.

I visited Madhubani, the largest district in Mithila, again in May 1968, when the drought relief project had been in operation for several months. The landscape of Bihar through which I traveled was harsh, gray, cracked, and desolate, and the heat remorseless. The dust and sun, the absence of water, and disappearance of green from the landscape left a monstrous tonal uniformity. The need for the worship of fertility and water, of tree and sap became understandable. Entering the villages of Madhubani (literally "forest of honey"), the landscape altered. There were a few dust-heavy trees and a total absence of running water, but the courtyards of the huts were freshly plastered, and colors flowed in streams from doorways. Old women, young women, and girls were bent over paper, painting with bamboo twigs and rags. The colors, deep earth-red, pink, yellow, and black were laid out in little bowls on trays of *sikki* grass.

In the paintings I had seen at the commencement of the project, the line of the drawings was hesitant. Years of abstinence, of poverty, of dreary monotony had clogged the stream; eye and hand had to be freed of the years of sterility. Within five months, the situation had changed. A sense of pride and joy had already permeated and transformed the women of Mithila. A simple dignity was visible, a poise, and a supreme self-assurance.

The paintings varied from village to village, from woman to woman. Jitwarpur appeared to be the stronghold of the Brahmin painters, Ranthi the stronghold of the Kāyastha artists. Some of the women emerged as masters of their art. In time they started signing their paintings with their names. Jagdambā Devī of Ranthi village, Sītā Devī from village Jitwarpur, Gaṅgā Devī of Chiri village, Mahā Sundarī Devī of Ranthi village, Ookhā Devī of Jitwarpur, Yamunā Devī, the Harijan painter from Jitwarpur. It was an individualistic work, recognizable by style and character.

In a few of the paintings vertical and horizontal lines were used to divide the paintings of incidents separated by time and space. The juxtaposition of minute figures of man, animals, and birds with towering forms to suggest and establish scale and convey the vastness of nature, a device used often in miniature painting, is also visible in these Mithila paintings. Though drawn on a miniature scale, some of the paintings have the spatial quality of frescoes. In these paintings there is a total absence of the tragic and the anguished, an absence of the anxieties that are central to the contemporary situation. And this was in the midst of the grim tragedy of drought.

The Maithils are Śakti worshipers; Bhagavati Gauri is their *kula devatā*. Schools of *tantric* ritual flourish. Vidyāpati's lyrics of passion and physical love saturate the countryside. The *Bhāgavata Purāṇa* is familiar to every Maithil house, and Mithila, the birthplace of Sītā, has ancient associations with the *Rāmāyaṇa*. These streams were the source material for the paintings of Śiva-Śakti, Rāma-Sītā, Kṛṣṇa-Rādhā, Rāvaṇa, and Hanumān.

Before bazaar colors started to be used in the paintings, paint was prepared at home. The black was made from burnt *jowār* or *kājal,* yellow from turmeric or from *chūnam* mixed with the milk of the banyan tree, orange from the *palāśa* flower, red from the *kusum* flower, and green from the *bilva* leaf—a tradition of brewing magical colors from plants that has remained unchanged from the time of the writing of the *Śāradā Tilaka* in the eleventh century. A cotton rag tied to the tip of a twig is still used as a brush by these women painters. The main lines of the painting are drawn in black and the twig dipped into the liquid color to outline and fill in the forms. Separate twigs are used for separate colors.

In Mithila, women of all communities paint. Three schools of painting can be seen. They are composed of women of three different castes, the Kāyastha, the Brahmin, and the Harijan, and can be distinguished by their use of color and of theme.

The paintings in an earthen palette of ochres and umber-browns, dust-pinks, dull turmerics, and earth-reds by Kāyastha women have fine black outlines. Here the emphasis is on volume and depth. Colors are laid on in broad sweeps of the brush. Ornaments on cloth or background are discarded; there is an absence of *alaṅkāra* as tree, bird, or foliage. The paintings are elemental energy forms, abstracted of all details. There is a stark austerity in the paintings, an unfolding energy and a sense of magic that possibly has its source in *tantric* ritual and worship.

The bodies of the gods and goddesses in these somber paintings are foreshortened and at times distorted. The hands and fingers are often left unfinished. The nose is pointed and merges into the forehead. The heavy, swinging, plaited hair ornamented with pompoms has a sinuous snake-like movement. The eyes are open. Even though most of the faces are in profile, the eyes are drawn in a frontal presentation. As in all rural art forms, the eyes are the source of Śakti; they are the central point of power. The pupil within the eye is placed after the painting is complete. It is the placing of this *bindu* within the eye that generates communication with the beholder. To the Maithil women, to place the mark of light before the completion of the picture would be destructive.

With every painting the goddess is born anew. She springs to life, energy-charged, filling the earth and the sky in a hundred forms. In one painting of the goddess as the Aṣṭabhujī Vindhyavāsinī Durgā, drawn by Ookhā Devī in energy-charged brown ochres and blacks, the goddess explodes onto the paper and penetrates all points of space. Serpents, vibrant with phallic energy, encircle her. Her archaic face is grim. At her waist is the mysterious triangle. She is many-armed, incandescent, the source of all color and the form of no color. The lady rides the tiger. The animal has a human face. Every hair on his body is taut and electric with the energy of the goddess.

In another painting, the goddess, as the *jogan,* the ancient witch, is conceived with a bird face, reminiscent of very early terra cottas. The dark, beak-nosed mother stands shrouded in brooding mystery. She is without attributes. She stands with arms outstretched. The eye of the sacred goddess of Mithila is drawn in full relief on the profile of the face. Her four hands are empty. On her head is a crown of lotus petals, at her waist is the triangle of energy, between her legs, the line of the serpent.

The *jogan* appears in another painting by Bhagavatī Devī, painted in pale almond tones. The hair of the mysterious mother is pulled back tightly and tied at her neck. Her nose is beaked; her hands are like flippers. The undulating form of a serpent lies beneath her.

The goddess, as Kālī, is painted in the color of the *nīlotpala,* the blue lotus. She is five-headed, eight-armed, six-legged. The iconography of the painting is of great antiquity. The red tongues of the goddess emerge from her gaping mouths. The red of her tongue is clearly defined against the stark blue of the body. In another version of the red-tongued mother, she strides across the canvas. Her hair is heavily plaited. Around her neck is a garland of skulls, on her waist an apron with projecting blood-stained hands. She also has the sacred triangle and *bindu* of power.

In a Maithil painting by Ookhā Devī, painted in sun-faded yellows, saffrons, and browns, Śiva appears as the *yogī,* with rhinoceros *kuṇḍala* in his ears and the face of a tiger on his loins. The ash-smeared god is in cosmic movement. He flies in the atmosphere, levitated by the fierce exploding energy and power of his *yoga.* Around him, moving in whirling, sun-charged movements, are the *ḍamaru* (drum), the trident, serpents, and flowers.

In another painting, Śiva sits cross-legged, his hands like flippers, his feet foreshortened. Serpents surround him and nestle around his throat. His heart is a blazing lotus of power.

A painting, in burnt umber outlined in black, depicts a four-armed Kṛṣṇa dancing his victory on the *nāga* king, Kāliya. The face of Kṛṣṇa is sharply angular and is sketched with a minimum of lines. His squat Ahīr body is massive; he dances in abandon. Kāliya is five-headed, with wide-open eyes that are fixed on the divine child. The serpent bears the marks of the *aṣṭadala,* the eight-petaled lotus, the symbol of the goddess. His sinuous form frames the dancing boy. The *nāga kanyās,* the *nāga* girls, float in the waters.

In the second group of paintings, by the Brahmin women of Mithila, the quenched ochres and earth colors of the Kāyastha paintings are replaced by a vibrancy of rich, madder-red, orange, and turmeric yellow, with touches of green and pink. The lines of the paintings are bold and confident, enclosing and strengthening the pools of color. Energy and passion find expression in the use of red and yellow as monochrome washes over the large surfaces of the paintings. Color creates the mood; it establishes the pulse and tempo. It also divides the space and provides the background for human forms, birds, animals, and plants. The use of deep pools of red concentrates the energy and acts as a coalescing factor, binding together various elements.

There is little in the present environment of Mithila that could provide the stimulus for this unbounded knowledge of color. *Bhāng* mixed with milk is drunk by the men and women of Mithila at the time of seasonal festivals and rituals. It is at this time that paintings appear on the walls. Is there a quickening of the visual nerve, a heightened sight, a rising of fluids that fill the eye with color, making these penetrating visual statements possible?

For want of what O Bhairo
are thine eyes red?
For want of what are
the lips dry?
For want of Gaṅgā thine
eyes are red
For want of *bhāng* are
thy lips dry.[5]

The women of Mithila uniformly wear cheap, white, cotton sārīs, yet the women in the paintings are resplendent with reds, yellows, blues, and saffrons. The *ghāgrā, cholī,* and *oḍhani* of the goddesses are decorated with dots, flowers, and lozenges. The *oḍhani,* richly ornamented with floral and geometric forms, stands out stiffly from the heads of the women, forming a background against which the figures are projected.

The idioms, the themes, the stylization of Mithila paintings are ancestral. They are from the *paramparā,* the time immemorial of the Maithil woman's past. She is the channel through which this inherited knowledge flows, is transformed, and made radiant and auspicious in the energy of the present. The central theme of the paintings is love and fertility. Passion, love, and desire are reduced to symbols to suggest and evoke the mood, to create the atmosphere and environment.

The elephant, the fish, the tortoise—animals symbolizing power and fertility, are drawn with extreme care. The tiger decorated with stripes, chevrons, or stylized floral forms emerges from bowers of flowering trees. In one of the paintings, a snarling tiger turns on his hunters. Men, holding guns and dressed in the garments of soldiers of the East India Company, surround him. Minute lines are drawn to delineate the hair on the neck and tail of the animal.

Paintings illustrating stories from the *Bhāgavata Purāṇa* are frequent. Kṛṣṇa is often depicted: Kṛṣṇa stealing the clothes of the *gopīs,* leaving them naked and vulnerable, subduing and dancing on the serpent in the water, stealing milk and curds, or with Rādhā dancing the mystic *rāsa maṇḍala* dance. A theme that is constantly repeated with great lyrical beauty is one in which the child Kṛṣṇa is shown caressing a calf.

Dev Kant Jha, a Brahmin youth from Jitwarpur, has painted a *kalīya mardana,* in which Kṛṣṇa leaps in wild abandon over the five-hooded cobra of the dark waters. Kalīya, the serpent king, his undulating body taut and virile, rises between the outflung legs of the squat Ahīr youth. Surrounding and gazing at Kṛṣṇa are two *nāga kanyās,* serpent girls, half-woman, half-serpent forms, daughters of the cobra king. The lower parts of their bodies are two cobras with raised hoods that join and penetrate the navel of the serpent maidens. An extraordinary motif of eyes, the symbol of the *yoni,* painted on the *oḍhanīs* that cover the heads of the *nāga kanyās,* is curved below their bodies, providing a background of concentrated red color. The painting is charged with erotic symbolism. The five-hooded, rising cobra between the outflung legs of the Ahīr youth and the eyes on the cloth are a visualization of phallic desire. The coiling, serpent bodies of the maidens express awakening passion, while the heads of the cobras penetrating the navel of the maidens is symbolic of *mithuna,* or union.

Kāma, the bodiless god of love, is reborn in the limbs of Kṛṣṇa of Mithila, in the *rāsa*-filled body and the fluid, slender limbs that, like the arrows of Kāma, pierce and intoxicate. In a group of paintings delineating the many moods of Kṛṣṇa, Sītā Devī, of village Jitwarpur, has painted a long-limbed, slender Ahir lover, blue-bodied, with lotus eyes, holding the flute as if it were the bow of the god of love. The tender form of Rādhā reaches to her beloved. The mood is saturated with the ethos of Vidyāpati. These are masterpieces of the rural tradition, expressing an intoxication of love and life manifest in wildly blooming flowers, flying birds, and in the eye-to-eye confrontation of lovers.

Very elaborate and richly patterned line drawings in black and *geruā* earth-red are the creation of Kāyastha women of Ranthi village. Drawn on walls, they appear on the earthen wall within the *khobar,* as the backdrop to the worship of the goddess Gaurī. The *sarovara* (pond), a drawing of the cosmic waters, decorates the western walls of the *gosāinghar.* The fish, the tortoise, the frog, and the crocodile, denizens of the waters and symbols of fertility, appear on the walls. On paper, as diagrams of fertility, drawings are placed in baskets, along with the turmeric and *kum kum* that form part of the bridal dower.

The masters of the craft, when drawing the diagram, use a twig or a coarse thread drawn from an old *sārī,* as the brush.

The thread or stick is dipped in liquid *kājal* and firmly sweeps across the paper to create the circle and the straight line. The line of the drawing is supremely confident; it never hesitates, nor is it altered. There appears a deep understanding of the ancient belief that lack of care in execution of form results in a diminishing of power. The manner of outlining forms is strangely reminiscent of *kanthā* embroidery, a form of quilted embroidery widely practiced in Bengal and by the women of Mithila. Gaṅgā Devī, a Kāyastha painter from Rasidpur village and a great master of Maithil line drawings, illustrates episodes from the epics and *Purāṇas* in black and red lines. The quality of epic narrative and illustration is evident. The gods and heroes enact their archetypal roles in the unfolding drawing. Kṛṣṇa plays the flute in an urn-shaped, heavily flowering *kadamba* tree, while another Kṛṣṇa rescues Draupadi in the Kaurava court by raining an unending flow of variegated, patterned clothes, to drape the captive queen's body. A *gopī* dallies with a heifer on the banks of the Yamunā. The rippling waters are suggested by the use of finely hatched lines; delicately drawn ferns and flowers nestle on the river banks. In a corner of the drawings sits Śiva, the *yogī,* and a head of Gaṅgā with a massive nose-ring rises delicately from Śiva's matted hair.

Surrounding the god are flying serpents, birds, and a bending tree heavy with fruit. All the seasons mingle to provide ornament, to give texture, to fill the canvas, and to create a sense of lushness.

Mahā Sundarī Devī of the Ranthi village draws long-limbed bodies of *gopīs* surrounding the *kadamba* tree on which Kṛṣṇa sits playing the flute. It is eternal spring, and the air is heavy with fragrance.

The rural arts of Mithila are unique, for here coalesce a comprehension and knowledge of Sanskrit learning and culture, its vocabulary and iconography, *tantric* ritual and magic, and the distortions and robust vitality inherent in the rural perceptions of the visual arts.

In the use of deep pools of red as background to define, enclose, and create space and as a device to concentrate attention on central figures; in the stylization of form, in the angular projection of the *oḍhanī,* in the delineation of the nose and eye, in the ornamentation and presentation of the braided hair, in the use of scattered flower, bird, and serpent to fill empty spaces, is projected a sophisticated understanding of the structure and the raw material of painting. And perhaps they provide a clue to the provenance of some early miniature paintings, in which a rural idiom of color and distortion are used to illustrate lyrical court poetry.

It is likely that ateliers of painters from Mithila had flourished in these regions during the fifteenth and sixteenth centuries. While women painted on paper and on village walls, it is likely that their husbands worked as painters at the courts of the Karnataka and Oinwār rulers, and even traveled to the royal Muslim courts at Jaunpur. It could only have been in areas free from the insecurity and terrors of invasion that the profoundly lyrical *Gīta Govinda* masterpieces of the Prince of Wales Museum, Bombay, could have been painted.

The *Gīta Govinda* masterpieces demanded royal patronage and an environment drenched with the ethos of the Rādhā-Kṛṣṇa creed and painters familiar with the *alaṅkāras,* the *bhedas,* that enrich the Rādhā-Kṛṣṇa dialogues, a refuge where the arts of literature, music, and rural theater flourished.

It was in Mithila that Vidyāpati created his lyrics of an eternal spring, where the loves of Rādhā-Kṛṣṇa quickened the soil.

In our two hearts
Those shoots of love
Opened with two or three leaves.
Then grew the branches
And the clusters of foliage
They were covered with flowers
And scent lay everywhere.[6]

A young radiant Maithil girl must have been the poet's inspiration for Rādhā, as she could have been for the taut beauty of the *Gīta Govinda* paintings.

Today I saw her going—
Her beauty stayed,
tied to my heart.[7]

Years after the drought relief program, paintings continue to transform the mud huts of Mithila. The verandahs, the ***khobarghar,*** the ceremonial room of the bride and bridegroom, the *gosāinghar,* the room of the gods, have been painted with loving care. And the mood accentuates the transitory. These too will fade and disappear. Unlike most rural areas, where a proliferation of art forms outside their traditional ritual context has led to rapid deterioration, in Mithila some women painters are emerging skillful and supremely confident.

A woman painting a cow allowed by mistake a blot of color to fall. She gave a cry; before she could act to erase what she thought was a mistake, her husband, who watched her, said, "Why do you start? When you hold the rag of color in your hands, you are Brahmā; whatever you do is right." It is in such resources of understanding and vision that the rural arts have their foundation.

Recent research among the painters of Mithila has brought to light a third school of painters belonging to the Harijan community. Both men and women paint. A few specimens of this school had been discovered earlier: elongated horses and elephants in black, stark paintings on mud walls, with no symbols or figurative drawing surrounding the main form. With patronage, a new style, an individual vision and perception are emerging. The paintings recount the adventures of a mythical ruler, Raja Sailesh. Legends from the Hindu pantheon have entered the pictorial vocabulary of these Harijan painters: Mahishāsuramardini, the goddess, destroying the buffalo demon; Kṛṣṇa dancing on Kāliya, the dragon, who dwells deep in the dark Yamunā waters. Trees, birds, or symbols as devices to fill space are absent. The black line outlines human and animal figures. The red of a parrot's beak, used sparingly but with an instinctive understanding of color as counterpoint to the black line, accentuates and energizes the bodies of animals, of gods and goddesses. These are paintings by unknown masters, an emergent perception that was hitherto denied expression. The exploitation in form, color, line, and narrative imagery has confidence and power.

The *Maṇḍalas* and Magical Drawings

Maṇḍala, meaning an orb or circle,[1] symbolizes wholeness and the outer visualization of cosmic energy. Whether drawn on the earth, on walls, on paper, on cloth, or engraved on metal, as a symbol of mysterious power, *maṇḍalas* were man's earliest attempt to communicate concentrated, nonverbal meaning. *Maṇḍalas* were born of ancient man's perceptions of the cosmos and of the magical processes of birth, death, and existence—imponderables that could only be explained or revealed nonverbally through geometry and the magical abstractions of mathematical form.

The primeval urge for the auspicious and for protection against the unknown and the malevolent had demanded from the earliest times the tools of *maṇḍalas* or *yantras.* The *yantra* was the concrete form of the *mantra* and could be used both for protective and for evil purposes. *Rakṣā mantras* and *dhāriṇīs,* incantations and spells, ostensibly without meaning, formed an integral part of magical rituals of protection. *Mantras* were said to be either masculine, feminine, or neuter. Masculine *mantras,* with their *yantras,* were used as charms and in witchcraft, while feminine *mantras* were used as protective amulets against diseases.[2]

A *mantra* was either awake or asleep; when aroused from sleep to bear fruit, it had to be calm and uniform. There were *yantras* in the form of *kavacha* (armor) to give protection, *astra* (weapons), visualized as arrows, and *vidyut* (lightning).[3] *Yantras* in the form of magical winds were visualized as a closed diagram of coiled serpents.

The contours of the *yantras* and the *maṇḍalas* are determined by the need to give visual form to the magical spell and to concretize the exploding energy of the ritual gestures. The magical diagrams created by the ritual act, when awakened and made operative by incantation and ritual gesture, could create, enclose, protect, and destroy energy. Certain elements were common to all forms of *maṇḍala* diagrams. These hieroglyphs of *tantra* and magical ritual, the *vrata* and *utsava maṇḍalas*, more commonly known as *aripans, alpanā, sathiā, chauka,* shared a common need for symmetry. The circle, the triangle, the square, the hexagon, and patterns which evolved from these simple structures formed the basic elements of all magical drawings. Another common feature in the *maṇḍalas* was the gateway, the opening that surrounded enclosed energy-charged space. These doorways were guarded by sound forms, *mantras,* and by invisible *kṣetrapalās* and *dvārapalās,* guardians of gateways and spaces. The entry into the heart of the diagram, into the sanctity and security of the *maṇḍala*, was through the *mantra* and *mudrā,* spell and magical gesture, revealed to the initiate.

The antiquity of the *maṇḍala* diagrams is evident from their emergence as fully developed symbols on the seals and amulets of the Indus Valley and on the rock paintings of the heartlands of India. One of the earliest and most powerful of the *maṇḍalas* is the *sarvatobhadra.* Regarded as the source of all *yantras* and *maṇḍalas,* it symbolizes the energy of the goddess and the explosive energy of the rising sun made manifest through abstract form. A paradigm of supreme potency, the *maṇḍala* is formed of forty-two crosses (*svastikās*) linked together. The main arms of the diagram encompass the four cardinal directions; the diagram is considered auspicious in its northern, southern, eastern, and western regions.

The *Agni Purāṇa* describes the drawing of the *sarvatobhadra maṇḍala.* In the ritual, the votary at sunrise offered worship to the virgin goddess of energy in the east. The *sarvatobhadra maṇḍala* was then to be constructed as follows:

> First a square should be drawn, which should be divided into nine chambers, by drawing two straight lines across it, running from the east to west, and two straight lines drawn from north to south. The number of such lines should go on increasing till a quadrilateral figure of a hundred and fifty chambers should be inscribed within the greater and the exterior square. Then the four corners of the exterior quadrangle (*pīṭha-kṣetra*), should be marked down, each such corner having been made to consist of three of the above-said interlinear chambers. The *vīthīs* or the causeways of the mystic quadrangle, should be made to extend over two lines beyond the exterior boundary of the *maṇḍalam,* which should be made to occupy a space of two *padas,* reckoned in proportion to the entire area.
>
> The lotus delineated within the inscribed quadrilateral, should be marked with white powder, the petals with yellow and the pollen with a variegated hue. The *vīthīs* or the causeways, should be marked with red-coloured rice powder, while the door should be coloured with the same substance, like the complexion of the god Lokeśa.[4]

The *Śāradā Tilaka,* written in the eleventh century, describes the drawing of the sacred diagram in five colors—the white of rice, the red of the *kusum* flower, the yellow of turmeric, the black of burnt cereal-ash, and the green of the leaves of the *bilva* tree.

One of the most potent forms of the *sarvatobhadra* was the *chitra bandha,* a parallelogram used in poetics, that had letters of the alphabet arranged in absolute symmetry, rendering the diagram immune to penetration by forces of evil.[5] The *Agni Purāṇa* describes the *chitram* as an arrangement of words in the shape of a lotus or a sword. The letters placed in the petals of the lotus when read in the natural order conveyed one meaning and when read in an inverse order conveyed another.[6]

The *sarvatobhadra maṇḍala* is drawn today around the *tulasī* plant, by women, at the time of the *durgā pūjā* festival. To draw the sacred diagram, the Maithil woman places one, three, five, seven, and nine vermilion dots (*bindus*) on the prepared space. These dots are placed in a formal arrangement of two triangles, one with its apex pointing towards the sky, the other towards the earth.

It is on these *bindus* that the *sarvatobhadra* is drawn. All the main *yantras* emerge from the amalgam of geometric forms that can be structured on the *sarvatobhadra.* At the corner of each Maithil *aripan,* four *yantras,* evolved from the *sarvatobhadra,* are placed: the *trikoṇa,* the *ṣaṭ koṇa,* the *aṣṭa koṇa,* and the *Śrī Yantras.*[7]

The supreme symbol of the virgin goddess and of the rising sun is the *sarvatobhadra.* The expression of these two great energy forms is integral to all *maṇḍala* and *vrata* pictographs. The goddess is *chakra rūpā,* in the form of a circle, and the word *maṇḍala* is itself another word for the sun, the exploding, life-giving orb.[8] The *aṣṭadala,* the eight-petaled lotus, an archaic symbol that first appears in a seal of the Indus Valley, also symbolizes the virgin goddess and the sun, in *vrata* diagrams of the northern river valleys. In the *chakrabedha* ritual, *durgā* is visualized in the form of five circles. In the *magh maṇḍala vrata* to the sun, observed by women in West Bengal at the time of the winter solstice, five colored powders are used to draw the sun, a diagram of five circles. The first circle is drawn with the green of the powdered leaf, the second with yellow turmeric, the third with the black of powdered burnt rice, and the fourth with the red of powdered brick. The fifth is drawn in a circle of powdered white rice. A circle is placed on the top of the *maṇḍala,* and this is covered with red brick powder. Magical songs (*chhandas*) are chanted at the time of drawing the diagram. The first chant is one of the triumph of the sun over the winter of long nights; the second celebrates the marriage of the sun with the moon in spring; the last rejoices at the birth of spring and its marriage with the earth.[9]

Very early representations of the evolving *sarvatobhadra maṇḍala* diagram have been discovered among two rock paintings at Beri Beri, Panchmari, in Madhya Pradesh. The earlier painting is in a deep red-ochre *geruā* wash. The arms of the diagram are composed of several triangles in the shape of the *Śrī Yantra,* the triangle of the Śakti. That the diagram is a sacred, magical form is evident from the posture of the figures that surround it. The long-limbed human figures wear towering, feathered headdresses and appear to be dancing with upraised hands. Another figure with identical headdress watches with hands upheld in awe. Above the *maṇḍala* drawing is a man holding a club. He is running and is followed by a cock and three other animals. Ahead of him are six faintly drawn images that suggest shafts surrounding the mystic form.[10] In the Gond legend of Lingo Pen there is a description of Lingo and the first animal sacrifices to the newly created Gond gods:

> Then Lingo said: "Come, O brethren, we cannot find god anywhere, let us make a god, and we will worship him."
>
> Then all the Gonds with one voice said: "Yes, O brethren, bring a goat, five years old, a crowing cock, one year old, a three-year-old calf, a cow . . . " Then Lingo, became a man devoted to god, and moved and jumped much; Lingo was in front, and behind were goats, cocks, a calf.[11]

Is the scene, depicted on the rock paintings, the first illustration of this legend? The cave drawing appears charged with energy. Near the diagram are strange horizontal and vertical lines indicative of great winds or of lightning and rain.

In the other drawing, also from the same cave of Beri Beri, Panchmari, the *maṇḍala* appears again in the form of a cross, three of the arms of which are filled in with horizontal lines. In the fourth arm are what appear to be pronged lines, exploding with life and movement. Seven figures surround the *maṇḍala,* approaching it from the four directions. The figures, in postures of urgency, are swept toward the magical cross. They are dressed in animal skins, and their hair is bound in topknots. Four of the figures hold what appear to be trees; in one of them the roots are visible. The bisector of two lines establishes the crossways, the points where the tracks of nomads met. From the stone age, these crossroads have been the sites where the mothers were worshiped through magical ritual and sacrifice.[12]

By the time of the *purāṇas, yantras* and *maṇḍalas* existed to delineate all of the main gods. The *maṇḍala* of Hari is described in the *Agni Purāṇa* as a vast circle holding a great, sixty-two-petaled lotus, on which rested twelve fish, inscribed within a square with the word *bhadra* (auspicious) written in the four quarters. The diagram had two, four, or six doors opening in all directions, each with a guardian that also acted as the adornment of the gateway.[13] *Maṇḍalas* existed in the *purāṇas,* for the worship of Śiva, as Rudra and Bhairava, and for the goddess in her manifold forms. The *mantra* of the goddess Gaurī, *"Om Hrīm"* (Obeisance to Gaurī), written within the *Śrī Chakra,* the mystical hexagonal diagram, within which a triangle with a three-petaled lotus rested, was a symbol of sexual union. It enthralled and ravished lovers and filled the person who recited it while in the act of love with beauty, passion, and poesy. It was considered to be the manifestation of the half-male, half-female forms, the *ardhanarīśvara,* Śiva and Gaurī made one in eternal union.[14]

The *saṭ chakra* diagrams of *haṭha yoga* and *tantra* were representations of the sensitive psychic centers within the human body. These psychic centers were the resting places, the *chakras* or *pīṭhas,* of the goddess as energy and were located as strategic points along the spine. There were seven *chakras* symbolized as lotuses. Within six of these, Śakti, the goddess, rested; in the seventh Śiva rested. It was through these *chakras* that the dormant "Kuṇḍalini, the serpent of energy that lay coiled around the *mūlādhāra,* the *chakra* that was placed within the generative organs, awakened and, lifting her head, travelled upwards along the spine, piercing and awakening the lotus *chakras* of the body, till she reached the *brahmarandhra,* the thousand-petaled lotus, the abode of the male Śiva, situated in the scalp."

Each of the *chakras* was a microcosm that contained the cosmos. Liberation was obtained by piercing the sheaths of the six *chakras.* The symbolism was tensely visual and aural. Each *chakra* contained its own sound form. A vast and complex symbolism pertaining to the goddess and her manifestations as geometric form, color, and sound centered around the visualization of the *chakras*. The imagery was sexual; the lotus became identified as the *yoni;* the *chakras* became the *pīṭhas,* the sacral altars, where the union of Śiva and Śakti, the mystery that transformed and transmuted, was manifest.

At the base of the spine was the *ādhara,* the *mūlādhāra.* Situated within the *lingam,* the male generative organ, it was visualized as a four-petaled lotus, crimson in color. At the center of the lotus was a yellow square, the seed of the earth. Within the square was a red triangle resting on its apex—this was the *yoni,* as *kāmākhyā,* "fine as the fiber of a lotus stalk." Within the *yoni* was the self-existent *lingam.* Coiled eight times around it was the Kuṇḍalini, the female serpent power, "the world-bewilderer," she who was the source of sound, to be meditated upon in the form of a girl of sixteen.

The *svādhiṣṭhāna,* the six-petaled lotus, was in the region of the anus. It was of a vermilion color; within it was a white, watery region, in the shape of a half-moon. The *maṇipura,* the ten-petaled lotus, was at the region of the navel; it was the color of rain clouds. Within the pericarp of the lotus was a red triangle, the seat of fire and the sun. The *anāhata,* the golden, twelve-petaled lotus, the color of the *bandhūka* flower, rested within the heart. The pericarp was a smoke-colored hexagon, the region of *vāyu,* the winds. Above it was the *sūrya maṇḍala,* the triangle, lustrous as ten million flashes of lightning. In the throat was the sixteen-petaled *viśudhi* lotus, smoky purple in color; within the pericarp of this was the ethereal region, circular in shape, white like the full moon, inscribed with a triangle. Between the eyebrows was found the white two-petaled *ājña chakra.* Within the pericarp of this resplendent lotus was a triangle of the color of radiant flame. In the hole in the skull, in the silent spaces of meditation, was the *brahmarandhra,* the thousand-petaled lotus, resting in supreme emptiness. Lustrous and whiter than the full moon, its filaments were tinged with the color of the young sun.

The *saṭ chakras,* the cosmic *maṇḍalas* of *yoga,* permeated the Indian landscape and appeared not only at the courts of kings but also in the humble dwellings of village India.

In rural societies, in the Rahasya Vidhis, the *chakrapūjā* and *bhagapūjā* rites of the *tantrikas,* the diagram (*yantra*) became identified with the female generative organ as the goddess Bhaga or Kāmākhyā, the eye of love and creation, the doorway to the womb, to the secret places in the female body where life originated. In the temples of the goddess, the *Śakti bhumis, yoginī yantras,* the *maṇḍalas* that formed the essential abstraction of the sacred female form, were drawn on a background structure of *bindus;* the *yantra* was then placed below the anthropomorphic image of the goddess.

Diagrams to the dead, *srāddha maṇḍalas,* form part of the ceremonies that free the dead from their ghostly state and give them the status of the *pitṛs,* the ancestors. These diagrams act as magical tools through which the dead are contacted and empowered to participate in living rituals. In Rajasthan, *srāddha maṇḍalas,* known as *sanjh-ka-koṭ,* are drawn in the form of a parallelogram with four gateways. The drawing of the *maṇḍala,* and the filling within it of objects familiar to the dead one, is continued for a fortnight, from the day of the full moon to the *amāvāsyā,* the day of the darkest moonless night. Only virgin girls fill the *sanjh-ka-koṭ.* They light a lamp every evening during the ritual and sing songs. On the day of the full moon, images of the sun and the moon are drawn within the diagram. On the first day of the waning moon, a wooden stool and a *pachita,* a dice game played on a cloth in the form of the crossroads, is drawn within the diagram. On the second day a *torana,* an auspicious and protective hanging of cloth or flowers, is drawn or placed. On the third day a plate of *ghebar* (sweets) in the form of a spiral is placed. On the remaining days the following objects are drawn or placed within the diagram, in this order: on the fourth day, a fan; on the fifth day, the *svastikā;* on the sixth day, five *kumaras* or unmarried young boys; on the seventh day, the top of a water jar; on the eighth day, the couple—the faithful wife, or the *satī* and her dead husband; on the ninth day, nine images of old hags; on the tenth day, the auspicious bird and the crow; on the eleventh day, images of the mother-in-law and the wife; on the twelfth day, milkmaids carrying buttermilk; and on the thirteenth day, a pair of *yajñopavīta* (sacred threads used in initiations). On the fourteenth day, as the time approaches for completing the *koṭ,* all the remaining symbols are crowded in. These include headless warriors, the water carrier, the sweeper and his wife, *sādhus,* drummers, the plaintain tree, and the date palm. On the fifteenth, the *amāvāsyā* day, the diagram is complete, and on the sixteenth day, the *koṭ* drawing is destroyed.[15]

The *Vrata Maṇḍalas*

There are over two thousand *vratas,* many of them linked in origin to the spells and hymns of the *Atharva Veda* and the *Strī Karmāṇi* rituals described in the *Kauśika Sūtra.*[1] Some *vratas* are integral to the great festivals and are common to the whole country; others are particular to local areas and are receptacles of ancient autochthonous rites. In none of them do priests participate. *Vrata* worship is open to women, unlike the rituals of the *brahmanic pūjā.* In areas where the *vratas* retain their magical nature, *chaddhas* or spells and incantations accompany the liturgical drawings in a secret initiatory language. One role of these women is to draw *vrata* diagrams on the floor and walls.

The archetypal diagram is the channel through which the energy of living things, the storehouse of nature, can be tapped and made operative in rites of transformation. Nurtured on archaic homeopathic magic, the root of *vrata* ritual lies in the belief that desire, when visualized and made concrete through *maṇḍala* and activized through spell and ritual gesture, generates an energy that ensures its own fulfillment. The diagrams are symbols through which the memories of the race are abstracted and preserved, to be communicated in group participation as visual statements of thousands of years of man's history. Through the diagram the participant seeks protection from the malignant forces of nature, disease, and sorcery.

In Bihar, the *vrata* diagram (*ālepan*) is known as *aripan*. It is known as *alpanā* in Bengal, *osa* in Orissa, *chowka* in Uttar Pradesh, *mehndi maṇḍana* in Rajasthan, *sathiā* in Gujarat,[2] *raṅgolī* in Maharashtra, and *kolam* in Tamil Nadu. Strangely enough, the making of these diagrams is referred to as writing and never as drawing or painting. This is possibly evidence of its archaic hieroglyphic origin. The *Gṛhya Sūtras* and the *Manu Smṛti,* manuals dealing with *saṁskāra* rites and the *vrata* observances, obligatory for any Hindu householder, enjoined the drawing of *maṇḍalas* by women in rituals connected with *bhūmi śhobhās* and *gṛha pūjās,* the worship and adornment of the earth and the home at the time of celebrations of pregnancy and birth, *yajñopavīta* or initiation, and marriage.

The *vrata kathās* that today accompany these diagrams, tales lauding the value of the observance and vows and the perils faced by those who neglect to observe them, are later accretions intended to stabilize the magical diagram and to give new interpretations to the imponderables. The *kathās* have become vehicles through which the *brāhmanic* tradition has sought to strengthen its moral and ethical codes that relate to the duties and obligations of women. They deny a woman initiation but leave to her the peripheral rituals. The magical nature of the original act of invocation and transformation persists, but the legends and myths are heavily overloaded with *brāhmanic* conditioning.

In Mithila, the *aripans* focus around passion, sex, and fertility. The day of puberty, of marriage and the subtleties of sex and loveplay, are interpreted through diagram, ritual, and *mantra.* Vibrant circular forms of the *kamalban* and the *bānsa,* the forests of lotus and bamboo, illuminate the *khobar,* the bridal room of a Maithil hut. This is an appropriate diagram to adorn the bridal room, for the lotus has archaic symbolism linking it to the earth, to the waters, and to fertility. As diagrams of the generative organs, the female is an open lotus, the male is the bamboo. The meeting of the two symbolizes sexual encounter and union.

In the *khobar* drawings the seven heads of Gaurī, resplendent with nose rings, are inset within a circle of seven lotus blooms. The heavy stem of the bamboo splits the circular form. Surrounding the diagram are the auspicious marks to protect the bridal couple: the bride seated in a palanquin, the sun and the moon, the *nava grahas,* the nine astrological signs, the Ṣaṣṭhī—the presiding divinity of childbirth who appears in all the diagrams of the northern river valleys from birth to marriage—the *maṭha,* an abstraction of a temple to represent the earth, and the *gaur,* the symbol of the goddess Gaurī as sexual love. In another fertility diagram, the fish and the lotus alternate to form the circle of fertility. At the center of the diagram is the radiant face of Gaurī.

In Bengal, the *alpanās* of Lakṣmī pūjā are drawn to ensure prosperity and beauty in spring, in autumn, and in winter. In spring, before the sowing of the seed, the *alpanā* to Lakṣmī is drawn in a tender green color. In autumn at the time of maturing of the harvest it is drawn in a vibrant yellow color, and in winter, at the time of harvesting, with the brown-gold color of the leaves of autumn. The most important festival is that which coincides with the *Durgā Pūjā* celebrations in late autumn.[3] Two forms of Lakṣmī are worshiped in Bengal, the one auspicious and uprising, the giver of prosperity, and the other Alakṣmī, inauspicious and malignant. Alakṣmī, the goddess of black magic and misfortune, is worshiped on the night of the *Kālī pūjā.* Numerous rites are enjoined for the clearing of the house of the goddess Alakṣmī before the auspicious Lakṣmī enters.

The *vrata* for Tusārī Pūjā, in Mithila, is performed at the *makara śaṅkrānti,* the movement of the sun into the northern constellation, and a diagram is made which is regarded as the dwelling place of the ancestral divinity of the Maithils, Bhagavatī Gaurī. In this diagram, three symbols of the *maṭha* (temple) are drawn, first with dry, white rice-powder, second with turmeric and rice-powder, and the third with vermilion mixed with rice-powder. The temples have a trefoil roof, forming the shape of lotus petals. Within the temples are placed the mark of the goddess, the Gaurī *yantra,* three triangles symbolic of three lotus petals welded into a single form. This *aripan* is written by women with the thumb and one finger.

The *Tusārī Pūjā* is performed at dawn by unmarried girls; the efficacy of the ritual is lost if the ceremonies extend beyond sunrise. Unmarried girls continue to perform this *vrata* until their marriage. The Tusārī rites are accompanied by the recitation of spells, performed on the white *yantra* for granting a loving husband, on the yellow for wealth and prosperity, and on the red for protection against disease. During these rituals the sun, the moon, and the planets are worshiped.[4]

It is a belief in Mithila that Śiva visits the virgin goddess at night, on the festival of *Gavahā Śaṅkrānti.* As a gesture of welcome to the wild lover, a *vrata maṇḍala* is delineated in the form of a lotus flower, within which two footprints are drawn; at times the figures of Śiva and Pārvatī replace the footprints. A bamboo, placed on the footprints of the great god, leads to the resting place of the goddess, the shrine within the hut. The sexual symbolism of the lotus and bamboo echoes the song of sexual love and fertility. On the right side of the diagram, five circles, symbolic of the goddess, are drawn by women with the help of three fingers. The circles, symbolizing the living energy-form of the goddess, are worshiped by maidens; only then, for the first time after the rains, can the fuel of cow dung be made and used by the village.[5]

One of the most charming of Maithil *aripans* is the *mohaka,* the "falling-in-love" diagram. This is written in the bridal room, the *khobar ghar,* and is intended to break down barriers and to awaken desire between the bride and bridegroom, who may be totally unknown to each other. The marriage rites of the Maithils are very elaborate and bound by ritual. In the *mohaka aripan,* two fully-opened lotus blooms are shown facing each other. The two lotus blooms are joined by a heavy bamboo shaft, tipped with two unopened lotus buds. The bride and the bridegroom sit facing each other before the diagram and feed each other rice and curds. The spell that accompanies the rites is from the *Atharva Veda.* The *Kauśika Sūtra* prescribes its use on the fourth day of marriage, when the husband and wife anoint each other's eyes and the bridegroom says, "Put thou me within thy heart, may our minds verily be together," and the bride, covering the groom with her garments, says, "I bridle thee with my Manuborn garment, that thou mayst be wholly mine, mayst not make mention of other women."[6] Women in Bengal have a *vrata,* similar in sentiment to the *mohaka,* known as the *subhāsinī vrata.* The ritual is performed at the house of the grandmother when the bride sees the face of her husband for the first time. The ceremony is tense with emotion, for it is after these rites that the beloved daughter leaves her childhood home and enters a new life among strangers. In the *alpanā* that accompanies the rites, seventeen birds with outstretched wings are depicted flying toward a lotus diagram. This is an abstract form of the virgin bride, drawn with vibrant lines that speak of the youth, the energy, and passion of the young maiden. Vermilion, ***kum kum,*** flowers, and fruits are placed on the diagram, and the goddess is worshiped.[7]

The ***ṣaṣthī aripan*** in Mithila is written at the time of the young girl attaining puberty. The rituals are performed on the fourth day after the girl has taken her ritual bath. For four days from the onset of menstruation, the girl is kept in ***nāga,*** a shelter built of the shoots of the bamboo and banana tree. The young virgin, awakening to desire, love, and procreation, is likened to the vital energy of the cobra. After the ritual bath of cleansing, a drawing of bamboo shoots is written on the maiden's forehead in ***sindūra*** orange, and her yellow ***sārī*** ornamented with paintings of the sun, the moon, the ***navagraha,*** the ***gaur*** (Gaurī), ***saṭhī*** (or ***ṣaṣthī***), and a diagram of the bamboo and the lotus. The virgin's relations gather and place paddy, rice, turmeric, betel nut, banana leaves, and coconut in the folds of her cloth. A clay image of a cow and a calf is then placed on the ***ṣaṣthī aripan*** and the ***pūjā*** performed. On the walls facing the ***aripan,*** auspicious images of the sun, the moon, and the planets are drawn in yellow color. Surrounding the empty space, enclosed within the ***aripan,*** are placed tiny dots, the seed and sperm of life. Within the space float numerous tiny lotus forms, driven by an invisible urgency. At the heart of the ***aripan*** is the vermilion ***bindu,*** the mark of the goddess. At the base of the ***aripan*** is a sharp-pointed flame, resplendent with a scarlet ***bindu.*** This is the point of ***kāma,*** the magnificent intensity of a virgin's desire likened to a strong flash of young lightning.[8]

With the first pregnancy, a new doorway to creation opens. Dangers lurk. The demand for ritual protection is heightened to ensure that evil eyes do not fall upon the seed within the womb. The Kāyastha women of Madhubani draw diagrams of protection from the first month of pregnancy. This continues till the nine-month cycle is completed. With the first birth pangs, a diagram of a labyrinth is drawn on a clay platter. At the center of the labyrinth the unborn baby is seen cradled. The platter is held before the expectant mother to help her in childbirth. The baby starts its journey through the labyrinth of the womb, to the only doorway, slowly opening, to once again enter the labyrinth of life. Birth was a journey from darkness to light, but still to be in a labyrinthine hold. The diagram of birth is painted with white rice paste. A similar labyrinth is drawn by the Bāul women singers of Bengal. It too symbolizes birth and entry into the world and its bondage.

In the Chattisgarh region of Madhya Pradesh, a *vrata* is observed known as *Hala Ṣaṣthī* or *Harchhaṭ*. For the ceremony women prepare a rectangular portion of the wall with cow dung. Over this a stylized image of the mother, *Harchhaṭ Mātā,* is painted. In the courtyard, a *chauka,* a square diagram establishing the four cardinal directions, is drawn to provide the *pīṭha,* or altar of the goddess. On it are placed seven earthen images of cows with calf, separated by an earthen mountain of a tiger made of clay. Before these images is placed the *kalaśa,* a water pot decorated with leaves. In the *Harchhaṭ* ceremony, a pit is dug. In it are placed freshly cut branches of trees, a *mahuā,* the *kāns,* and the jungle *ber.* An image of the goddess Gaurī, modeled out of cow dung, is placed within the *chauka* or altar. Other parts of the ceremony include the placing of seven kinds of parched grain in a leaf cup of the *mahuā* tree. This mixed grain is called *satnāj.* During the worshiping, bangles, vermilion powder, and a piece of cloth are offered to the branches of the trees. The women of the household eat no grain from a ploughed field on that day. The use of cow's milk is also prohibited.[9]

In another fertility festival, the *Gaurā Vrata* of Chattisgarh, women build, five days before *Dīwalī,* a small earthen rectangular platform called *chaurā* (*chabūtarā;* Sanskrit, *chatvara*). On it are placed seven varieties of flowers, the *tulasī* leaf, and some rice. Seven unmarried girls pound their grain seven times; the grain is then offered to the goddess on seven leaf cups. Offering songs are sung:

> A basket of leaves I offer O Gaurā
> Ray Ratan Durgā Ho Ray Ratan Durgā.
> Thy seat is of fragrant sandal-wood, Great is thy glory, O Gaurā
> Great is thy glory,
> Like the branches of the Karma tree
> Like the buds of the Karma,
> Like the flowers of the Paroda
> Such is thy glory, O Gaurā, Such is thy glory.
> Gaurā knows only the mango fruit, we desire the mango seed
> We beg for sons, we beg for grandsons for many births will
> We be grateful, will we be grateful.

The worship continues till the night of *Dhanterasa,* the thirteenth day, sacred to the goddess of good fortune. Songs are sung by women every night. Two days before *Dīwalī,* women go in musical procession to the house of *kumbhār,* a potter, who molds out of specially dug earth two icons of Mahādeva on a bull and Pārvatī on an earthen tortoise. On the night of *Dīwalī,* the images are brought away from the house of the potter after they have been worshiped by the potter and his wife, by women with dancing and music. The procession is known as the bridal procession of Mahādeva. During the procession men and women become possessed by various local *devatās,* Bhaironātha or Siddhnātha Bābā. On the way, people who have some unfulfilled desire offer a coconut to Mahādeva. The person on whom the coconut falls is expected to have his desire fulfilled. On returning home, the icons are placed on the specially prepared, rectangular, earthen platform, the *chauka.* The two unmarried girls who have carried the images make five circumambulations around the platform; this is known as the *kunwāri bhanwar,* the virgin circle. A design is then drawn on the platform in white rice-paste and four earthen pitchers filled with parched paddy are placed at the four corners; this represents the marriage bower. The icons are worshiped again and the sacrament performed. The next day it is married women that go round the images seven times in a ceremony known as *suhāgin bhanwar,* the circle of married women whose husbands are alive. Then the images are taken in procession for ritual immersion.[10]

Nāga Pañchamī, the day of the serpent, is celebrated throughout India by women on the bright or dark fifth of the lunar month of *śrāvaṇa.* Images of the cobra, which has ancient associations with magic, with medicine, with protection, and the power to bring rain and virility and images of the scorpion, the sun, the moon, the cradle, and the serpent goddess Manasā are painted within diagrams on walls and floors of village homes.

> As the black snake spreads himself at pleasure,
> making wondrous forms by the *asura's* magic, so
> let the *arka* make thy member, etc.[11]

In the legend associated with the rites of *Nāga Sādhanā,* the serpent worship to be performed at the time of drought, the king Guṇakāmadeva of Nepal is said to have approached sāntikara, the magician, who drew a great *nāgamaṇḍala.*

> This master, while using the proper incantations, drew a magical eight-petalled lotus flower, which he filled with gold and powdered pearls. He made therein the effigies of the nine great Nāgas, and by his spells induced them to occupy their proper places. Varuṇa, white of complexion, wearing a seven-jewelled snakehood, and carrying a lotus and a jewel in his hands, took his position in the centre; Ananta, dark-blue in the east; Padmaka, with his five hoods and of the colour of a lotus stalk in the south; Takṣaka, saffron-coloured with nine hoods in the west; Vāsuki, greenish with seven hoods in the north-west; Mahāpadma, gold-coloured in the north-east. Only Karkoṭaka, who was portrayed in blue colour like a human being with a snake tail, remained absent, as he was ashamed of his deformity and would rather expose himself to the deadly influence of the spell than appear in person.
>
> On the advice of Śāntikara, the king himself went to secure the help of the obstinate Nāga and notwithstanding his remonstrances, forcibly dragged him along by the hair. When the nine great Nāgas had thus been brought together, Śāntikara worshipped them and besought them to reveal unto him a remedy against the drought. Then they told him that he should paint their images with the blood of Nāgas, and for the purpose they offered him their own blood. As soon as the wizard had followed their instructions the sky darkened. Clouds overcast the celestial vault, and heavy rain began to pour down.[12]

In Mithila, the *Madhu Śrāvani Pūjā* is offered by the newlywed bride and groom on the *Nāga Pañchamī* festival. Women write serpent diagrams on five leaves of the *peepal* tree, and on the earth on both sides of the seated couple. The female serpent, Kusumvati, and the male, Voras, are worshiped during this ritual. The sun and the moon, the *gaur* (Gaurī), the *saṭhi* (Ṣaṣṭhī), and the nine planets appear as *bindus* (circles) on the left of the *aripan*. In some of the *aripans,* a *nāga bhāga,* two rampant serpents entwined in close embrace, are drawn to one side of the diagram. The striking head of the cobra forms the root of the *maṇḍala*. The imagery is intensely phallic. In the Deccan, the *Nāga Pañchamī* is celebrated on the fifth of the bright half of the month of *śravaṇa*. Serpents are drawn with red sandalwood paste on wood, and clay images of the cobras are molded and worshiped.[13]

The *Viṣṇudharmottara Purāṇa,* an ancient treatise on painting, mentions the making of *dhūli chitras* and *rasa chitras. Dhūli chitras* were outlined in wet colors. Both these processes are found in the *ālepan* drawings and the *vrata maṇḍalas*. The liquid color is known as *pithar* or *pithali* and is made by the mixing of rice or cornstarch with water. Before the *maṇḍala* is drawn, the earth or the floor of the house is freshly plastered with cow dung. The *maṇḍala* drawing is executed by women on the prepared space. The thumb and the first finger of the right hand are usually used to draw the *ālepan* diagrams. The *Devādaśa aripan* is an exception. This is drawn by Maithil women on the twelfth day of the observance of *śrāddha,* the ceremonies to the dead, before the shrine of the *kula devatā,* the clan god, in the *gosāinghar*. It is painted to the chanting of *mantras*. One finger of the left hand is used to draw a complete circle in white on the ochre color of the earth. The circle is empty of the *bindu,* the vermilion dot of energy. When the *kartā,* the main performer of the *śrāddha* ceremonies, goes to pay obeisance to the *kula devatās,* the *aripan* is effaced with cow dung, so that the eye on the *kartā* does not fall again on the *aripan* when the *karta* leaves the *gosāinghar*.[14]

Paintings as *Kathā*, or Story

Paper was introduced into India in the fifteenth century, at a time when the emergence of the vernaculars—Maithilī, Braj Bhāṣā, Avadhī, Deśī Bhāṣā, and Oriyā—had led to a great revival of storytelling in peoples' languages that could be understood throughout the countryside. Illustrated manuscripts appeared, rich in vernacular expressions and imagery, recording early oral and visual traditions. Art became transportable. It moved from walls and floors to scrolls, to folios, and to the traveling *paṭuās,* the itinerant painter bards. Paintings which had as their canvas the clay walls of village huts and the plastered walls of palaces, or which existed in the ateliers of monasteries, where illuminated bark-leaf manuscripts had been known from very early times, suddenly found mobility. Icons on paper and on cloth of the *purāṇic* gods and goddesses started being painted at centers of pilgrimage and were carried back by the pilgrim to be installed in the shrines of the *gṛha devatās,* the household gods. Villages of *chitrakāras* (painters) clustered around pilgrimage towns catering to the needs of the pilgrims. These *chitrakāras* also painted the stone, wood, and stucco images on the temple walls and painted as well the clay icons sold at religious fairs. The painted icons of Puri, Nathadvara, Tanjore, Kalighat, painted in pure primary colors, were carried in all directions across the country, weaving a tapestry and identity of common symbol, icon, and story.

A vast number of renderings of the *Mahābhārata, Rāmāyaṇa* and legends of *purāṇic* gods appeared in local vernaculars, absorbing into the stream of the story local folklore, wild and magnificent rural fantasy, and the heroic encounters of local warriors. The gods of the *purāṇas* fused with the local *grāma devatās;* their composite images with their wild passions and human frailties became familiar within the compass of the village viewer. A tender, often jocular, relationship between the gods and their devotees was established. Illustrated scrolls, in which the story unfolded horizontally or vertically, were carried by wandering *paṭuās* or *kathā-vachakas* to dwellers in village or forest. The *kathā* readings were rarely one-dimensional or restricted to the spoken word. They were integrated into dance, dialogue, recitation, and epic theater. Many of the wandering storytellers also practiced magic, astrology, and palmistry. Some of them were painters and musicians.

The transition from the extensive spaces of village walls to the limitations and confines of handmade paper led to a shrinking of scale in the paintings without a corresponding diminution of concept. The power and precision of brushwork, the sweep and curve of the line, the massive use of color, the stance and demeanor of gods, heroes, animals, and trees remained heroic, even epic. The narrative nature of the *kathā,* with its limitless interpolations of legends, myths, and other stories, extended to the illustrations. Like rural frescoes, the early manuscripts, scrolls, and miniature paintings were not enclosed within frames or borders, but overflowed the boundaries of the paper and the wall. The development of an incident was often related simultaneously within the same canvas, vividly reflecting the direct impact of the epic stage, where happenings separated by time and space occur at the same time at different levels of the stage, one episode coming to life and movement while the rest of the stage and its actors remain still.

In the early manuscript paintings, the script was used to support the painting and to provide visual accents. The sizes of the illustrations were determined by the space available on the page of writing. Perspective and shading suggesting distance and volume were totally lacking. There was also, as a rule, a complete absence of architectural detail.

By intention the narrative illustration projected swift and fleeting impressions. The eye and the ear of the audience rarely paused to minutely observe and assimilate. This led to an absence of detail and the use of pure washes of bold color, against which the images were projected. The bodies and faces of the gods, heroes, and beautiful women were painted to fill the canvas, the faces accentuated and the pupils of the eyes especially emphasized, to suggest life and power, leaving the hands and feet unfinished. This led at times to distortions—the protruding eye and the angular form were common.

In rural painting there was a sense of the inclusive, born of a direct perception of the environment, which entered and transformed the canvas. Symbols of parrot and *mainā* bird, bamboo and lotus, serpent, tiger and fish, and bow and arrow ornamented the *kathā* and the illustration. These symbols, impregnated with centuries of meaning familiar to the *kathā-vāchaka,* the painter and the audience, created the emotional mood and the ambience, making detailed explanation unnecessary. Communication was at many levels.

Many of the *kathā* readings, told through illustrated scrolls or puppets, were the enactment of rites to guard against drought. In Andhra and Mysore, the *tholubommalata* (leather puppet) performances were intended to ensure rain and a rich harvest. In Bengal and Bihar, the painters and storytellers were the itinerant *chitrakāras,* who combined in their hereditary occupation the arts of poetry, sculpture, and painting. The long scrolls (*paṭas*) they carried, painted on paper and pasted on to cloth for strength, were hung vertically on bamboo frames. The scrolls were from twenty to twenty-five feet in length. They were colored in warm sun colors, the brilliant reds and yellows of the noon sun and the blues of the sunset. Rivers wound in serpentine motion across the canvas; lines were fluid and luxuriant. The line of the creeper found expression in the curved rhythms of a woman's body, a clay water pot, or the *kadamba* fruit. It was a curvilinear art; the sharp accents of geometric figures of triangles and squares were missing. The canvas was illuminated by the lush, green environment of village Bengal. The story of the snake goddess, Manasā, and the legend of Gaurāṅga stories from the *Rāmayaṇa, Kṛṣṇa Līlā,* the triumph of Durgā, were told with grace and abundance and were chanted as the scroll unfolded to illuminate the song.

Many *paṭa* paintings were recordings of the seen and the heard. The *Rāma Yātrās, the Śiva Yātrās,* and the *Chaṇḍī Yātrās,* performed by traveling players who embellished the stories with their own experiences, gave body and character to the *purāṇic* gods. In Mymensing, Bengal, Śiva, the ash-smeared ascetic, appeared dancing to *ḍhāk* drumbeats. In the dances of Kalī, the terrible goddess of immense proportions wore a blue mask as she danced the *tāṇḍava,* one foot on Śiva's chest. The rhythm of the drumbeats echoed the roaring laughter of the primeval mother. The swiftly moving *yātrās* often ended in a frozen scene, a tableau. These frozen stills were recorded by the *paṭuā* on scrolls and walls.

The cult of the *baghai devatā,* the tiger god, extended over vast areas of the Himalayan foothills and the Ganges delta. Barakahan Gazi or Dakshin Rai in East Bengal was painted by Gaṇakas or Āchāryas. The paintings showed the Gazi riding a tiger, holding a rosary in his right hand and an *āsādaṇḍa* (two-headed axe) in the left.[1] At the end of the Bengal scrolls, the court of Yama Rāja, the god of death, where the evildoers of the world were punished, was painted. The *paṭas* of *baghai devatā* were carried by professional beggars of the Bed caste, who chanted the *kathā* of the tiger god and unfurled the scroll at village fairs, revealing the story.

The *jādū paṭuas,* magician-painters and brass-workers of the Santal Parganas, tribal converts who painted scrolls for the Santal tribe as well as for the dweller in the settled villages, had a repertoire which included paintings of Kṛṣṇa and Rādhā, the gods of the *purāṇas,* Santal heroes, kings, and Satya Pīr, the human-faced tiger god. In the Gazi scrolls, the spotted leopard replaced the tiger. Satya Pīr, the Gazi, who wore a pointed cap and beard was worshiped by both Hindus and Muslims. The Gazi scroll ended with the monkey deity, Haru Bonga, conversing with Sengel Bonga, a peacock.

The same *jādū paṭuās* of Santal who painted and told the epic stories also painted *jādū paṭas* (magical scrolls depicting the journey of the dead Santals through the devouring terror of the netherworld) for the Santal tribe. The Santals believed that their dead wandered aimlessly and blindly until the *jādū paṭuās* gave them *chakṣu dāna,* eyesight, by painting pupils and eyes into the portraits of the dead spirit.[2] The colors used in these paintings of the dead were muted earth tones of indigo, madder, burnt sienna, and ochre. The spaces in the scrolls were clearly defined, events being depicted in vertical arrangements to denote time. Line was precise and used with the utmost economy. There was an absence of the luxuriant curve of the creeper and woman's thigh, which gave way to austere forms in keeping with the theme, the mystery, and secret purpose of these paintings.

The *chitrakāras* or *paṭuās* of Kalighat, Bengal, were the creators of a series of paintings which have come to be known as the *kalighat* (bazaar) paintings. Painted on cheap paper and sold as icons at the shrine of the goddess in Calcutta, these paintings were in a flat watercolor wash. The shading used to suggest volume clearly indicates the obvious influences of Anglo India. Many of the scenes depicted religious scenes, but a large number of reproductions of fruits, flowers, fish, animals, and scenes of contemporary life formed part of their wares. Later paintings grew more topical and were often expressive of the reaction felt in some sectors of Bengal at the growing westernization of Calcutta society. Although influenced by the schools of Anglo-Indian painting, the *kalighat* paintings retained their vernacular roots. The line was a bountiful curve expressing endless rhythms of breast and thigh. The outline was firmly delineated. The brushwork was immensely confident; there was an absence of the inessential. The colors were the savage, glowing reds of the midday sun, the browns and intense green of the leaves of autumn, and the blues of water lilies.

Early *kalighat* paintings reflect the rural love of the dramatic and the urge of the Bengali towards religious ecstasy and passionate devotion. Many of the paintings illustrate stories from the epics and *purāṇas*. A towering figure of Hanumān, the devoted one, tears open his heart to reveal the incandescent images of Rāma and Sītā. A baby Gaṇeśa gazes with adoration at the face of his mother, the benevolent goddess. Nṛsiṁha, the man-lion, "he who is clad in living flames," drawn in fierce lines that sweep across the canvas, tears apart the demon being, portrayed as a dark aboriginal chieftain. Within the leonine face, the eye of Nṛsiṁha is a great lotus petal, his snarling teeth suggested by a few powerful strokes of the brush, his lion whiskers curled back in anger. An incongruous touch is the pointed shoe worn on the foot of the tribal king.[3]

Later *kalighat* paintings are dramatic statements on secular themes. A mustachioed husband in *dhotī* and *angarkhā,* with shoes on his feet and round earrings in his ears, is painted carrying an umbrella in one hand, while in the other he holds a chopper with which to strike down his "westernized" wife. His wife, in the strict orthodox tradition of Bengal, wears a simple *sārī* without a *cholī*. The only indication of her western conditioning is a handbag, which the artist places in front of her as a symbol of her degeneration. In another drawing a young woman, radiant with energy, tramples on her reclining lover. The dark coat of the lover forms a black pool of color in vivid contrast to the white, bold-black-bordered *sārī* worn by the soaring, splendid woman.[4] The *paṭa* painter has unwittingly interpreted an ancient theme familiar to the *yātrā* performances; in this painting of secular themes lauding the values of male supremacy, the dark, energy-filled goddess, Kālī, tramples and dances on the inert earthbound body of Śiva. "Ever art you dancing in battle, Mother. Never was beauty like thine, as with thy hair flowing about thee, thou dost ever dance, a naked warrior on the breast of Śiva."[5] Like the ancient god, the male figure in the *kalighat* painting is devoid of life and movement; it is the feminine, the sacred embodiment of energy, who by her touch awakens the lifeless, the inert, to new life and radiance.

In Andhra and Maharashtra, a tradition has long existed of wandering storytellers, the *chitra kathis,* who illustrated their recitations of the epics with paintings, with mime, and with puppet shows. A series of paintings that have come to be known as *pratisthana* paintings possibly represents the work of painters descended from artists at the court of the Vijayanagar kings. These illustrations are painted on a thick ivory-colored, handmade paper and illustrate local variations of the *Rāmāyana,* the *Mahābhārata,* and the legends from the *purāṇas.*

These paintings strongly resemble the Lepakshi murals and the *tholubommalata,* the flat leather shadow puppets of Anantapur district, Andhra. The leather puppeteers of Andhra and Mysore, who speak a corrupt Marathi dialect, are believed to have migrated to the south from Poona, Satara, and Belgaum during the sixteenth and seventeenth centuries.

The *Pratisthana* paintings of the eighteenth and nineteenth centuries are martial in mood. They represent a strong male-dominated culture. There are scenes of battle, of the hunting of savage beasts, of the destruction of malevolent female tree-spirits and demons. The male heroes, symbols of the *vīra rasa,* the heroic mood, are resplendent with bow and arrow, dressed in a tightly tied *dhotī* and long hanging upper cloth, and in some cases close-fitting coats. The women appear in subordinate roles; they wear a tight satin bodice and a *dhotī,* with a cloth at times draping their heads.

The colors used in the *pratisthana* paintings are primary—red, blue, and yellow. There is little modeling or perspective; the faces are drawn in profile, the features are sharp, the nose is pointed. As in all rural paintings, the eyes are depicted from a frontal position, even though the face is in profile. The colors are mainly used on the bodies of man and animal; the background is in a natural-color wash.

As in the *tholubommalata* leather-puppet performances, *pratisthana* performances were linked with ancient rain magic. They served as rituals to propitiate the rain gods. There is a recurrent focus on fertility, symbolized by the taut bow and swiftly flying arrows, shafts that pierce trees, shatter milk pots, and strike the bodies of women in the narrative of these paintings.

In a *pratisthana* scene illustrating the Kṛṣṇa cycle of legends, the young god has merged with Kāma, the god of love. The flute has been exchanged for a taut bow. Kṛṣṇa's weapons are the shafts of Kāma; he shoots his arrows and they pierce a palm tree and shatter the milk pots carried by milkmaids. Below Kṛṣṇa, a fish lifts its head from a pool of water. The phallic symbolism is accentuated by the way the bowstring unites with the bow, the way the trunk of the palm tree joins the palm leaves, and in the symbolism of the fish.

In a series of paintings on the exploits of Hanumān in Laṅkā, the erotic is given wild expression. Hanumān's tail is on fire. He escapes his demon captors and enters the households of Laṅkā, causing terror in the hearts of the demons dallying there with beautiful women. The tail of Hanumān, like a powerful, sinuous serpent, sweeps across the paintings. Hanumān is absent, but his tail, itself a phallic symbol, disturbs the erotic couples and fornicating demons. In another painting Hanumān, the valiant warrior roaring with the sound of Indra's thunderbolt, his arms raised in anger, stands before the sea. The wild fury of the monkey god is evident from his aggressive stance and the way that his tail sweeps the sea, seeking to destroy the fish, the sea serpents, and the other denizens of the deep. The spirit of the sea in human form stands with hands folded in supplication.

In another painting from the *Rāmāyaṇa* series, a mustachioed Rāma and a beautiful Sitā are depicted sitting in a pavilion within a forest playing *chaupar;* looking in from under the trees is a golden deer, the demon Mārīcha transformed. In the following painting Sītā points to the animal. The deer springs away in flight as Rāma, his arrow strung to shoot, is poised to pursue him. Another painting depicts Śūrpanakhā, Ravana's demon sister, who, insulted by having her nose cut off by an angry Lakṣmaṇa, turns into a demoness, uprooting palm trees and attacking Lakṣmaṇa. The heroic and demonic are boldly presented to an audience familiar with every nuance of the *Rāmāyaṇa* story. The actors, the paintings, and the audience enact their epic roles in a torchlit village square, sharing in the victories of Rāma, weeping at the agony of Sītā kidnapped by the demon king, enthralled by the exploits of Hanumān.

Another series of paintings illustrates local legends of the hunt and of wild women, the spirits and the guardians of impenetrable forests. A woman, her legs entwined in two interlocked palm trees, hangs suspended from the trees. She wears a tight bodice, but her lower limbs are bare, her *yoni* is sharply defined to resemble an eye. The hanging woman with wide open eyes, a dynamo of energy, is guarded by two hefty amazons dressed in tight *dhotīs* and bodices, carrying shields and curved swords. Though at first glance it appears as if the suspended woman is undergoing some form of monstrous torture and punishment, on closer observation the close and intimate link between the suspended woman and the trees is evident. The naked, suspended woman is a tree-spirit, an *apsarā,* a symbol of the explosive fecundity of nature. The frontal exposure of the woman's genital regions have unquestioned ritual significance. Nudity is sacred; it affirms and establishes presence. In archaic rituals, nudity has prophylactic virtue against all evil influences and is integral to rain magic.

The *bhopas,* the magician bards of the Bhils of Rajasthan, travel through the countryside with long painted scrolls, the *pabūjī kā paṭa.* The scroll is about thirty feet long; the illustrations to the story are arranged horizontally. There is no attempt at chronology. Bold colors are used in flat washes of red, black, olive, and yellow ochre. Surrounding the main figures are warriors, scenes of battle, cows and calves, lions and tigers, and episodes of heroic encounters. The central figures of the hero, Pabūjī Rathore, and his proud black horse, Kasar Kalini, tower over the rest of the figures. These scrolls (*phards*) replace the live performance.

The legend of Pabūjī, who lived and died in the fourteenth century, springs from the Rajput traditions of chivalry. The *kathā* recounts the story of the beautiful virgin-princess Deval Devī, an incarnation of the goddess, who rode a splendid black mare while tending her cattle in the desert of Marwar. Jind Raj, a baron of Jayal, saw and coveted the wondrous black mare, Kesar Kalini, but Deval would not part with it. Jind Raj threatened battle. Fearing for her life, Deval fled to the land of the chief of Kohlugarh, who gave her refuge and treated her like his own daughter. In gratitude and love, Deval gave her black mare to her foster-brother Pabūjī, the young son of the chief of Kohlugarh, whom Deval esteemed greatly. Pabūjī in turn promised to protect Deval and her cattle at the cost of his life. Years passed. A beautiful princess fell in love with Pabūjī as he rode on his resplendent black mare and wanted Pabūjī to marry her. He told her, however, that marriage was not for him, for he had pledged his life to protect Deval's cattle. The princess was adamant and so the marriage between Pabūjī and the princess was arranged. While the wedding rites were taking place, Deval's cattle were attacked by Jind Raj. Deval transformed herself into a bird and flew to Pabūjī and whispered in his ear as he sat in the marriage bower, reminding him to keep his word to her. Pabūjī left his bride and, astride Kesar Kalini, the black mare, rode with seven men against Jind Raj and his thousand soldiers and rescued Deval's cattle. Pabūjī was fatally wounded in the battle. He died soon afterwards, together with the black mare. His bride immolated herself as a *satī* and joined Pabūjī in heaven.

The performances of the *Pabūjī Ka Phard* are held at night. The *bhopa,* the magician-painter bard, and his wife, sing and dance before the scroll, while the relevant illustrations are illumined by an oil lamp held by the woman. The story is narrated in mime, song, and drumbeat. Interspersed with the story are acrobatic feats and magical interludes.

As well as being used by wandering bards and storytellers, painted scrolls were used in temples. These painted and printed temple cloths fulfilled the functions of frescoes on temple walls. In Nathadvara, Rajasthan, an important center of Vaiṣṇava worship, the subject of the painting centered around the worship of Śrī Nāthajī. His image, a black stone, squat and sculptured with massive compactness, appeared in the center of the painting. The face was featureless except for massive, silver-lotus eyes that focused and channeled the attention of the worshiper. A brilliant orange hue, filled with the energy of exploding sunlight, formed the background to the paintings. The deity in the painted cloths was adorned with the colors, flowers, and ornaments of the seasons, changing in harmony with the cyclic movement of nature. Around the dark deity were women and men worshipers; in some of the cloth pieces, a hundred, liquid-eyed cows surrounded the lord, taking the place of the *gopīs,* the milkmaids of Brindaban.

In south India, Andhra Pradesh, in Kalahasti, Nagappattinam, and Pallakolu, painted and printed cloths of mythological nature, known as *vasamalai,* extensions of the mural technique, which narrate stories from the *Bhāgavata* and other *purāṇas* were produced. These cloths were used for hanging on temple walls and as screens on wooden *rathas* that carried the icons of the great tradition in procession around the town.

The goddess Bhadrakālī occupies the center of one of these cloths. She is ten-armed and wears a check-patterned cloth as a *dhotī.* The mighty presence of the goddess fills the cloth. Her face is prominent, her eyes stare unceasingly. Serpents spring from her crown. Around her, the gods of the *purāṇas* and the *grāma devatās* act out their cosmic destiny. The head of Reṇukā is worshiped by women with lamps and flowers. Kṛṣṇa steals the garments of *gopīs,* the gods and the demons churn the ocean. A vast number of such incidents are placed on the canvas, arranged in horizontal panels, giving to the picture a compactness that suggests the complexity of life.

In another cloth, an infinite number of dots are used to add texture to the background against which incidents from the *Rāmāyaṇa* are delineated. The ten-headed Rāvana stands facing two ways, his earth-shaking stance suggesting the arrogance and fury of Laṅkā's lord. Hanumān, the favorite deity, appears as a black pool of color and overshadows the demons and the gods. Fish flow in streams. The flowering trees, under which Sītā sits, appear as fragile vertical lines suggesting the delicacy and beauty of the lady surrounded by demon hordes. The sense of epic landscape is evident.[6]

In Gujarat, *mātā ni pachedi,*[7] the cloth of the mother, recounting the exploits of the seven mother goddesses, is printed by artisans of the lower castes for use in the wayside shrines of the mothers, at the time of the *Navarātras,* the nine-nights-festival celebrated after the rains, when the earth and the mothers awaken. The printing and preparing of the cloth is by the alizarin processes wherein the earth, the waters, and the sun participate in a chemistry that transforms and brings to life the colors of the cloth, the blood-red, the black, and the white filling the center of the cloth. One of the seven archetypal forms of the mother rides a black male buffalo. From her crown springs sprouting corn. Surrounding her are her devotees, her son Gaṇeśa, the *buā,* her magician-priest, the sun and the moon, horses and their riders, dancing-girls, and milkmaids. In other forms she is Bahuchara, the four-armed goddess who holds a sword, a spear, a bell, and a cup of blood. As Ambā, the benign mother, she rides a camel; as Bhadrakālī, she is sixteen-armed and rides a tame buffalo. As Chāmuṇḍā, she rides a buffalo; as Kālikā, she sits on a cock. She sits on a peacock throne as Khodiyal, the lame mother. As Jogan, the ancient sorceress, she strides forth, the sacral trefoil crown on her head. The *buā,* the priests of the goddess, sing of the mothers' ancestry and their glory at specially constructed shrines in which a round earthen pot containing the *javarā,* tender, sprouting barley shoots, have been placed. The cloths of the mothers are hung around the shrine and form its roof. Within the shrine, placed in a horizontal line on the platform, grim abstractions in wood symbolize the mothers. They are triangular in shape, without eyes or faces, with protruding stumps as arms. Three forms of the primordial mother are manifest within the shrine: the uroboric Earth Mother, carrying vegetal life, sprouting corn, within her womb; the mother as geometric abstraction, blind, brooding, pregnant with terror and mystery, and the mother of human form, recognizable, with a sublime and radiant face, many-armed, riding the buffalo, the cock, the camel, and the peacock throne.

On the last of the nine sacral nights of the goddess, the *buā,* the magician-priest, drinks fermented rice wine and is possessed by the goddess. He dances and sings wildly and, wrapping the *pachedi* cloth of the goddess around his shoulders, he leads a procession to the riverside. Virgin girls follow him, carrying on their heads the earthen pot containing the sprouting corn. At the river bank they worship the departing mothers and the sacral pot is consigned to the waters.

The Pictographs of the Warlis, the Bhils, the Gonds, and the Śavaras

Earthen grainbins and the mud-plastered walls of huts are the canvas on which tribal people paint. The Gonds of Mandla paint in red and black on a white background; the Śavaras in white on the red-ochre-washed clay walls of their huts; and the Warlis and the Bhils of Maharashtra and Gujarat in white with touches of brilliant *geruā* red on the earth-color walls of their homes. The canvas has shrunk and the vast world of the tribesman, of mountain, forest, tree, and animal is compressed into a framework symbolized by the hut, the enclosed space within which the tribesman lives. On the "canvas" are elaborately drawn and ornamented dots, triangles, and chevrons; the ever-extending world of the tribesman enters the world of dream, of magic, of ghost and spirit, the world of bird and animal, the sun and the moon, man and woman, the motor car and the train. The descent from the high places, from the freedom of cave and mountain to the enclosed spaces of the hut built on flat lands, is evident in the drawings.

Like the rock drawings of their ancestors, the diagrams of the Warlis, the Bhils, and the Śavaras appear sacred, ritual-bound, but they are not icons demanding worship. The main purpose of these drawings is to promote fertility, to avert disease, to propitiate the dead, to fulfill the demands of the ghost-spirits who permeate the dream world of the tribe. By painting the picture and including the object desired, the result is achieved and the spirit is satisfied. Among the Gonds of Mandla and the Warlis of Maharashtra, the tribes who have had close contact with settled village societies, pictographs are also made to celebrate festivals and for aphrodisiacal purposes. It is the magician-priests of the tribes who paint the magical diagrams and the spirit-pictographs; the women of the tribe do not participate in the painting of the mysteries.

The Warlis, as a rule, do not enclose their drawings within a frame, but use the wall as a stretching canvas; the cracks in the clay walls create a textured rich surface. An unusual power and control of space and composition is evident in these paintings. Nothing is static; the line of the drawing is laid with nervous energy. The most significant of their pictographs is of the *pālạghat,* a *maṇḍala* of the corn goddess, wherein the sacred presence is drawn within a chevron-ornamented square.

The *pālạghat* is formed of two triangles, one pointed downwards, the other upwards in the manner of the *Śrī Yantra.* The triangle pointing upwards is the male element and is a symbol of the *pāla* (erect stone). The one pointing downwards is female and is the *ghaṭa,* the overflowing water pot of plenty, a symbol of the earth from which all life emerges. In delineating the sacred form the Warlis do not intersect the lines of the triangles ⧖ . It is this that distinguishes divinity from man, for in depicting the human form the triangles do intersect ⧗. A head, two hands, and two legs are then added to the geometric abstraction of both the sacral presence and the human form.[1]

The chevrons of the border of the *maṇḍala* form is the Hariālī Deva, the god of plants. Near the *maṇḍala* of the corn goddess, a headless warrior is painted, either standing erect, or riding a horse, with five shoots of corn springing from his neck. This archaic symbol expressing the cosmic cycle of death and life is known as Pañcha Sirya Deva, the five-headed god. This deity is worshiped only by women.[2] A metal image of this divinity with five human or animal heads and a rising phallus appears among the Bhils of Gujarat, where he is known as Pañcha Mukhī Deva.[3] The figure is often identified with Mahādeva. That the origins of this divinity stem from the fertility rites of agricultural magic, appears evident.

In areas where the Warlis have come in close contact with the culture of settled village societies, both men and women paint. The women painters have an exceptional sense of fantasy and magic. Recently they were given handmade paper and asked to paint whatever and however they desired. The results were paintings of strange significance.

A tiny, wrinkled lady created landscapes of uprising trees, painted in varied tones of white on an earth-colored background. The images from the Warli paintings could have been born of the *Atharva Veda* hymns, of the glory of virgin forests and the sacral spirit of tree-divinities, the homes of *apsarās* and the dancing, crested *gandharvas*. There was a primeval knowledge that each tree was alive, creating a luminous, light-filled world of splendid trees, hundred-branched trees with outstretched leaves, "fortunate, God-quickened, powerful." Horses and riders appeared in minute forms; hidden by the rising-resplendent trees, a startled deer confronted the hunters. In another painting, the old Warli woman had painted a canvas of forest trees in shrill tones of red against a background of muted earth tones. The trees filled the canvas, elongated forms creating the loneliness and the secret spaces of forests. The fine, vibrant leaves of the trees arose towards the sun, forming a fragile tracery—delicate and tender. Two of the trees were drawn with heavy, hanging fruit, accentuating the fragility of the surrounding trees. The number of humans and animals and birds had increased. Tiny images of the tiger, the deer, the hare, and the peacock were painted in deep tones of red; men carried burdens, but they were still free to gaze with wonder at the rising trees. The uprising immensity of the trees and the smallness and insignificance of man and animal reflected the mood of the painter. In a corner, out of proportion to men and animals, waited a brooding, brilliant red spider, a symbol of the unspeakable one—Thakramal Chatri—the great, malignant spider, who in tribal legend straddles the path under a dark sky, waiting for man. The spider is a symbol of the evil and of the primordial terrors that lurk as much in the primeval forests as in the subconscious of man.

In another painting drawn by the same wrinkled old woman, the forest had been cleared. The trees lay prostrate; the fields had been marked, boundaries established, and huts built. Everywhere man appeared. He had grown in size in proportion to the few standing trees, but everywhere man was bound, held imprisoned in the complexity of a settled culture. Huts were shown being built. A cross structure of bamboo formed the roof, within which man was caught and crucified. Labor had replaced the freedom of life in the forest. Yoked oxen carried man to the fields; solitary figures with raised arms were held within the confined spaces of their huts. An old man walked bent over his stick. Across the central spaces where the trees had been felled, the waiting spider had spun a vast web. The spider had disappeared, but the empty web, drawn in lines of white and black, lay waiting, a symbol of tragedy and anguish that perhaps is unsurpassed in tribal art. The spirit and mood, the deep subconscious stirrings of the *Ādim Vanya Jāti* people, the ancient dwellers in forests, caught in the suffocating spiral of civilization, was expressed in this painting with infinite poignancy.

Many Warli paintings appear at the time of marriages and at the celebration of the Gaurī festival after the rains, when the earth awakens to a new cycle of fertility. A moon-faced Gaurī is painted on a Warli wall painting, seated cross-legged within a square altar. Her two arms are raised in the sacral gesture that establishes the presence of the goddess. From her sacred head sprouting corn arises. Her virgin breasts are covered with necklaces. She is surrounded by symbols of fertility: a creeper luxuriant with flower forms an aureole around the goddess; ears of corn, fish with their interiors exposed revealing baby fish, and pregnant rabbits fill the spaces around the numinous form. The bodies of the animals are hatched with vertical and horizontal lines. Great care is taken by the Warli painters to delineate details of hair and feathers on the bodies of animals and birds. The sun and the moon, the two oil lamps, the foot of Gaurī, and the mark of outstretched palms protect the diagram and render it auspicious. A tree heavy with fruit and flower in the form of an *alepan* diagram is painted on the side of Gaurī, and a seven-petaled flower forms the *maṇḍala* of fertility under which the goddess is seated.

A number of pictographs of the Warli depict dance. Human forms are constructed with utmost economy of line, with the awareness of the relationship of line to background surfaces. Dancers blow the *dobru* (*ḍamaru*), an archaic instrument found among most tribes of western India; men beat the drum and hold hands in circular formations. To primitive man, dance, accompanied by chants and rhythmic sounds, was the magic that set hidden forces into motion. These were the *karma* dances of tribal India, dances in which "the men leap forward to a rapid roll of drums, then bending low, the women dance, their feet moving in perfect rhythm to and fro, until the group of singers advances towards them, like the steady urge of wind coming and going among the treetops and the girls swing to and fro in answer."[4] In one of the pictographs three dancers leap into space. On their heads are wildly fanciful headdresses, one with uprising sheaves of corn, another with five heads of horses, and the third with dancing human figures. No such headgear is worn by the Warli dancers of today. The illustrations possibly express the exploding energy of the earth and relate to an archaic past when the Warlis were children of the forest, free of care, a world where plant, animal, and man were in intimate communion and relationship.

THE BHILS

The *buās,* the magician-priests of the Bhils of north Gujarat, paint sacred *pithorās* of horses and riders on mud walls within the Bhil hut in red, yellow, and black. The sacredness of the images is suggested by the tautness of line that delineates each man and animal. Every equestrian group is given the separate name of a Bhil deity. One horse and rider is designated Ganhotra Bāpā, from Ganapati, the elephant-headed god; another is Rājā Bhoj; another becomes the Pithorā Deva. In some areas the horses are painted without riders. Within the framework of the *pithorā* are painted the sun and the moon, yoked bullocks, elephants, tigers, peacocks, and curious horse carriages. Like the Warli paintings, a headless figure is invariably represented with five heads of sprouting corn emerging from the neck. In one insignificant corner of the *pithorā* a copulating couple is depicted as an emblem of fertility and life. This composite drawing forms the Pithorā Deva.

As part of ancestor worship Bhil *buās* also make a liquid paste from *javāra* (*joār*) grain and spit it onto the walls of their huts, to make shadow outlines of the palm of their hand, or a sickle. These symbols protect the huts from malevolent forces of the known and unknown world.[5] The wall at the entrance of the Bhil hut is coated with cow dung, and three images of humans, two in an erect position and one in an inverted position, are sculpted in low relief. These figures are worshiped by the *bhopa,* the magician-priest of the Bhils.

Before the *gotra,* the ancestral shrines of the Bhils at Poshena near Ambaji in Gujarat, mysterious paintings of elongated ghost-like figures, painted in tones of white, are drawn by the Bhil magician-priest. The figures hold flowering plants in their two hands; their heads are covered with cowls; only the eyes appear, hollow pits of death. From the heads tendril-like forms float, images of sprouting corn. From the dead ancestors arises continuing life. The figures are surrounded by living things, by birds and flowers, and are enclosed within a framework of chevrons.

THE GONDS

Verrier Elwin in his book, *Tribal Arts of Middle India,* has written in some detail of the festival of *Ate Kaniya.* This birthday of Kṛṣṇa is celebrated by the Gonds of Mandla by painting Kṛṣṇa of Brindaban on the walls of their huts.[6] The frescoes celebrate the various *līlās* of Kṛṣṇa: Kṛṣṇa plays the flute, roams with cowherds on the banks of river Yamunā, dallies with *gopīs*. The drawings are geometric in form, in the severe tribal idiom. Young boys and girls make offerings to these pictures.

The Pradhans tell a story of Kṛṣṇa and Arjuna. When Arjuna saw his friend Kṛṣṇa's stupendous success with young women, in contrast to his own hopeless, unrewarded passion for Subhadrā, he grew depressed and jealous. He retired to the forest and on the walls of his hut painted the first originals of the pictures made in a thousand homes today, exclaiming: "O Kṛṣṇa, you are loved by seven hundred, but not a single one loves me." Kṛṣṇa's heart was touched by the prayer and the pictures, and he granted his friend's wish. He brought Arjuna and Subhadrā together.

THE ŚAVARAS

In the *purāṇas,* the Śavaras are called the Vindhya Maulikas, the wanderers in the Vindhyas, an ancient tribe mentioned in the *Rāmāyaṇa* and the *Mahābhārata.* Appearing in the epics as a primitive people dwelling in thick forests, wearing leaves for garments, they rise to power and emerge into history, as rulers of vast tracts of territory in the heartlands of India. In the seventh and eighth centuries, they appear in Mirzapur, in Uttar Pradesh, in Ganjam, Keonjhar, and Puri in Orissa, and in Andhra.[7] The cult of Jagannātha is closely linked with ancient Śavara cults. In the following centuries the fortunes of the Śavaras declined—they were defeated in battle, lost their kingdoms, and disappeared again into the forests, to continue life as primitive hunters and wandering cultivators. For many centuries after their defeat, the Śavaras continued to influ-

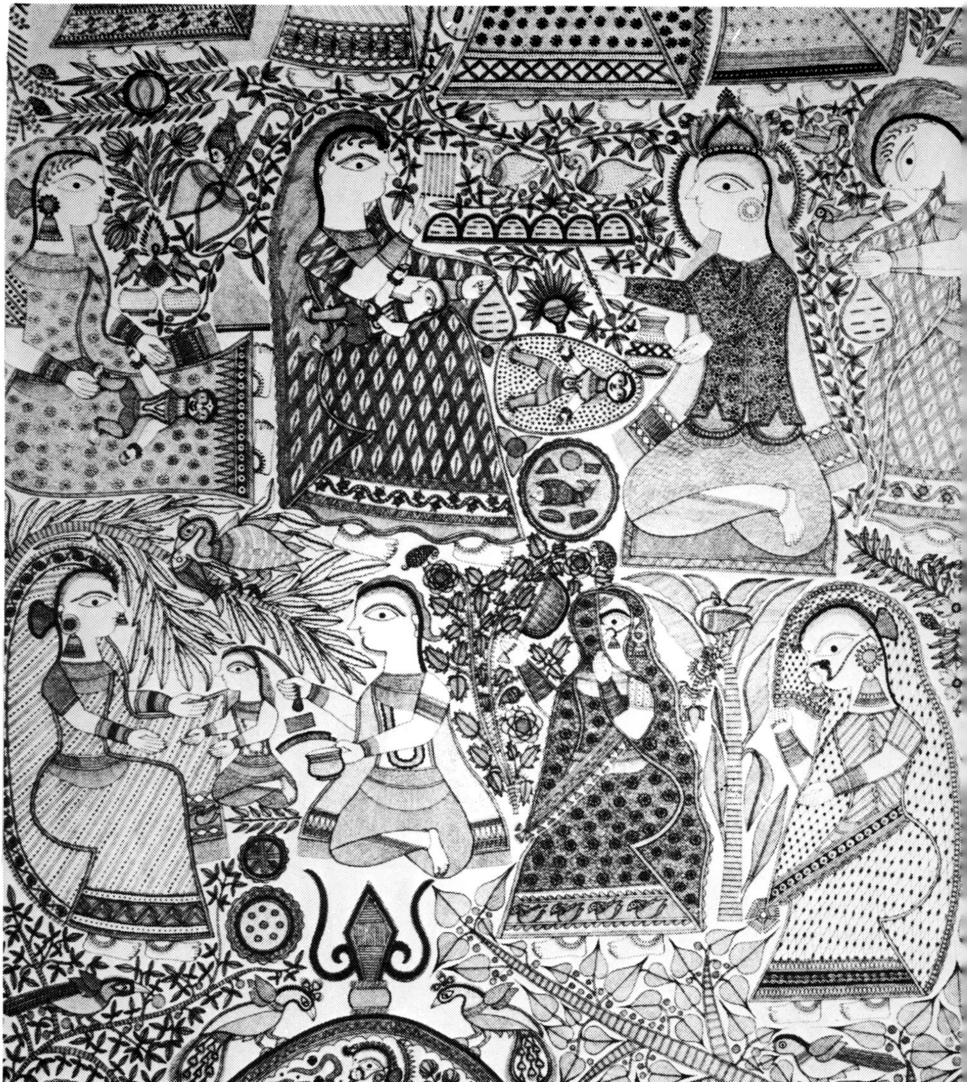

42. Part of a large black-and-white drawing illustrating marriage and birth. Ganga Devi from Ranthi village, Mithila, Bihar, 20th century.

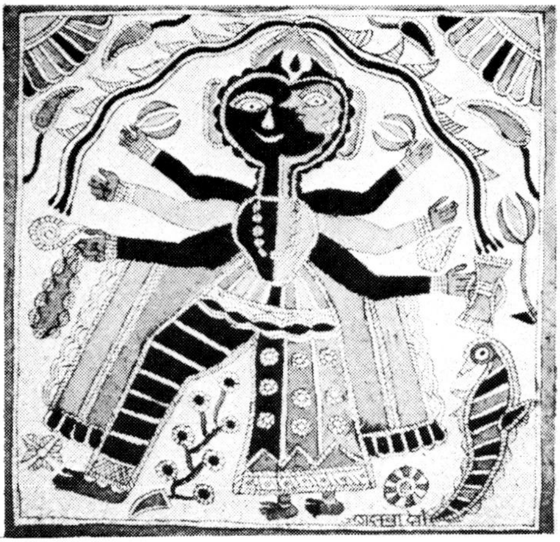

43

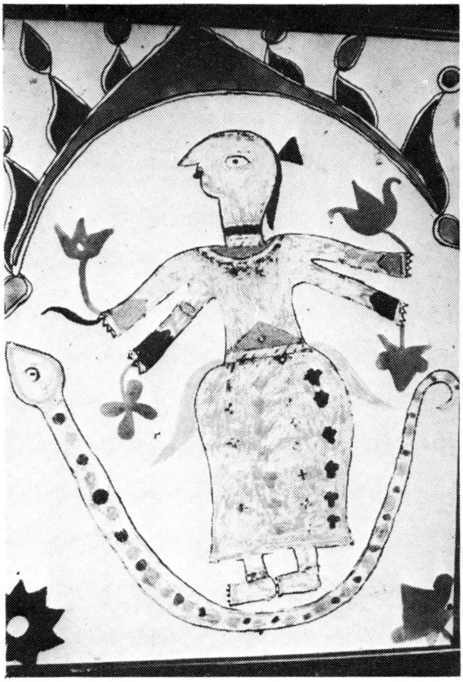

44

45

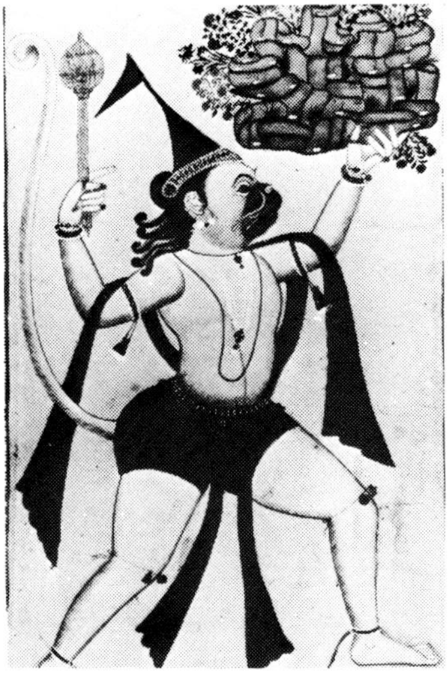

43. Kālī-Gauri, the biform image of the goddess, holding within her the two aspects of the Mother as darkness and light. Painting of straw board. Jagadamba Devī of Ranthi village, Madhubani, Bihar, 20th century.

44. Jogan, the bird-faced divinity, with her hair tightly drawn back from her face. At her waist is the mystical triangle. A snake is coiled beneath her feet. In the Ganges valley the Jogan is known as Nona or Lona, the Jogan. Jamuna Devi, a *Harijan* painter from Jitwarpur, Madhubani, Bihar.

45. Hanumān, the devotee of Rāma, as inspired by Tulsidasa's *Rāma Charita Manasa.* Kotah, Rajasthan, 18th century.

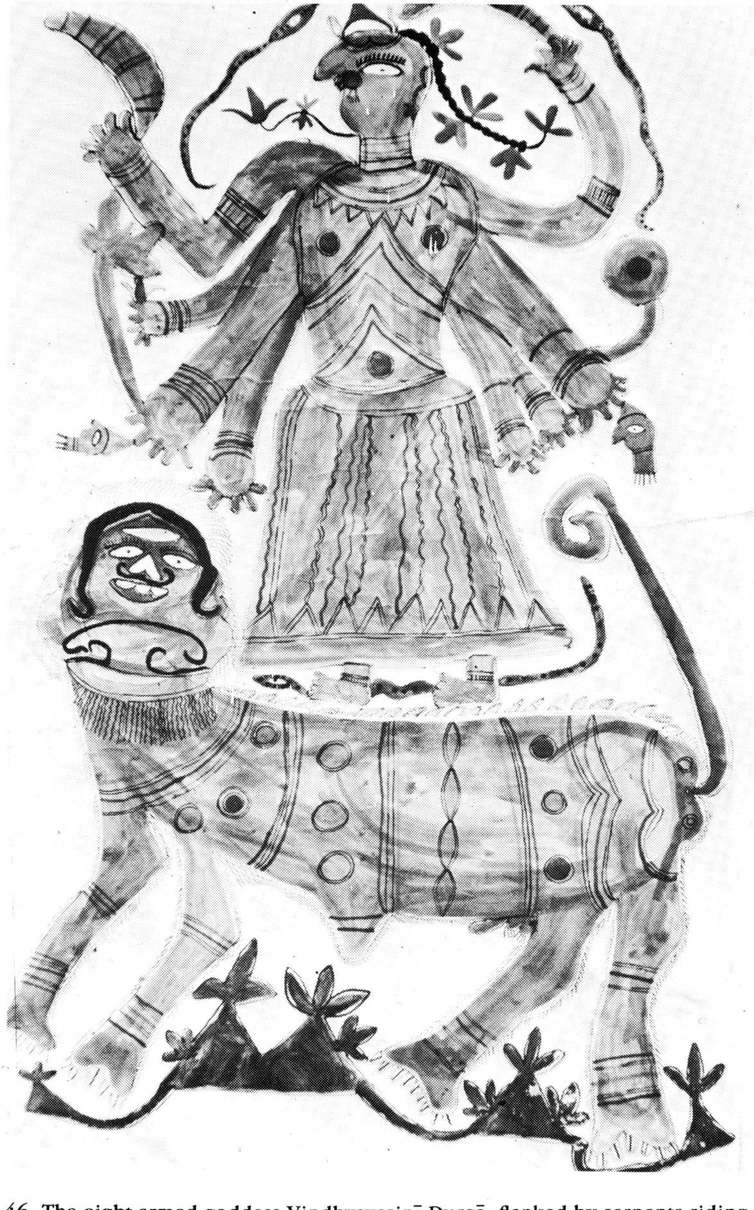

46

46. The eight-armed goddess Vindhyavasinī Durgā, flanked by serpents riding the human-faced tiger. Ookha Devi, Jitwarpur village, Madhubani, Bihar, 20th century.

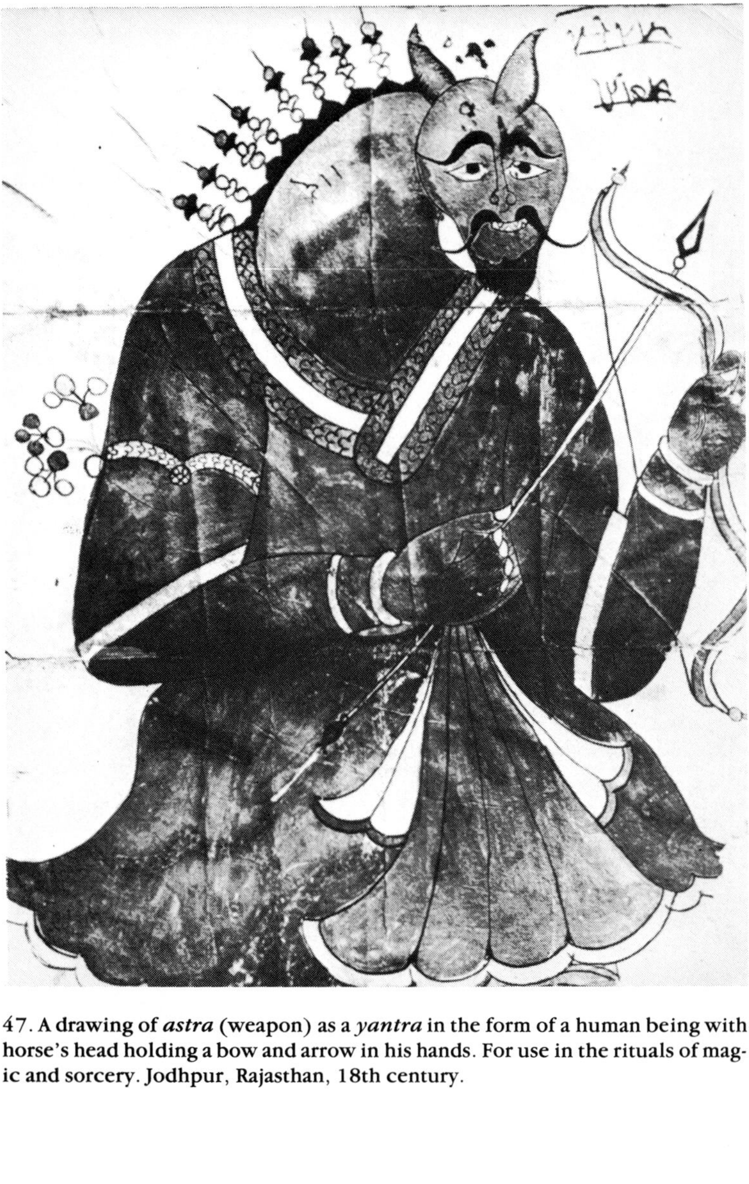

47

47. A drawing of *astra* (weapon) as a *yantra* in the form of a human being with horse's head holding a bow and arrow in his hands. For use in the rituals of magic and sorcery. Jodhpur, Rajasthan, 18th century.

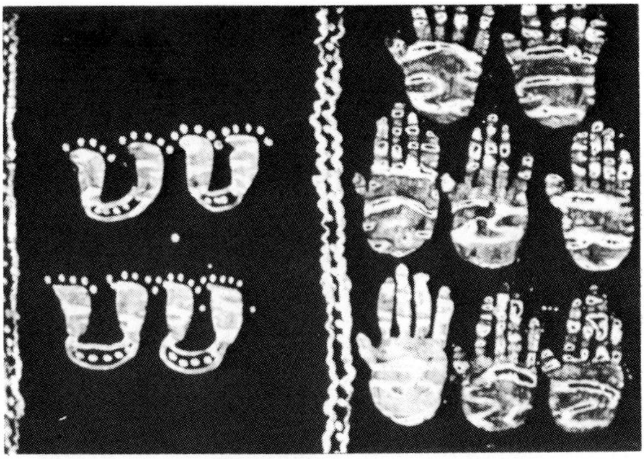

48

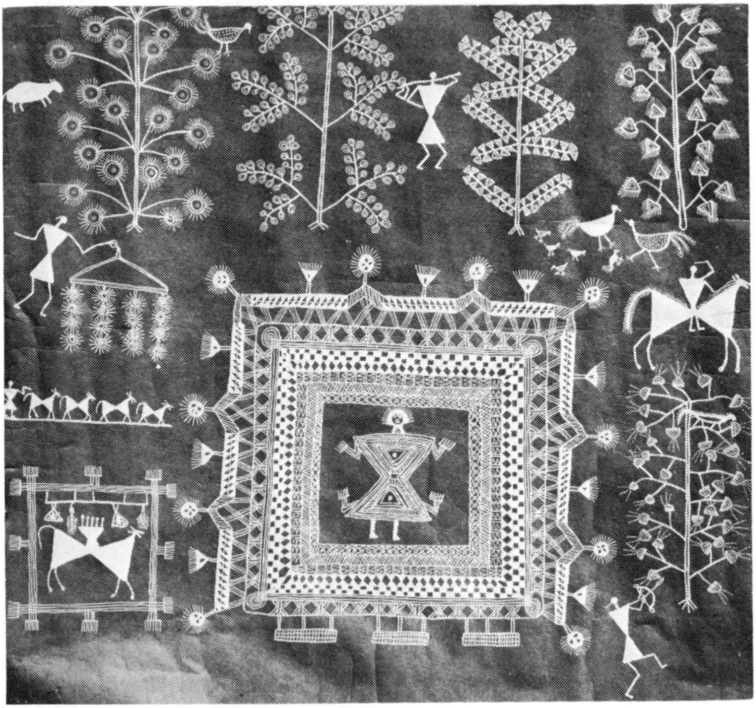

49

48. Osa drawing showing palms of hands and footprints. Painted by the wife of Mohan Mehra, weaver from Sonepur, Orissa, 20th century.

49. Pālaghat or Kansari, the corn Goddess, enclosed within a square *maṇḍala.* To the left is the Pañcha Sirya Deva riding a horse, a headless figure with five sheafs of corn sprouting from his neck. Painting on paper by Jivya Soma, Ganjad village, Thana district, Maharashtra, 20th century.

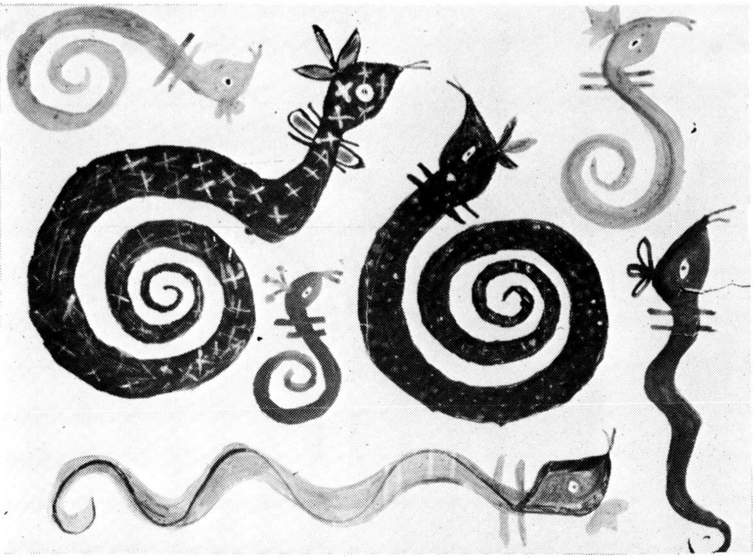

50

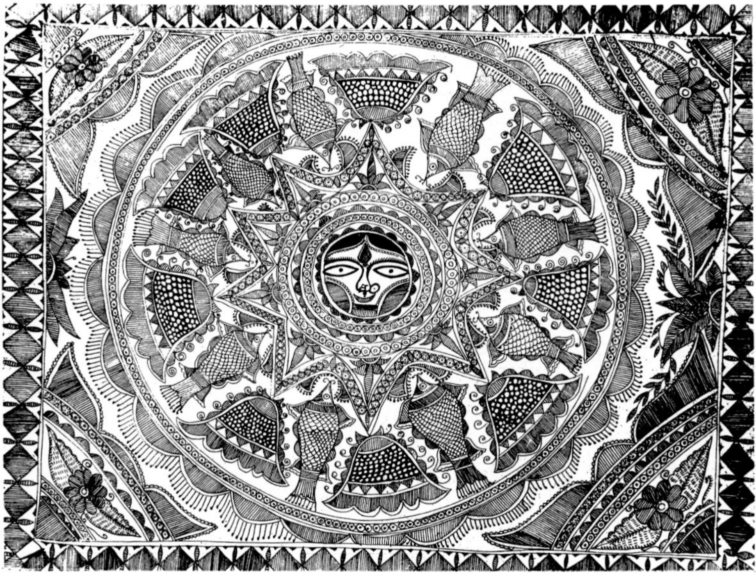

51

50. Serpents. Paintings on the walls of a *Harijan* hut. Uchet, Madhubani, Bihar, 20th century.

51. A fertility *aripan* from Mithila, Bihar, written in the ***khobar ghar,*** the bridal room. Symbols of the fish alternate with the lotus. At the heart is the head of Gauri. Drawing on paper by Maha Sundari Devi of Ranthi village, Madhubani, Bihar.

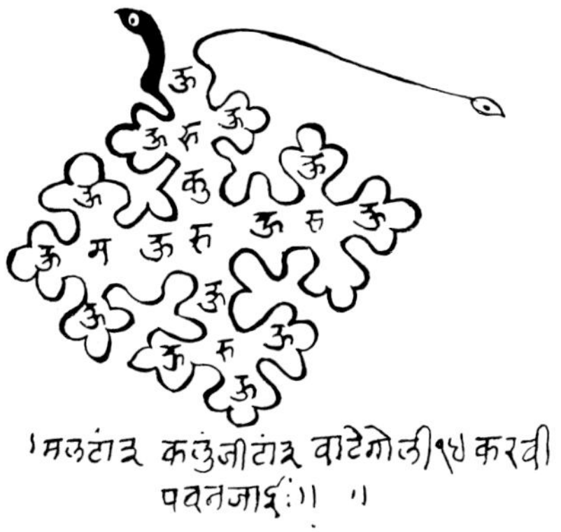

52

52. A drawing of an *astra* (weapon) as Pavan Jādu, the striking magical power of winds, visualized in the form of a serpent. Jodhpur, Rajasthan, 19th century.

53. A *Sūrya maṇḍala* of the sun. A cobra with raised hood and two leaves sprouting from its tail symbolizes the exploding energy of the sun, the waters, and life. Drawing on paper by a weaver of Varanasi, 20th century.

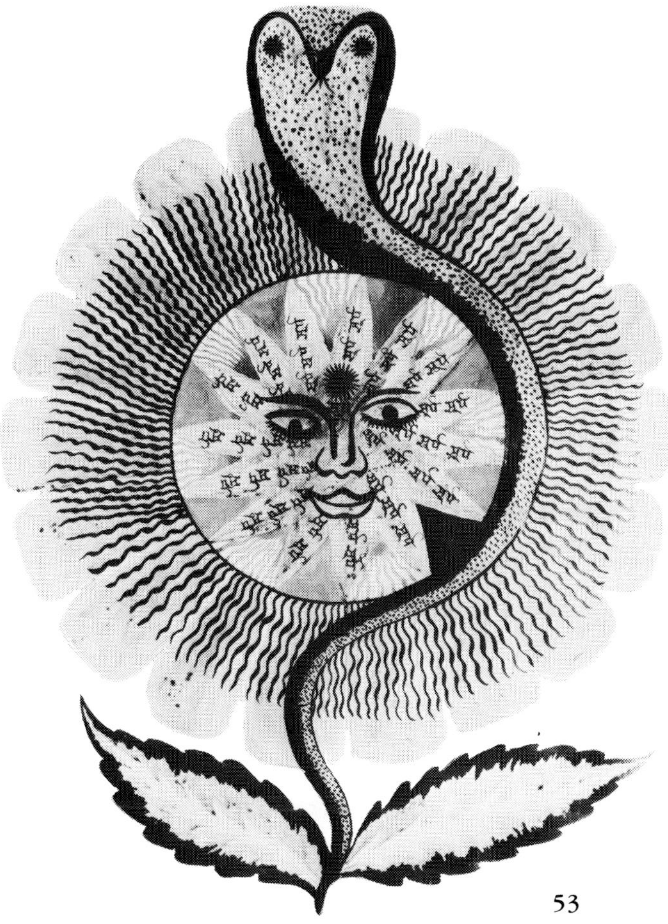

53

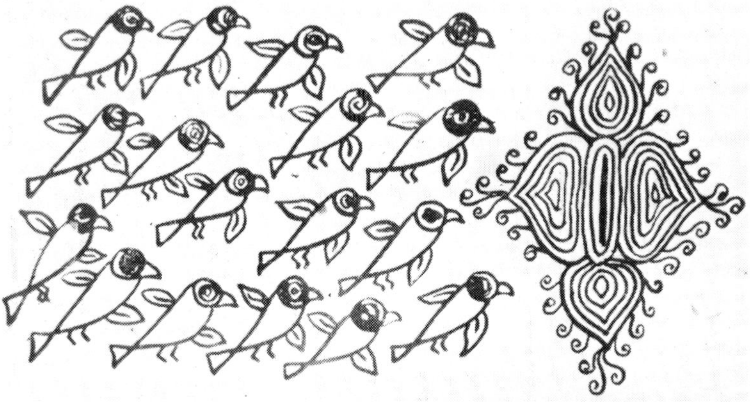

54

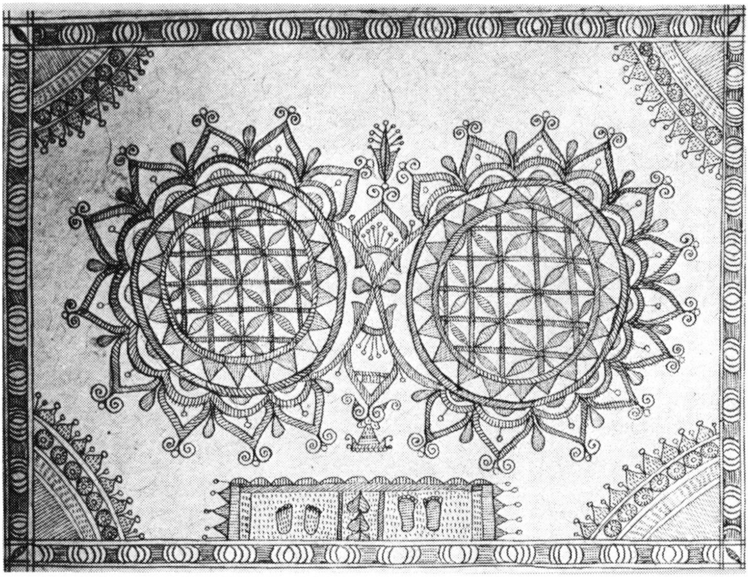

55

54. Subhāsinī *alpona,* drawn at the time when the bride leaves her father's home. Bengal, 20th century.

55. Mohaka *aripan,* written to the chanting of *mantras* on the fourth day after marriage. Sīta Devī of Jitwarpur village, Madhubani, 20th century.

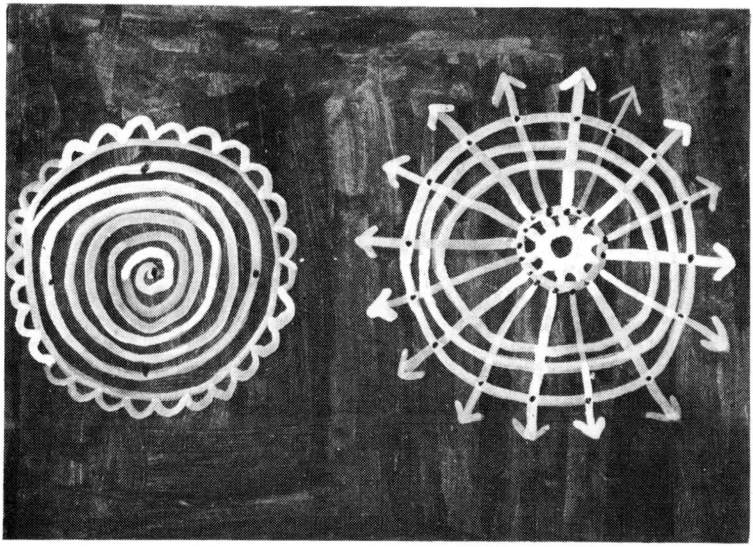

56

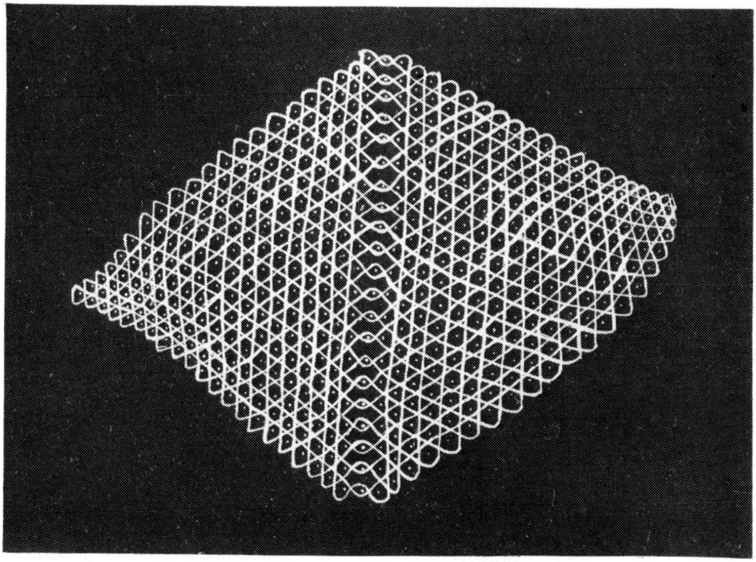

57

56. A spiral convoluting inwards symbolizes the sacred female principle as "the great coiled one." The virile male principle is visualized as a circle radiating outwards with arrows flying from the central core. Used in *tantric* rites. Painting on wall. Barohi Jha, Jitwarpur village, Madhubani, Bihar.

57. *Kolam,* drawing on the earth, two triangles interlink to form a *yantra.* Drawn by the women of the weaving community of Tamil Nadu to ward off the evil eye, 20th century.

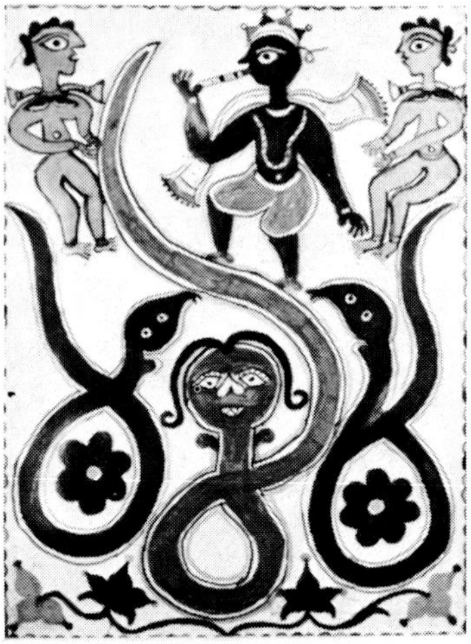

58

58. Kṛṣṇa plays the flute and dances on the human-faced Kāliya, the serpent king of the Yamuna river. Flanking Kṛṣṇa are the *naga kanyas,* the daughters of the serpent king. Painting on paper, Madhubani, Bihar, 20th century.

59. Hor Rāja, leader of Santal tribe. By Rajaram Chitrakār, Tesjuri village, Jamtara subdivision. Santal Parganas, Bihar, 1944. India Office Library, London.

60. Kṛṣṇa playing on his flute to two *gopīs,* while below, baby Kṛṣṇa is seated on his foster mother Yasodā's lap. By Babulal and Surendra Chitrakar, Ranga village, Raj Mahal subdivision, Santal Parganas. Bihar Archer Collection, London.

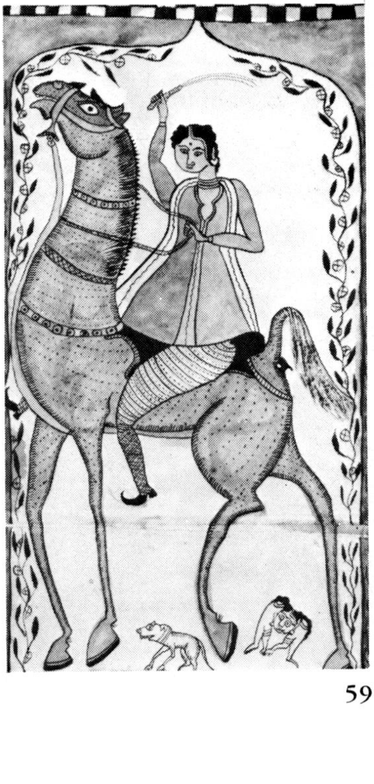

59

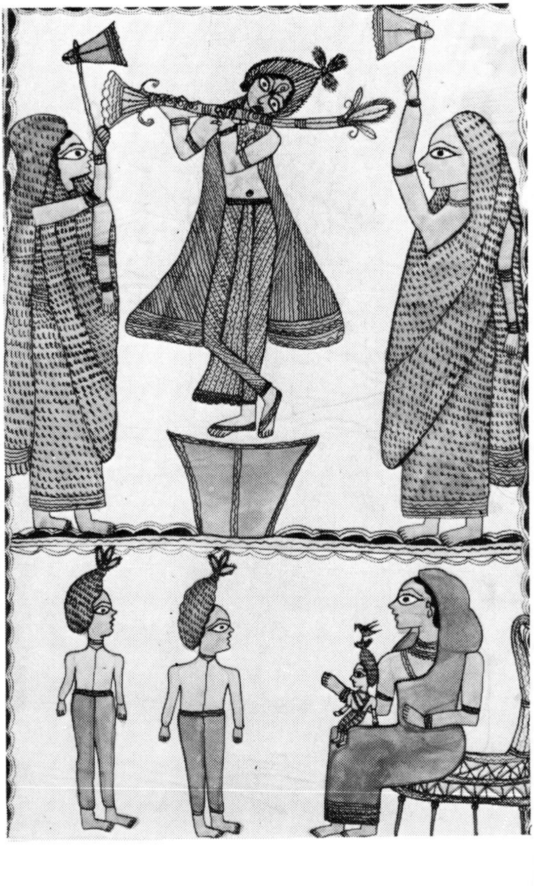

60

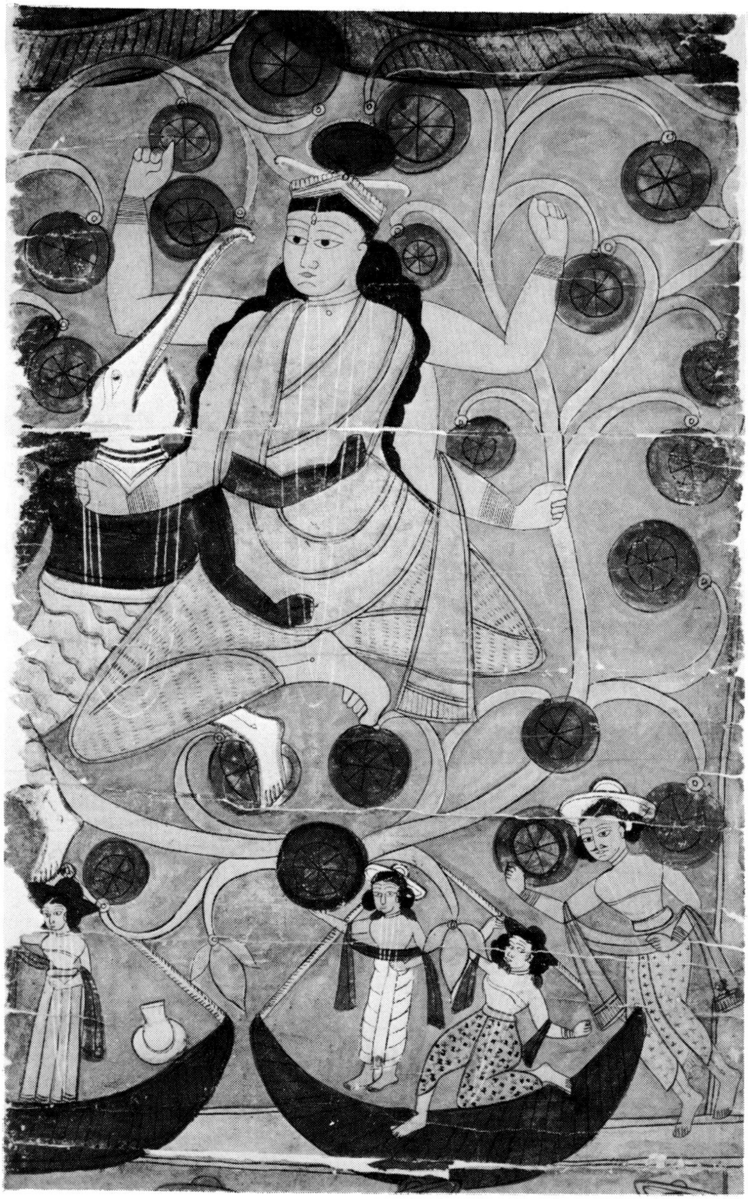

61

61. Jarano Pat of Sakti, Gouache on paper, Birbhum, Bengal, 19th century. Courtesy: Philadelphia Museum of Art.

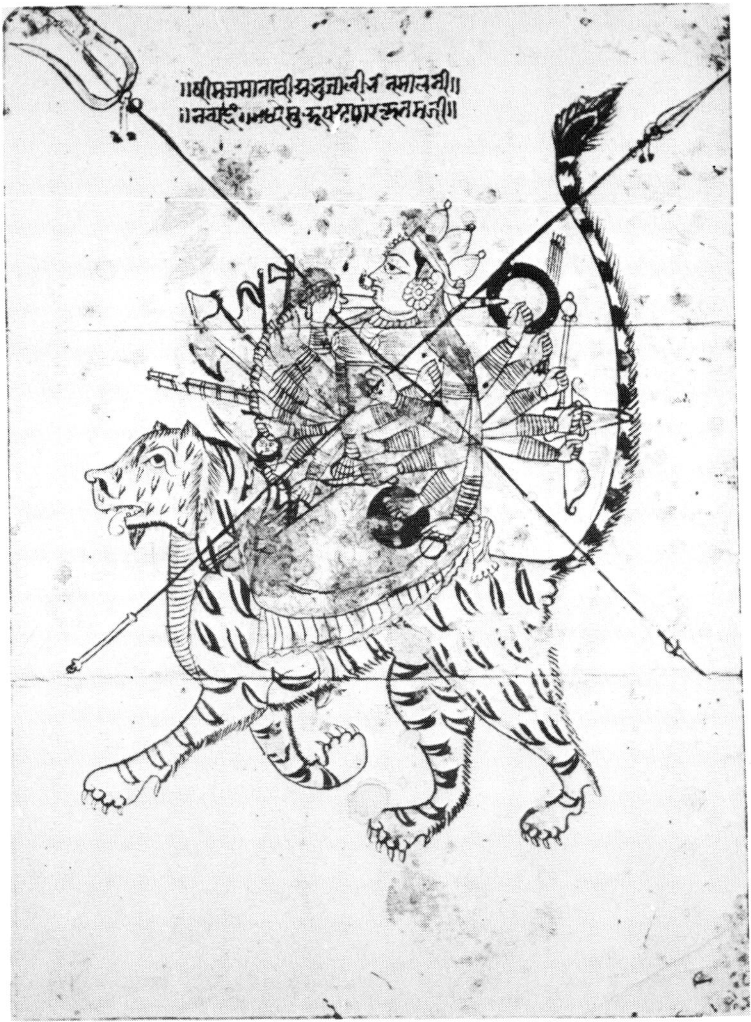

62

62. The resplendent twenty-armed goddess in her militant role as warrior, riding the tiger. Drawing on paper, Rajasthan, 18th century.

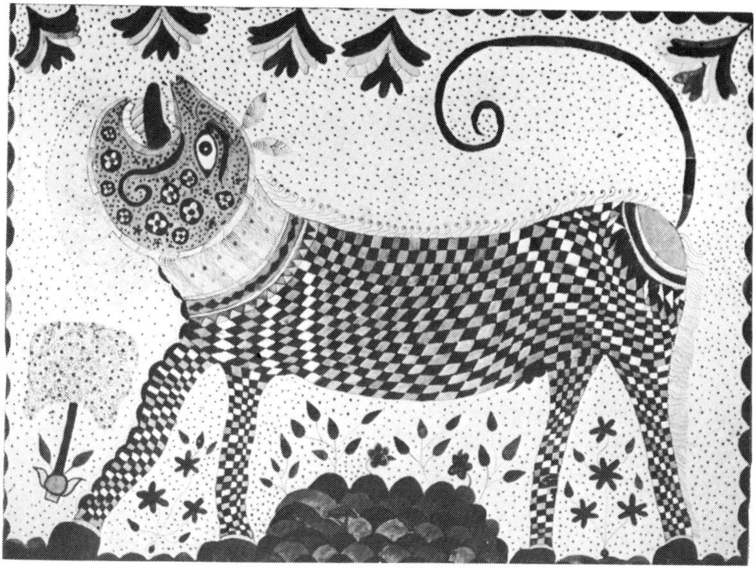

63

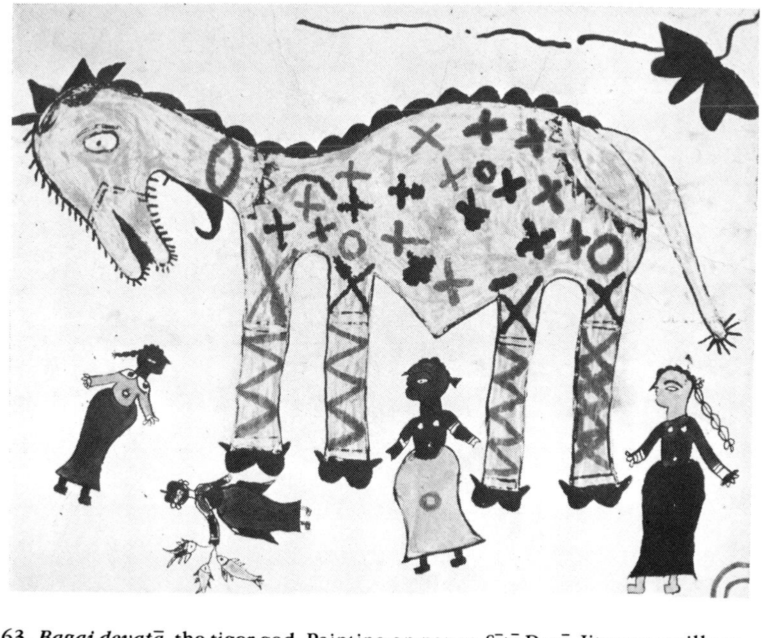

64

63. ***Bagai devatā,*** the tiger god. Painting on paper. Sītā Devī, Jitwarpur village, Madhubani, Bihar, 20th century.

64. A horse. Jamunā Devī, a *Harijan* painter of Jitwarpur, Madhubani, Bihar, 20th century.

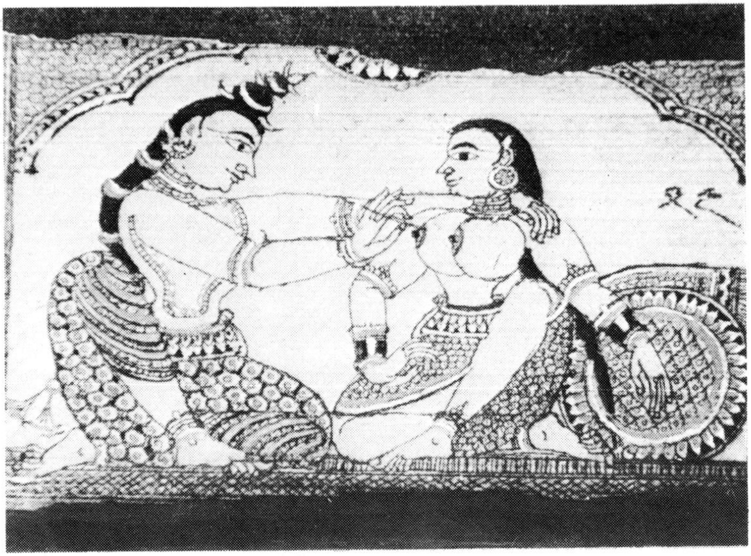

65

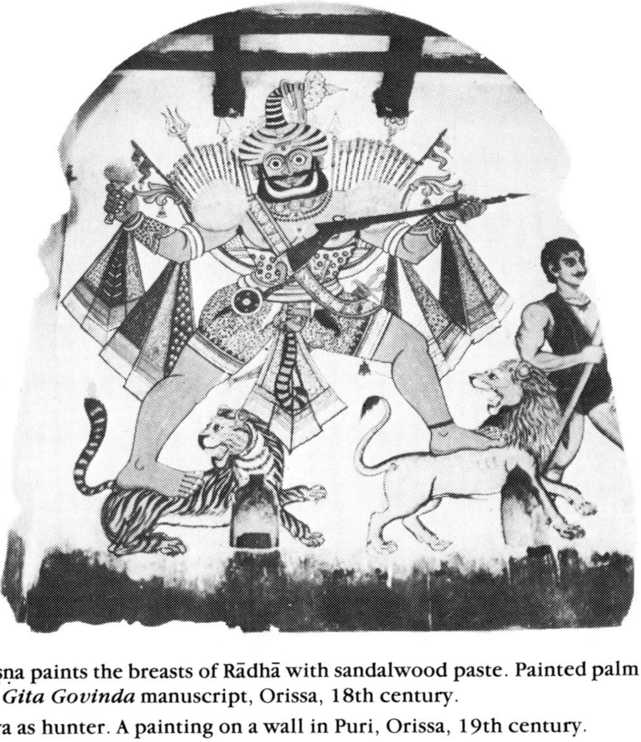

66

65. Kṛṣṇa paints the breasts of Rādhā with sandalwood paste. Painted palm leaf from a *Gita Govinda* manuscript, Orissa, 18th century.

66. Śiva as hunter. A painting on a wall in Puri, Orissa, 19th century.

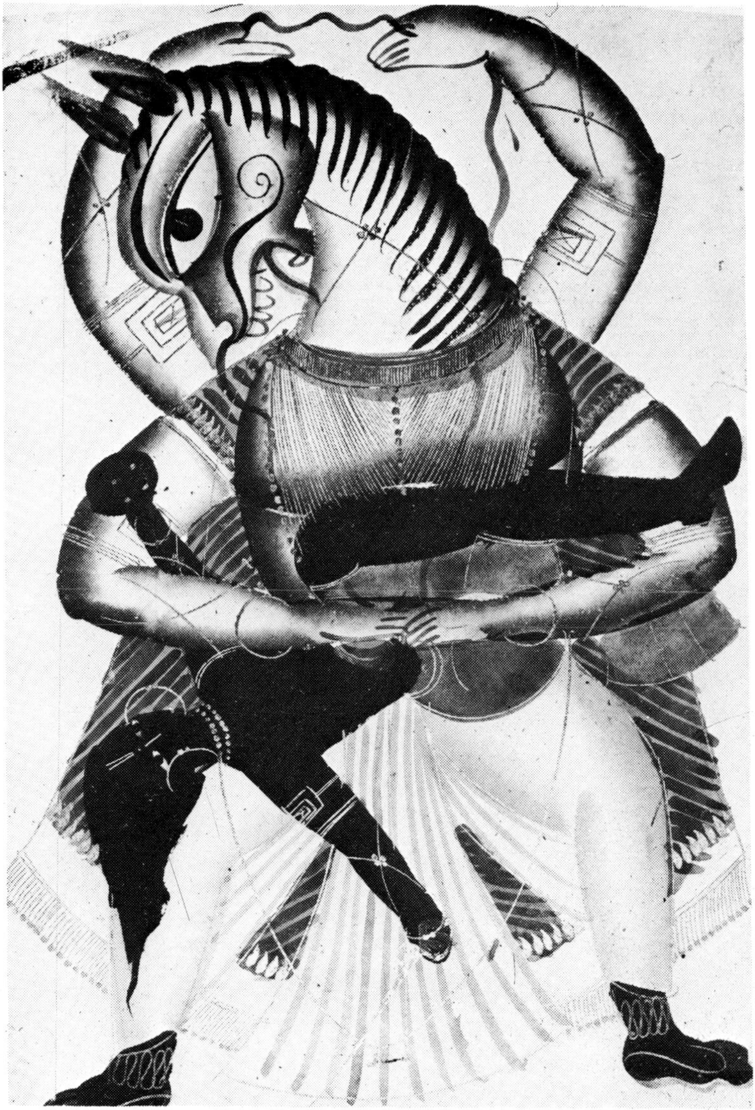

67

67. Narashimha, the half-man, half-lion incarnation of Visnu, destroying the demon king. Kalighat, West Bengal, 19th century.

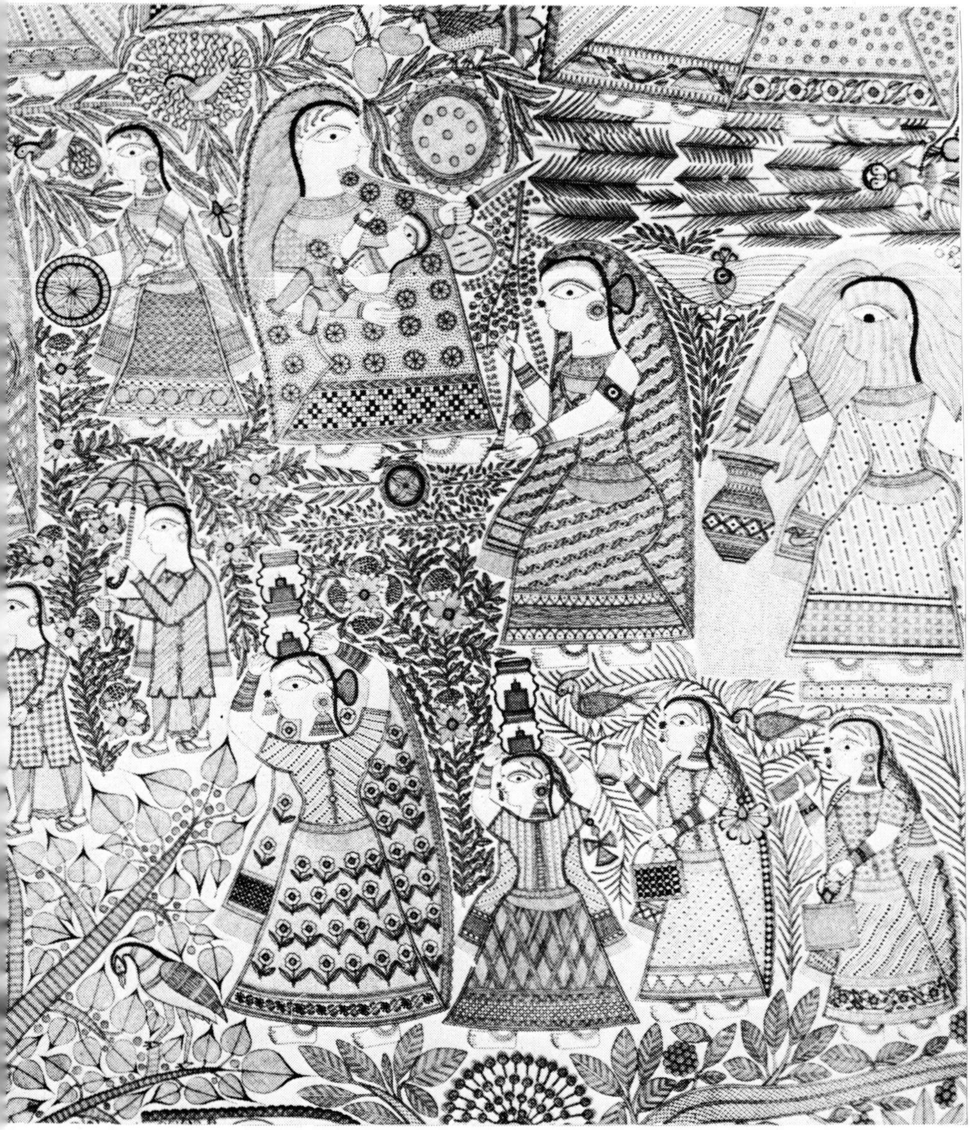

68. Part of a large black-and-white drawing illustrating marriage and birth. Ganga Devi from Ranthi village, Mithila, Bihar, 20th century.

ence the life and art of the peoples of central and eastern India.

The Śavaras were reputed to be great magicians, with a knowledge of witchcraft, astrology, and palmistry. They practiced medicine and had archaic knowledge of herbs and of *mantras* to induce healing. The Śavaras give no anthropomorphic forms to their gods. Their *sonum,* ancient ancestor-spirits, appear in the form of sacred pots smeared with turmeric and filled with rice, chiles, garlic, and salt. These pots are hung from the roof. The sun god, Uyungan, is considered a great deity; he is the creator, the life-giver of seed.[8] A solar eclipse is regarded as the swallowing of the sun by the primordial snake. The sun, the moon, and the planet Venus are visible and so are drawn by the Śavaras on the walls within their huts. The diagram of the sun is held sacred but is never an object of worship. When the Śavara priest, during his rituals, chants the incantations that are references to the sun, he does not look at the picture of the sun, nor are there any offerings made to its sacred form.

The Śavara artist is usually also the magician-priest, the *kuranmaran. Ittal* (ritual fertility diagrams) are part of the normal obligations of the tribe and are renewed year to year. *Ittals* are drawn when the magician-priest diagnoses the cause of disease or disaster to be the presence of a ghost or spirit or *deotā (devatā).* The fantastic, potent dream world of the tribesman finds expression through the *ittals.* Many pictographs are associated with the spririt world and the propitiation of the dead. The ghost, met in a dream or trance, makes demands on the attention of the dreamer; these demands are met by projecting the object demanded in the *ittal* painting. Like the rock paintings, from which they emerge, the culture portrayed in the Śavara paintings is male-dominated. Scenes of hunting, riding, and other male occupations predominate. There are no female forms, no focus on the female principle. The *ittal maran,* the creator of the *ittal,* paints with a twig splayed at one end. Visible in these drawings is the tribesman's fear of empty spaces. "The space is filled with horses and riders, monkeys climbing or perched on trees, the sun and the new moon, the elephant, the deer, the tiger, the peacock and dancing human forms; and, when the space cannot hold any more forms, drawings of trees, motor cars, trains, all the moving and static objects of the Śavara environment, appear around the framework." [9]

The Śavaras are not horsemen, and yet their *ittal* diagrams picture many valiant horses and riders. These are the ***kitting,*** the mysterious riders who are regarded by the Śavaras as their masters. They are mythical heroes who, according to Śavara legend, came to rescue the Śavaras from persecution and later left the country by sea, abandoning them.

Who were these mythical riders on horseback? Were they bands of Aryans who pushed deep into the heartlands of India? The frequent appearance of horses and riders and chariots in the rock paintings of central India and in Śavara *ittals* would suggest the presence of some ancient horse-riding tribes who mingled and dwelt among the local primitive communities. Rural and tribal myth abounds in descriptions of heroic figures appearing on horseback to rescue the oppressed, later to be deified and installed and worshiped as cult objects.

The Rural Gods—Sculpture

The making of icons in India has a very early origin. Pāṇini writes in the fifth century BC that metalsmiths in village societies existed as distinct from the *rāja Śilpīs,* the sculptors of the king.[1] Patañjali, writing three hundred years later, speaks of the Maurya kings who encouraged the manufacture and sale of images of Śiva, Skanda, and Viśākha to augment revenues for the state. Two forms of icons were available, the likeness of the gods, made and offered for sale, and consecrated images for worship. In the one the image remained just a likeness, in the other the image was the godhead incarnate.[2]

It is idle speculation to determine the period when the cult image appeared in rural shrines. Unlike certain other primitive societies which have survived isolated from the germinating currents of the world, the tribal population of the heartlands of India has for numerous centuries been exposed to the culture of settled village societies. It was in this confrontation, in the fusion of the culture of the tribesman, the nomad, and the dweller of the settled village, in the integration of sacred purpose and ritual, of myth, magic, and technology, that the cult icon emerged to give rural arts splendid significance. According to the *Smṛti Purāṇa*

Samuchchaya, grāma devatās are to be found in the dwellings of savages, in the villages of peasants, in the tents of Ābhirs, among hunters, in bazaars, among cultivators, in carpenters' shops, on the roads, and in the houses of weavers.

The earliest movements toward creating form were when, to the aniconic stone smeared with orange *sindūra* vermilion eared with orange *sindūra* vermilion paste, silver eyes were placed, painted, or affixed. In rural tradition it is the eyes that establish the fount of energy. Before the eyes open, the gods are in deep sleep and lack *śakti,* power. In Tamil Nadu at the shrine of Mariammā, the ancient Āyī, the gift of eyes, the *kanmālā* (eyes made of flowers), is offered to the deity by her devotees.[3] In the northern river valleys, the sword, used to sacrifice animals before the goddess, is said to have a life of its own, and eyes are painted on its blade with vermilion. In village shrines in Rajasthan, Madhya Pradesh, and Gujarat, on the *samādhi* of Ram Deo Pīr, on the scarlet-coated stones of Bhairo (Bhairava) and Kālī, and on the seated Jain Tīrthaṅkara images, the great silver lotus eyes stare unceasingly, creating a perceptive field of energy and magic.

The anthropomorphic form, the cult image as mask or icon, was the product of the artisan of the little tradition: the rural potter, the *kumbhāra;* the metal worker, the *ghassia;* the carpenter, the *suthār;* the goldsmith, the *sunār.* In tribal society, the artisan structure was absent, and the functional needs of the tribe—the pot, jewelry, cloth, agricultural tools, and ritual objects—were provided by craftsmen who lived within the tribal environment. In the northern river valleys and in the central highlands, craftsmen rooted in the traditions of settled village societies absorbed the rhythms of the inner and outer world of the tribesman, his view of the cosmos, his dream fantasies, his terrors, his poetic imagery, and his protective rituals. In time it became difficult to distinguish the craftsman from his tribal patron.

The same craft tradition that created the tribal icon was also the source for the icons of the settled village. In the dim past, in the hands of the image-maker, the gods of the tribe and village fused and mingled; myths gained dimension, and the great overhanging formless presence, the deity of primitive man, was given tactile form and supporting legend. Cleansed by sacrifice and ritual performance, the hand of the craftsman used material and technology to create form and distortion. Strength and power were achieved by the inward thrust of the sculptured form. Detail distracted from mathematical compactness and lessened power, and so was avoided. There was a total lack of concern with the abstract problems of light, air, and space; no attempt was made at aesthetic evaluation. The strict disciplines of measurement and proportions of classical art as laid down in the *Śilpa Śāstras,* ancient texts recording the canons governing classical art, had no relevance to the sculptured forms of the rural godlings. Live myth and the immediacy of the perceptive processes alone gave form, dimension, and meaning. Images were made for worship within the village shrines or the home, for protection, for use in sorcery and magic, to harm the enemy, and to transfer and transform energy and power.

The mask of the divinity which appeared over aniconic stones was a major step towards the formulation of the anthropomorphic image of the godhead. These masks were intended to safeguard the worshiper from confrontation with the naked presence, from the awesome emanations that projected from the sacred stone. Metal faces of the goddess and Bhairava, her male counterpart, were cast in the lost-wax process and installed in village shrines to cover the phallic stone *lingam* and the ancient stones of the dread Mothers.

In Maharashtra and along the Kanara coast, the stone *lingams* of the divinity were covered by metal masks of the *vīras* (heroes): martial faces wearing helmets of varied metal chieftains. The only point of identity in the facial types was the third eye of luminous seeing, the sacral mark of Śiva, the ancient lord of the autochthons, that appeared on the forehead of the masks. In the shrine of Narashiṁha (Nṛsiṁha) in Yadagiripalli, Nalagonda district of Andhra Pradesh, cut within a rock cave, the head of the lion-headed incarnation of Visnu is covered by a silver mask with prominent eyes and snarling mouth.[4] In Varanasi, Kāla Bhairava, the main guardian and protector of the city, wears a round, shining metal mask over the original, uncarved stone. The mask is benign, and the eyes are prominent. Garlands of marigolds around the neck of the mask create a vast orange corsage; white cloth is stretched tautly over the stone.

In the coastal regions of Mysore and Kerala, metal masks of the goddess Bhadrakālī, her tongue outstretched and her eyes blazing, are placed over the wooden carved face. In parts of Maharashtra, the sacred stone of the goddess daubed with *sindūra,* the vermilion of sacrifice, is only exposed on the *sasthī,* the moonless night, when the mask and the garments are removed and the stone of the divinity confronts the worshiper. On all other nights and days the face is veiled by the metal mask and the body covered with cloth.[5] The goddess Sambalesvari, the primitive goddess of the tribes of Sambalpur, wears a thin, hand-beaten metal mask that outlines the form of a bird's head, through which the slightly protruding stone daubed with *sindūra* thrusts itself. The rest of the stone is covered with a checkered cloth, spread on either side. On the top of the mask, looking grotesque on the stark abstraction of the ovaloid bird face, are tiny metal wings and a small Romanesque crown. The beak projects as a stump at the base of the face, and a filigree nose ring sharply accentuates it. The impression created is of brooding mystery. To accentuate these grim and fantastic aspects, live beetles, the attendants of the sacred one, crawl over the metal face and body.

In the highlands of Kulu and Kangra and in the Simla hills, *grāma devatās* were conceived as flat discs of metal, cast as severe abstractions of the human form, with boldly finished projecting faces. The names of the *devatās* varied, but the manner of their delineation remained identical; in effect they were metal counterparts of the sacred, formless stones wearing the metal masks of divinity. The icons cast in the *cire perdue* process have distorted faces, prominent eyes, pointed bird-like noses, and strange, indrawn, smiling lips. The faces range from grim primitive masks of the netherworld to gracious faces of smiling divinity. One of the icons has the face of the first androgynous ancestor, the ancient seer who wears on its forehead the mark of the *yoni*. The eyes of the *devatā* pierce and penetrate, cast spells, and see into the unknown nature of things. The smiling face is a reservoir of unanswered questions. Another icon is round-faced and reflects the benign and the protective. Serpents invariably appear, in sinuous movements at the base of the icons. The breasts of the *devatās* are cast as tiny buttons; coiled metal spirals form the earrings and the headdress. Centuries of worship have worn the metal; and patina enhances its beauty. These *devatās* of the northern highlands never appear alone, but in groups, their faces shining from amid brightly colored cloths, as they are carried in palanquins to the site of the festival.

Unlike the transient clay images of the *grāma mātrkās,* the village mothers, with their mysterious links with the earth and its cyclic laws of appearance and disappearance, the images of the *vīras,* the deified heroes, and the *kṣetrapālas,* the protectors and guardians of field and womb, are carved in stone or wood. Rising like pillars towards the sun and sky, these carvings are deeply rooted in the earth: the vertical lines, the tense geometry, the harsh simplicity of the flat planes give to these heroic forms the sanctity of the immovable and the eternal.

Vīra, meaning hero, the word used for the ancestors, the valiant warriors who were killed in battle while protecting women, fields, and cattle, is also the word for the *siddhas,* the enlightened ones, the alchemists, *yogīs,* and magicians who were conquerors of body and mind. Both were deified and worshiped in the form of the *vīrakals* and the *palia* stones. The *vīra* cult has very ancient origins.[6] The two rampant tigers protecting the Earth Mother, from whose womb plants sprout, and the two male cobras protecting the *yogī,* pictured in the Indus Valley seals, are indicative of the archaic role of the *vīras* and the *kṣetrapālas.* Many ancient elements fuse into creating the images of the protectors and guardians. Ancestor worship of the heroic dead, the *burā pura,* or the *āyī vadil* of the Bhils, worship of the great magician seers, and the rich and wondrous symbol of the *yaksas,* denizens of forests and rivers, familiar from the *Atharva Veda* and the *purāṇas,* with their vertical male bodies and their mysterious means of transforming themselves, all contribute toward the iconography. At first regarded as malevolent beings, at some stage the role of the *yaksas* underwent a significant change; they fused with the *kṣetrapālas* and the *vīras,* to emerge as the guardians and the protectors of the earth and the goddess.

The *yakṣas* are mentioned in the *Vamana Purāṇa* as the four guardians of the holy land of Kurukṣetra.[7] They were also the protectors of the waters and keepers of the sacred springs, asking the dread riddle to the stranger who came as a pilgrim to the waters. Any failure to answer correctly was punished by the ritual sacrifice of the pilgrim himself.[8] In an ancient Buddhist text of the third or fourth century AD in the *Mahamayurī Mantra,* three *yakṣas* are mentioned—Khandaka, Vīra, and Nandī. These continue today to fulfill their ancient role as protectors of the lands of Maharashtra, Karnataka, and Andhra, maintaining in their rituals and imagery elements of their mysterious origins.[9] Khandaka, the patron *yakṣa* of Paithan, who becomes Khandobā, the virile warrior, the god of shepherds, is widely worshiped in Maharashtra. The attendants at his shrine are tribal priests and frenzied women priestesses. He appears in metal icons and amulets, dressed as a Rajput chieftain, riding a horse. His wife is Mhalsā, a dreaded demoness and a harbinger of destruction. His enemies scatter before him, a dog runs beside him. Khandobā's sylvan ancestry is evident from the branch of leaves he carries in one hand; in the other he holds a sword denoting his warrior nature.

The Yakṣa Nandī, the bull, becomes Nandikesvara in Karnataka and Andhra, where his worship fuses with the cult of the *vīra saivas* and with the worship of Bāsava, the founder of the *liṅgayāta* sect. As one of the *bhutas,* the terror-inspiring ghosts of Śiva's army, his worship penetrates deep into the Kanarese districts of Mysore. In a forest shrine at Mellakettu, the main deity is Nandikesvara, depicted as an elongated wooden bull. In the same shrine, he is also conceived as a standing human figure, with a bull's head.

The Yakṣa Vīra, who becomes Birobā or Vīra, the shepherd's god, is the patron deity of the Dhangars, the fierce nomadic people of Satara in Maharashtra. The chosen ones of the Dhangar tribe are also known as *sids* or *vīras;* they are descendants of families whose ancestors had sacrificed their sons to the cult of the great Yakṣa Vīra.[10] In some shrines Biroba is transformed into Maskobā or Mhasobā, the buffalo *asura* chief, reborn after his destruction by the goddess.[11] As Maskobā or Mhasobā, he is worshiped in the form of a *lingam* smeared with oil-soaked *sindūra.* The nomads regarded him as the god of fertility. His shrines take the form of clay dolmens, "soul houses," similar to specimens found in Songarh Vyara in Gujarat and in the Ayanar shrines of Tamil Nadu.

In Karnataka and Andhra, the cult of the *Yakṣa Vīra* fuses with the worship of Vīrabhadra, the general of Śiva's army of *bhūtas* and *ganas.* Here Vīrabhadra assumes the role of *kṣetrapāla* or *kṣetrapati.* The Vīrabhadrasvāmī stone image at Karivi, in the Mahubabad, subdistrict of Warrangal in Andhra Pradesh, is five feet high, with twelve arms and a grim, awe-inspiring face. The legend surrounding his worship claims that only bachelors were permitted to perform his *pūjā,* till the image of Bhadrakālī, his consort, was installed within his shrine.[12] At Mellakettu, on the Kanarese coast, Vīrabhadra, the *kṣetrapāla,* carved in wood, sits at the doorway of the shrine of Bhadrakālī. Beside the martial god sits a ribald image of a monkey fingering his genitals to ward off the evil eye.

Ancient bronze images of the *kṣetrapālas,* dating back to the first and second centuries BC, have been found at Kausambi. Cast in solid metal, the squat ithyphallic figurines, fierce shafts of virility and power, have an earth-directed stance. The tradition of casting metal icons of the *kṣetra devatās* by the *cire perdue* process continues. Among the Bhils and Kolis of Thana and Nasik, the metal icons of the guardians and protectors are identified with the *burā purā* of *āyī vaḍil,* the ancestors, and are worshiped in forest shrines. Here ancestor worship fuses with the cult of Śiva, lord of the forests, claimed by the tribes of Maharashtra and Gujarat to be their first ancestor. The solid casting of the metal icons captures the quality and potency, and in-drawn energy emanates from the dense molding of face and torso.

The Panchamukhī Deva, the five-headed god, has a squat massive body abstracted to form a triangle, from which his head, arms, and legs project. The five heads have animal and bird faces. The phallus is accentuated. The symbols carried are phallic in nature: the stick, the knife, or the sword. This *devatā* is identified with the ancestor, but also with Śiva Mahādeva. In one variation, the form of the godling is androgynous: the great phallus hangs to touch the earth and the rounded breasts appear within the body triangle. In one hand is the male stick of fertility, in the other a coiled spiral, the symbol of the female. In another icon, the five-headed one, holding a sword and a shield, rides a bull.

Among the Bhils of Chota Udaipur in Gujarat, the male ancestor is visualized as a standing wooden figure installed in a jungle shrine by the carpenter priest. Clay animals, the elephant and the tiger, are offered to this anthropomorphic cult image. Similar wooden figures, *vetra,* are also found in the Surat district of Gujarat. The pillars are carved from a single piece of wood, cut from a living tree. In the Mirzapur district of Uttar Pradesh, and in the bordering areas of Bihar, the Ahīr hero, Bīra Kaur, killed by a tiger while protecting the buffaloes of his tribe, appears as a vertical male figure carved in stone or wood.[13] In Bastar, Thakur Deo, the male Bhumi Raj, lord of the earth, worshiped by the Gonds, is molded in clay. He holds the stick of fertility in one hand, while in the other he holds the cup, the female symbol of the *grāma devatā.* A stone plaque dug from a field in Maharashtra shows the *Kṣetrapāla,* a squat-bodied abstraction formed of two ovaloids, holding a digging stick in the right hand. The *lingam* is prominent and touches the earth.

The horse and rider is rural India's symbol of the great hero. The potent image moves through the primitive mind and finds form in stone-carvings, wooden memorial tablets, and brass icons. In numerous images of horse and rider the figures merge into a single composite form, male, masterful, auspicious, and protective. The horse and rider is the symbol of the hero killed while protecting field or cattle; it is also the symbol for many of the minor village gods. Khaṇḍobā of Maharashtra rides a horse; so do Vireśvara and Mallanā, the forest gods of Andhra. The Brahmā *bhūtas* of the Kanarese coast, *devatās* born of the fusion of Brahmā's skull with the *nāga devarū,* the snake godlings,[14] ride horses with garlands of shells round their necks and with flying serpents in their hair. At the shrine of Mhasobā in the Satara district of Maharashtra, an image of a horse and rider is identified as Bhairava.[15] In the districts of Cutch, monumental heroes and riders in stone commemorate the Jakh heroes, possibly *yakṣas,* who came from afar to save the people from the tyranny of the local king.[16]

In a solid bronze casting of the second or third century AD, the Vīra, holding the stick of fertility, rides a galloping ram. The object is three inches in height. The virile power in the thrust of the man-animal shaft is reflected in the cobra, with head raised to strike, that springs from the warrior's loin. The phallic imagery of the raised head of the cobra, a substitute for the erect phallus, appears in another archaic solid bronze casting of a man with two bulls yoked to a plough, found at a chalcolithic site of 1500 BC in

Daimabad in the Aurangabad district of Maharashtra,[17] a ritual object of great antiquity and power.

In the early beginnings of this era, the cult of the ***vīras,*** the ***yakṣas,*** and the ***kṣetrapālas*** fused into the worship of Śiva, the non-Vedic god of the autochthons. Khaṇḍoba, Mhasobā, Ayanār, Śāṣṭā, Mallanā, Brahmā, Bhūta, Vīreśvara, Gaṇeśa, Hanumān, and Bhairava are all emanations of Śiva, the supreme god. Enshrined at the entrance of villages, these godlings stand eternal watch as guardians and protectors. They ensure fertility, destroy enemies, avert drought, and guard against demons, ghosts, and the malignant spirits that dwell in trees and at crossroads.

The Faces of the Mothers

A painting from the village of Jitwarpur, Mithila, by Jagadambā Devī, a worshiper of the goddess Gaurī, elaborates the bi-form image of the goddess holding within her body the dread intensity of the moonless night and the brilliance of the rising sun. The squat black goddess encompasses the canvas and the universe. Her face, a massive circle, is painted in a frontal position: mirrored within the smoke-dark luminosity is the delicate-faced profile of the golden one. The left eye of the black goddess is the left eye of the fair lady. The black image is virile, massive, powerful; the form of the fair one is slender, virginal, fragile. This image of the goddess Gaurī—both male and female, black and white, squat and slender, tender and terrible, lover and devourer—permeates the tradition.

It was in Onkāra Māndhātā, the ancient Mahiṣmatī, on the rugged highlands of the Vindhyas overlooking the Narmada River, that the most ancient legends of the goddess coalesced. It was here that mythical birds, dwelling in a cave, recounted the exploits of the virgin goddess, the Devī Māhātmya, to the silent sages of the Vindhya forests. According to the *Mārkaṇḍeya Purāṇa,* the *asuras* took possession of the mountains, the netherworlds, and the waters. The gods, in fear, turned for succour to the transcendental goddess, "She the limits of whose hands and feet were everywhere; whose eyes and head and mouth were everywhere; whose ears and nose were everywhere."[1] While the divine ones were engaged in reciting their hymns of invocation, Pārvatī Gaurī came to the river Gaṅgā. Hearing the chants of the gods, the smoke-dark lady of the beautiful brow asked them to whom the hymns were addressed. Without waiting for a response, the goddess answered herself. Out of her body there came forth Śiva Kauśikī, the fair, incandescent virgin goddess, lovely of form, and she said, "This hymn is being addressed to me." After the emergence of the fair one from the sheath of Pārvatī Gaurī's body, Pārvatī became black. She was henceforth known as Kālikā.

The beauteous Śivā Kauśikī, the luminous goddess, was attacked by the demons Chaṇḍa and Muṇḍa. Angered at the threats to her person, the lady's fair countenance grew as dark as ink, and from her forehead, wrinkled with frowns, there issued Kālī Chāmuṇḍā, she of monstrous countenance, the color of collyrium, skeleton-bodied, with dry withered breasts. Kālī was hollow-eyed and wide-mouthed. Her skeletal body was covered with tiger skin, a garland of skulls hung around her neck. As Kālī emerged, she sprang into the sky and struck the earth with her two hands. By that noise all previous sounds were drowned out. Kālī Chāmuṇḍā then fell upon the Dānava hordes and crushed them. Chaṇḍa and Muṇḍa were killed. As Kālī battled, cries at once mournful and terrifying, the *Bhairavanādinī,* arose from her throat.

The flowing stream of the *purāṇa* continues the legends of the goddess. It relates the emergence of the terrible Śakti of Chaṇḍikā, howling like a hundred jackals, and of the Mothers, the seven female Śaktis of the *purāṇic* gods, with the attributes of their male counterparts. Taunted by the demon Śumbha for having battled with the strength of others,

Durgā Kauśikī smiled secretly to herself and drew the multiple forms of the female divinities into her breast, till she alone remained. Then the goddess speaks, "I who with my divine power appeared in many forms have now drawn all that is me, into me. Truly I am alone."

The cosmic role of the merging goddesses as enacted in the Devī Māhātmya was ancient and primeval. Deep in the ever-receding past, earth-born energies had taken female form. From the Vindyas, the heartlands of India, rose Kālī, Āryā, Vindhyavāsinī Durgā, the primeval Earth Mother of the autochthons, virginal, dark as a blue-black cloud with the energy of the rising sun. She was naked, *aparṇā,* without her covering of leaves. Wide-hipped and full-breasted, she was also described as having a body of a serpent. The flowers of the *kadamba* tree and the scarlet hibiscus clustered behind her ears, and peacock feathers crested her hair. A lotus, a bell, a noose, a bow, a great discus were held in her many hands. As the goddess of the tribal Śavaras, she who dwelt in the Vindhya mountains was surrounded by fowl, goats, sheep, and tigers.[2]

From the northern highlands, from Hinglaj and Kāmrūpa, emerged Nanā or Nonā, Koṭṭavī or Kauśikī, the ancient one, with a fully mature anthropomorphic form, with the symbol of serpent and bird interwoven into her image. Potent with magic and witchcraft, mysteries linking her to her Babylonian sisters, Nana, Inana, Ninhursag. She appeared as the naked goddess, fair of face and body, "golden-eyed with half-opened eyes, grey-eyed."[3] Goddess of sexual love and war, she was manifest as the militant bison-horned lady dressed for battle, holding a shield and wearing alien garments. Legends surround her battle and victory over the Asurā, the buffalo-headed demon. She appeared on Kushāṇa coins riding a lion and wearing a lunar crescent on her forehead.[4]

The temple of Hinglaj Mātā in Baluchistan, where "the goddess from afar" sought her resting place, was one of the four original Śakti *pīṭhas* established at the four cardinal points of the country. It was a site of great antiquity, a civilization possibly coexistent with that of the Indus Valley civilization. It is likely that the same elemental female energy of Hinglaj was manifest in Kāmarūpa, Assam, as Kāmākhyā, another very early Śakti *pīṭha*. Sacred to the sexual organs of the goddess, she is worshiped in Assam in the form of the great *yoni*. The shrine of Kāmākhyā in Kāmarūpa is famous for witches, for *tantric* practices, and all manner of rites connected with sexual love. At Kāmarūpa, Kāmākhyā is also known by the name of Nonā or Naina Yoginī. In the plains of Uttar Pradesh and Bihar, Nonā Yoginī is further transformed to Lonā or Nonā Chamārin or Jogan, the archetypal witch of overpowering beauty who, with her spells and incantations, seduces men, destroying their will.[5] The goddess who dwells in Hinglaj in Baluchistan is also known as Koṭṭavī, a name identical with that of the Tamil Nadu goddess Koṭṭavī, whose worship spread from Baluchistan to Maharashtra, to the South, to Rajasthan, and the Himalayan highlands.[6] The linking of the goddess of Mesopotamia, Baluchistan, the Punjab hills, Bihar, Kāmarūpa, and the lady of Tamil Nadu, is of significance, indicating ancient migrations of peoples and cultures and the permeation of the most isolated parts of the countryside. The formless, generating, pulsating energy of the Mothers, in the hands of the craftsman, found powerful image and tactile shape.

Another death-dealing form of the goddess, *Mahā Mārī,* is the most terrible of all terrors. As the manifestation of the cataclysmic anger of the Earth Mother, embodying dread disease, destruction, and death, the skeleton-bodied lady appears with terrible features, a complexion black as the darkest night and bloodshot eyes. She is the goddess of infernal sound, with a diabolical laughter that reverberates through the atmosphere. She wears garlands of dead human bodies, a waist-chain of human hands. Clad in the coils of serpents, in garments of raw hides, she appears to her devotees roaring, laughing, yawning, and dancing.

In the later *tantras,* the goddess is described as being of terrible face, fiery, three-eyed, with full and erect breasts. On her body are marks of the *yoni.* Naked, she dances her cosmic dance in cremation grounds, on the inert body of Śiva, as *Mahākāla,* unending time. Then in ecstatic union with Śiva, she creates the universe.

The *Agni Purāṇa* details the rites of worship of Mahā Mārī, the sister of the lord of death, Yama. The votary paints an image of the goddess with three faces and four hands. The first or middle faces of the goddess, painted pale smoke-black, has a look that would devour anyone gazing at it. The second face, to the right of the first, should be painted a pitch-black complexion, with a blood-smeared tongue, protruding teeth, and a hungry look. The third face should be painted white. The goddess Mahā Mārī is to be worshiped with perfumes, scented flowers, honey, and clarified butter.[7]

As they traveled along the ancient primitive tracks, the prehistoric routes of migration, the thrusting powers of the goddesses met and mingled and gained common identity. In their journey across the great land mass, as they absorbed into their identity the massive earth *Mātṛkās,* virgins yet mothers; the water and vegetal spirits, the *apsarās* and *yakṣinīs;* the serpent-headed *nāginīs,* the female ghosts, the *bhūtinīs;* the blood-thirsty *ḍākinīs;* the *yoginīs* or the *jogans,* the practicers of magic, the forms of the sacred one underwent continuous transformations. A composite form of the female energies emerged as Mātā or Devī. Neither male nor female nor neuter, incandescent with power and mystery; intimately linked with earth, water, vegetation; she held within her sacred auspicious being the secrets of life and destruction, fertility and death.

When she entered the *purāṇic* pantheon the virgin Earth Mother became Durgā, and, changing with provenance and tribe, her names and anthropomorphic forms are legion. The killing of the buffalo Asura Mahiṣa provides a common myth, the Devī Māhātmya, the *tantras* and the *purāṇas* a common art and liturgy.

In another manifestation as Umā Gaurī, the goddess's abode shifts from the densely forested Vindhyas to the snow-clad peaks of the Himalayas. Burned by the austerities of the fierce fire of *yoga,* she is *tapta kāñchana varṇābhā,* the golden one, of the color of the conch, the jasmine, and the new moon.[8] Her autochthonous, cloud-dark complexion transmutes to the golden , sun-skinned, color of Aryan pride; her virgin state ceases. She is Pārvatī, the lover of Śiva Mahādeva, the mountain god, and appears in domesticated family scenes in a thousand mountain landscapes, on paper, on walls of Himalayan homes, and on embroidered cloths as the wife of Mahādeva and the mother of Gaṇeśa and Skanda. The goddess is closely connected with vegetation and the earth.

The *Atharva Veda* equates plants with the goddess, "as a goddess upon the goddess earth was thou born, O Plant."

In the *Mārkaṇḍeya Purāṇa,* Durgā says, "Next, O ye gods, I shall support the whole world with the life-giving vegetables, which I shall grow out of my body. During the period of heavy rains, I shall gain fame as Śākambharī [the herb-bearing or the herb-nourishing]."[9]

The earth was Gandhavatī, the holder of fragrances, "which growing herbs and plants and waters carry, shared by *apsarās,* shared by *gandharvas.*"[10] The deified vegetation energies that were absorbed into the archaic composite form of the virgin goddess provided meaning to many of the rituals that surrounded the worship of the ancient one. The symbology and rituals of the *durgā pūjā vrata* and the *kumari vratas* of the northern river valleys drew their resources from the dread *apsarās* familiar from the *Atharva Veda.*

Trees were not only the homes of the female deities, but also contained their essence and divinity. The *Bhaviṣya Purāṇa* enjoined the worship of the *bilva* tree as Durgā. The tree was invoked: "Come, you are to be worshiped as Durgā." The tree was then adorned and made auspicious by the use of *mantras,* and an abode for the goddess was built out of clay, sandalwood paste, river pebbles, coriander seeds, *dūrvā* grass, flowers, fruits, curd and *ghee,* the *svastikā,* vermilion powder, conch shells, collyrium, *rochana,* mustard seeds, gold, silver, copper, lamps, a mirror, and a platter. Images of clay were made and installed in the shrine. Worship was offered to the clay image and to a bundle of nine plants. Durgā was invoked to enter into the plants.

For nine days a clay image was worshiped as the goddess and on the tenth day the clay image was immersed in a tank or a river.[11] The animals, which were sacrificed to the goddess accompanied by loud-throated incantations, were always the male of the species; the offering of the female was forbidden.

The sacred female has been associated with trees and plants for centuries. The *brihad gaurī vrata* describes rites in which, at moonrise, young virgins collect a plant called *durli* with its root and place it on an altar of sand. They worship the plant as the goddess, with flowers, with incense, and with archaic spells.[12] Among the villages of Maharashtra at the harvest festival of Gaurī and Gaṇeśa, the image of Gaurī is conceived of as a bundle of wild flowering plants. Nine plants are gathered by women to form the body of the goddess. Her vegetal form is then clothed in auspicious garments. A brass mask of Gaurī, ornamented with a nose ring and a necklace, is placed on the image, and the form of the goddess installed on a stool before the doorway of the house. Underneath the stool an auspicious square diagram, the *pīṭha* (altar) of the goddess is drawn. A virgin girl is made to stand on the diagram and worshipped along with the plants. As the girl, accompanied by the plants, enters the house, the mark of Gaurī's foot is drawn in red and the girl is asked, "Gaurī, Gaurī, whither have you come? Gaurī, Gaurī, what do you see?" The girl and the plants are taken from room to room in the house, special attention being given to the central room where the bride lives and babies are born. The plant goddess as Gaurī is worshiped for three days and is then carried by an old woman to the river where the vegetal image is immersed in the waters.[13] The image of Gauri continues the identification of flora with the goddess, incarnately.

The *Agni Purāṇa* maintains that the *oṣadhis* (medicinal plants) were *madhumatī,* full of honey, and were to be deified and worshiped as the Mothers. The *Agni Purāṇa* gives the names of charmed drugs and vegetables to be collected during a lunar eclipse and to be placed within amulets to ensure victory in battle. These magical plants bear the names of the Mothers—Mahākālī, Chaṇḍī, Vārāhī, Iśvarī, Indrāṇī, Valā, Garuḍī.[14] The magical sap within the plants that was the essence and blood of the goddess later gained anthropomorphic form. Images of vegetal divinities having the attributes of the goddess, with bodies formed of leaves, replaced the living plant as talismans of protection. The

Atharva Veda mentions these sacred *yantras* as the leaf amulets which the gods deposited hidden in the forest trees.[15] Numerous silver amulets from tribal areas in Maharashtra and Gujarat, engraved with leaf-bodied images of Durgā riding the tiger, the boar-headed Vārāhī, the malevolent Mhālsā with her dog, Chaṇḍī, holding a severed head, Kansāri, the corn goddess of the Bhils and Kolis, holding sheafs of millet in her outstretched hands, are worn by village men and women. These amulets are also placed along with the brass images of the tribal gods within the sacred basket, the *devra,* and worshiped.

At the time of the *kushāṇas,* the *matrs* (Mothers) underwent further transformations. They appeared as the zoomorphic forms of the *osadhis* (healing plants) with animal or bird face—Bidalī, the golden-eyed cat-faced mother;[16] Sakuni, the bird-faced one; Ajamukhī, she with the goat's face; Sarpamukhī, the serpent-faced one; and Mahiṣī, she of the buffalo head. A medallion of the horse-headed mother, surrounded by plants and carrying a child in her arms, is sculpted on the railings of the great *stupa* at Sanchi. Numerous *kushāṇa* clay images from Mathura show the *matrs* seated in a straight line, with animal or bird heads; some of them carrying babies on their laps. An early bronze image from Kausambī from the second century AD shows the *mātā* as Siṃhamukhī,[17] lion-faced; in her lap is a baby with human body and the face of a lion cub. In the district of Warrangal, Andhra Pradesh, the village Mothers continue to appear in archaic zoomorphic form: Pochamma takes the shape of an elephant, while Salatammā is manifest and worshiped as a tigress in several forest shrines.[18]

To perform the magical act of healing and protecting, the female principle of divinity has to undergo the magical processes of transformation. Being a composite of human, animal, and plant, she is potent with energy and charged with a power to heal and transform. In time, in contact with the great tradition, her form once again changes. The animal part of her being takes independent form as her *vāhana* (vehicle).[19] She appears accompanied by beast or bird. The plant elements within her become manifest in the lotus held by the goddess and in the plants that explode around her and clothe her body.

We have already noticed the links between the virgin Earth Mothers and rituals of fertility. Sītā, born of the furrowed earth, symbolized the archaic Earth Goddess of fertility and ploughing and was invoked according to the *Artha Śāstra* at the time of planting of seed. Her disappearance into the earth may also be a primeval myth to symbolize earth sacrifice. In the *Vedas, sītā* is the furrow which bears crops for men. The derivative meaning of the word *rāma* is linked to agricultural activities. The Peruvians styled their great harvest festival *Ramasitao.*[20] Sītā's marriage to Rāma, of the solar race, is possibly an ancient myth of the mingling of the earth-worshiping people and the sun-worshiping people.

Numerous legends exist of the marriage of the sun god to the earth goddess, symbolizing the fusion of patriarchal and matriarchal societies. Khond bards tell of the cataclysmic war that broke out between the male and female divinities when Tari Pennu, the earth goddess, the ancient first one, married Baora Pennu, the sun god. Baora Pennu decided to create man on the earth and vegetation to sustain him. Tari Pennu grew jealous and placed her hands on the earth and said, "You shall create no more." So Baora took the sweat of his body and threw it on the earth saying, "To all I have created." Thus arose love, sex, and the continuation of the species. The earth goddess grew angry and, rebelling against Baora, introduced disease and death into the world. A cosmic war broke out between them. Their battle raged fiercely through the earth, the sea, and the sky. Their weapons were the mountains, the meteors, and the whirlwinds. The Khonds are divided between those who hold that Baora, the male god, won and others who maintain that the goddess, Tari Pennu, was triumphant.[21]

With the ending of the virgin state of the great Earth Mother, many of the *mātalas* were tamed. The attendant male protectors and guardians of the field and earth, the *bhairavas,* the *kṣetrapālas* and *bhūmipālas,* became the consorts of the goddess. In time they were to become independent deities of agriculture, while Mātala, the Earth Mother, came to be identified with Durgā. In the interior sanctuaries of the northern river valleys and central highlands and in the deep south, however, the worship of the grim virgin Earth Mother, holding the noose and the cup of blood in rituals connected with fertility and death, continued, independent of the male gods.

Seemingly contradictory elements coalesced in the worship of the Mothers. The inherent powers of awe-inspiring creation, fear-inspiring destruction, and the strength of maternal protection were worshiped. They were manifest as female forms dwelling in trees; as the terrible mothers of disease; as the witch, the *jogan,* and as demonesses devouring children and attacking pregnant mothers. They were also invoked as the benevolent female deities, as nature goddesses and protectors of children.

According to the *Mahābhārata,* Skanda, born of the seed of Śiva and the forest mothers, divided the *skanda mātṛkās* into Śiva, the auspicious, and Asiva, the inauspicious. The *Mahābhārata* describes the malevolent Rākṣasī Jarā as feeding her five hundred children on the children of the people of Magadha. In the *Vāmana Purāṇa* the *yakṣī* Ukula Mekhalā is a blood-thirsty *rāksasī* that devours pilgrims. The *nāgins,* serpent deities, were destructive of embryos; so were the *kumārīs* and the *skanda māṭrkās.* Rites and formulae are prescribed for driving away these malevolent mothers and demonesses.

In Bengal, the cult of the fierce mothers was concentrated in jungles or solitary places outside the village. This deity was either Rūpaṣī or Guṇḍi Ṭhakurāin, the old woman of the tree trunk, or Vana Durgā, the goddess of the forests, the mother of the demons, *dānavas.* The worship of the dread mothers was identified as the *sheora* or the *sakot* tree, a crooked thorned tree associated with the spirits of the dead and unredeemed.[22] Women were the priestesses in the worship of the *vṛkṣa māṭrs,* the mothers dwelling in trees. To ensure safe childbirth, women tied rags of cloth dipped in turmeric to the branches of trees, applied vermilion paste to the roots, and worshiped the tree. No branch of the tree was ever cut for fear of calamity.

At some stage the role of the terrible Mothers underwent a radical transformation. From devourers and destroyers, they emerged as sustainers, protectors, as *gṛha devīs,* household goddesses. Hārīti, a blood-thirsty *rakṣasī,* the mother of *yakṣas* and the destroyer of children, was converted by the Buddha and became the benevolent goddess Hārīti—a savior of children. The malevolent deity Ṣaṣṭhī, regarded as a monster in the *Agni Purāṇa,* was transformed into the protectress of children, to be worshiped on the sixth night after childbirth. In time, Ṣaṣṭhī worship came to represent the defensive powers of the Mothers; it was a women's rite from which men were excluded. In the *araṇya ṣaṣṭhī vrata,* associated with the goddess Ṣaṣṭhī, women with fans and arrows wander in forests; they live on lotus stalks and roots; they worship Skanda and Vindhyāvāsinī Durgā and pray for the protection of children.[23] In Mithila, Bihar, the symbol of Ṣaṣṭhī appears in all the *aripans,* the *maṇḍala* drawings that form part of the protective rituals that permeate the life of the householder. To propitiate the goddess Ṣaṣṭhī, women in Rajasthan walk in the woods eating herbs and worshiping the goddess. In Maharashtra, the goddess Ṣaṣṭhī assumes the name Satavai, yet she remains a primitive and malevolent Mother goddess. Skanda, the son of Śiva, is Ṣaṣṭhīpriya, the beloved of the goddess Ṣaṣṭhī, and in the *Devī Bhāgvata,* Ṣaṣṭhī is portrayed as the wife of Skanda. In Kerala, serpents, closely associated with Skanda, are worshiped on the *ṣaṣṭhī,* the sixth day of the lunar month. In rural ritual all over India, however, Ṣaṣṭhī remained virgin, and rites sacred to her are performed by female-worshipers at crossroads on dark, moonless nights.

It is likely that the transformation of the malevolent female spirits, the *dākinīs* and *yakṣinīs,* into protective goddesses was achieved by means of magical *yantras.* In Andhra, with the fusion of the gods and goddesses after the conquest of the Ishvaku kingdom by the *brahmanic* Pallava dynasty, the *tantric* Mahāyāna goddess Tārā, widely worshiped in the region, was transformed into the many *durgās* of Andhra.[24] Kanaka Durgā, the golden one of Vijayawada, one of the most ancient and most renowned, is five-faced with eight arms. She holds the attributes of the goddess and with her trident pierces the buffalo, Asura. The legends surrounding her maintain that the goddess had a wild and ferocious death-bestowing face, and her votaries, confronting her and the fire of her eyes, were doomed to die. Sankaracharya visited the place and, to save Durgā's worshipers, created a protective talisman, installed it to the left of the image, and thus transmuted the face and being of the divinity, rendering it protective and compassionate.[25]

At Vilakatti, in Mahubabad Taluk of Warrangal district in Andhra Pradesh, Mutyallammā, the *grāma devatā,* is worshiped under a *thakkali* tree. To transform the ferocity of the wild mother, the *grāmsuttalu yantram,* a talisman, is buried under her image. This magical talisman is the tool that transforms the violent, ferocious nature of the goddess's energy into a protective energy. She can then become the guardian of the village.[26]

The great *grāma devatās* of south India—Mariammā, Elammā, Gaṅgamma, Bhadrakālī, Pidarī—are mothers, yet virgins. They are worshiped outside village walls with turmeric, *kum kum*, and animal sacrifice. Many legends bestow on these south Indian goddesses a northern Himalayan ancestry. Savadammā, the goddess of the weaver caste in Coimbatore, is said to have come from her original home in the Himalayas, to defeat the *raksasas,* the destroyers of men. The myth associated with Kanniha Paramesvarī, the goddess of the Komatis, regarded as an incarnation of Pārvati, the wife of Śiva, outlines the story of a Komati girl in whom the goddess had taken birth. This low-caste girl was beautiful and was desired by the barbarians. A battle between the Komatis and the outsiders led to the victory of the Komatis, because of the presence among them of the incarnated Pārvatī. But the Komatis, after the victory, doubted the chastity of the goddess and made her go through the ordeal of fire. She did so and disappeared into the flames. Her last words commanded the Komatis to worship her.[27] Mariammā, the goddess of smallpox, claims descent from Bhagavān, the Ārya, the northern stranger who impregnated Ādi, the dark *pariah* girl of luminous beauty. Of this union was born Mariammā, the mighty goddess of the Tamil countryside.

Mariammā, the Mahāmārī of the *purāṇas,* has her counterpart in the northern river valleys, where the goddess of destruction is Marai; in Maharashtra she is Mārī Āyī. The home of Mariammā, the red lotus lady of Tamil Nadu, is the *neem* tree. She is also found on crossroads, in fires, and on burial grounds. The geometrical forms of the triangle, the square and the hexagon are her symbols. Mariammā is red-faced; her eyes are liquid with poison to destroy those who laugh at her. Her hair is braided with five hundred hooded cobras. She enters the bodies of young girls and makes them whirl around in wild, ecstatic ritual dances. She is regarded as the mother of the *kannimārs,* the seven virgins. Her stone image never leaves her temples, but, at the time of her festival, a procession image is carved in the wood of the *neem* tree or molded into shape by the potter, and carried by the magician-priest as he dances among the devotees. Poturājā, the king of the buffaloes, the herald of the dread mother, is her chief devotee and priest. At the time of her festival, a *pariah* called Vīravesin takes the place of Poturājā and performs the sacrifices before the image of the goddess. The priest is also a sorcerer and possesses potent spells and charms.[28]

Pidarī, one of the most malevolent of the *grāma devatās,* is widely worshiped. Before her shrine are often found the *neem* and *peepal* trees entwined in sacred marriage. A richly decorated bull is sacrificed at the annual festival of the goddess. The ritual is enacted at midnight on a dark night, by the light of torches.

Another goddess of composite form is the Durgā of Tamil Nadu. She is portrayed with the head of a sheep.[29] The *Atharva Veda* refers to the sheep-headed goddess,[30] and the Ashutosh Museum in Calcutta has a water jar of the sixth century AD in the shape of the goddess with the head of a sheep, clutching a babe fiercely to her breast. At Kantillo, in Orissa, where the image of Nīla Mādhava, the Jagannātha of Puri, was originally said to have been enshrined and worshiped, a Śavara, a sheep-headed *grāma devatā,* holding the cup of the Mother, has been cast by a *ghassia,* a metal craftsman in the *cire perdue* technique—witness to the continuity and strength of the visual tradition and its roots in the prehistoric past.

In Kerala and on the Kanarese coast, the ancient Tuluva worship of ghost and malevolent spirits has fused with the worship of the *purāṇic* divinities, and in the process the *purāṇic* gods have assumed the terror-inspiring distortions of the Tuluva gods. The gods and heroes, the *bhūtas* or ghosts, appear with elaborate headdresses, costumes, and painted mask-like faces; the evil elements being characterized by the black complexions, with cone-like headdresses and strange bulbous noses. The worship of Bhadrakālī Bhagavatī, the awesome goddess in her destructive form, is widespread and is closely associated with the worship of serpents. Weird dances bring to life the terrifying goddess, serpents, gods, and *bhūtas,* inspiring and supplying the visual vocabulary to woodcarver and stone craftsman.

During the festivals to Bhagavatī, the goddess dances before her devotees holding the sword of death in her hands. Strange masked presences circumambulate the stage. The goddess is manifest through the *vellicapad,* the descendants of ancient dancing priests, who get possessed and roar and dance the *therayattam* and the *tiyattam,* the most important of the ritual dances to the goddess, and enact the grim legends of the Mother.[31]

In south Kanara, dances center around the worship of the *bhūtas* as malevolent ghosts and spirits. The dancers' wives recite the legends of the *bhūtas* to the sound of weird piped music. The priest-dancer receives the traditional sword and reenacts the legends before the *bhūta* shrines. He wears an elaborate headdress, his face is painted, and he is clothed in the traditional Tuluva dress, which is similar to that worn by *kathākālī* dancers.

One of the most important of the dances is the *vaidya* dance intended to propitiate the serpent god Subha Rāya, a manifestation of Subramaniam (Subrahmaṇya). In a clear space a great *maṇḍala* (*nāga bandha*) is drawn of Mahā Śeṣa, the serpent god, an intricate pattern of interwoven serpents in black, white, red, green, and yellow. The Brahmin priests dressed in red, with wildflowers in their hair, represent the serpent god Subraya Devaru. In front of Subraya Devaru stands a dancer dressed as half-man, half-woman. The musicians sing songs, play pipe music, and beat the cymbals and *ḍamaru,* the drum, in grim orchestration. At night in the light of flaming oil lamps, the male-female dancer and the serpent god go around, delineating the intricate form of the *maṇḍala.* The serpent god and the hermaphrodite dancer, the supplicant and lover, advance and retreat. After hours of courtship, the serpent god is pleased and there is union of the god and his devotee.[32]

In an interior *bhūta* shrine at Mellakettu in Mysore, the image of Bhadrakālī riding a five-headed bull appears in painted wood. Oil lamps illuminate her face, red with *kum kum* powder and garlanded with wild jungle flowers. Fierce silver eyes pierce the gaze of the worshiper. The heads of the bull face various directions. The goddess is surrounded by the *bhūtas,* wooden figures with grotesque animal and human faces, some tall and soaring, some holding the head of their dead enemies, others squat and gnome-like. Images in wood of the Mothers are included among the *bhūtas.*

A vast number of painted wood carvings of the goddess Bhagavatī, serpents, masked gods, and demons adorn village shrines in Kerala. In one of the images, the eight-armed goddess with protruding fangs tramples on an *asura.* The many arms of the goddess create a whirlpool of movement, an aureole within which the full-breasted goddess dances to the sound of her own cries as the death-dealing Brahmanādini. Surrounding her are the Mothers: one with outstretched tongue and shriveled breasts, the other full-breasted and taut with youth. In another image of Chāmuṇḍā, she is surrounded by serpents with hoods raised to strike. She sits on her human-headed *vāhana.* The goddess is eight-armed. In one hand she holds the head of Chṇḍa; the others hold a trident, a goad, and the other attributes of the goddess. Her arms and the striking serpent heads create the circle and spiral within which the goddess is manifest.

In another extremely significant wood carving, the *Śrī Chakra,* the *yantra* of the goddess is manifest in human form. A great aureole of flame forms the body of the divinity. At the heart are the two triangles in union, forming a six-pointed star, at the center of which is the *aṣṭadala,* the eight-petaled lotus, a symbol of the sexual body of the goddess; centered within this again is the *bindu.* The head of the anthropomorphic form of the *yantra* is heavily bearded, with jutting fangs. The face with its headdress closely resembles a *kathākālī* mask. Near the feet of the divinity is a tribal woman holding a cup in her right hand; with the other she holds the arm of a young boy.

Clay Images of the Mothers

The tradition of hand-molded clay images of the *mātalas,* earth mothers, has continued unbroken for eight thousand years. From the food-cultivating communities of Zhob and Kulli, to the urban civilization of the Harappan cities, to the chalcolithic cultures of the Deccan plateau, to contemporary hamlets throughout the country, archaic mask-like figurines with schematized bodies have been molded. The mastery of material and the maturity of techniques used in the hand-molding of the early terra cottas indicate the ancient origins of icons of the earth mothers.

Recent finds indicate that the earliest human figurines come from Mehrgarh, a series of villages situated in the Kacchi plain of central Pakistan, at the point where the Bolan River descends from the mountains. Mehrgarh is a site which shows continuous settlement from a ceramic pre-6000 BC to the beginning of the second millennium. At every strata mother goddesses have been found. The earliest, dating to the sixth millennium BC, sit with legs and hands joined, with featureless faces with huge vacant eyes that stare blindly. Later, toward 2600 BC, the mother, slender, long-limbed, proudly stands erect, holding a nursing baby. Her vacuous eyes still dominate her face, but now she has a flat broad nose, and elaborately-styled shoulder-length hair. She wears a pendant and has coils around her neck.

Fired or left unbaked, depending on the rituals for which they were intended, these icons of the Mothers, the holders of the secrets of the earth, epitomized magical rites of agriculture, fertility, life, and death. At the time of sowing of seed and harvesting and in rituals to the dead, icons of the virgin Mothers were made of clay, installed, worshiped, and then cast into the waters, or offered to ancient sites of the goddess—to caves, clearings in forests, or to trees—or abandoned at village boundaries. By their very nature impermanent, the earth mothers could not be kept under a householder's roof, except for short ritual purposes.

Three forms of the Mothers are observable from the earliest times. At Zhob and Kulli, in Baluchistan, early settled agricultural village communities of the third millennium BC, the form of the sacred female was molded only down to the waist. The breasts were superimposed in the form of clay pellets; the pelvic triangle and the legs were missing, invisibly held embedded in the earth, the womb, of which the Mother was an indivisible part. The sacred Mothers from Kulli, with elaborate head drapes, have gaunt skeleton faces and deep, death-filled crater eyes. In one icon the woman holds two babies in her arms.[1]

At the cities of the Indus civilization (2500–1700 BC), the Mothers appear with the sacral face of divinity, molded with deep concern, with the ancient brooding shamanistic face of the seer, elaborate ritual headdress, serpentine form, long slim legs, and slender hips. The ornamentation on ears and neck, the virgin breasts, and the girdle that holds the cloth that covers the waist are formed of clay withes, appliqued on to the body of the divinity. As the timeless, nude Earth Woman, she appears through the centuries headless, sightless, with outstretched arms, the universal gesture of the sacral female in all archaic civilizations. Free of all inessential detail, the awesome lines of her body are tightened and her form abstracted in sacred austerity, as in the early images from the chalcolithic finds of 1200 BC from Nevasa and Bilwali Dhar on the Deccan plateau. She appears with bird, animal, or human faces, pinched into shape by hand; with clay pellets applied to eyes, mouth, and breasts; with outstretched arms and a hole for the genitals. In later forms the thighs and breasts of the sacred lady grow rounded and heavy; she becomes synonymous with the vessel of plenty; her heavy girdle accentuates her pubic triangle.

In her manifestation as the Great Mother, creator and destroyer, she is conceived in the northern river valleys as a woman with virgin breasts and massive thighs, holding a baby in one hand, and a cup of blood to fecundate the earth in the other. These fired clay images of the Mother date from around the second century AD. The conception is monumental. The body is molded by hand; the texture of the clay is uneven. The massive arms have withes of clay coiled around them. The body and ornaments are pitted with holes. The face of the mother is a grim mask: the eyes are elongated, the nose is a bird's beak, the breasts are immature, and the feet point backwards, indicating links with rituals of death, magic, and fertility. In one of the icons from the Farakka barrage, the face of the mother, with her timeless, passionless mask gazing into eternity has given place to a terror-devoured face, with eyes poignant with the knowledge and agony of death. The arms and legs of this image are broken. A strange, horseshoe-shaped clay strip rests over her breast.

In south India, excavations of ancient dolmens of the first century AD have revealed elongated female forms, hand-molded in clay and sun-dried, forming lids to funerary urns. The body of one of the images is a flat skeleton-like vertical slat of clay; the breasts are clay pellets; a hole accentuates the genitals. The figure is seated on a stool; the arms are broken. The head of the Earth Woman is tilted at an angle; the neck is lean, taut, and stretches upwards; the face is a skull; the eyes are gaping hollows. Hatched lines define the girdle and the neck rings. As in all forms concerned with grim ritual purpose, these terra cotta figurines are powerfully formulated and carefully executed.

An unbaked clay figurine of a nude headless woman with squat body and outstretched arms, placed within a tiny womb-like clay urn with a lid, from Inamgaon, a site on the Deccan plateau, dating from 1200 BC, is indicative of links of the Earth Woman with magical rituals of death, burial, and emergent life. The exact purpose of this image is not known, but a study of contemporary village rites suggests its function and purpose. At Sonegarh Vyara in the Surat district of Gujarat, baked clay images of a nude, animal-faced woman, with outstretched arms, tiny breasts, and a hole for the genitals, are placed within a lidless urn and then offered to the sacred sites of the goddess, as wish-fulfillment vows against death and disease. These icons also figure in ancestral rites to the dead. At times the Gujarat female figurines hold embryonic babies.

Metal Icons of the Mothers

The existence of a vast number of metal icons of the Mother Goddess, squat vernacular distortions, with thick lips and ancient deep-set eyes, or with extremely slender serpentine bodies, ovaloid faces, and pointed noses and chins, indicate the multiple ethnic elements that have gone to build the composite entity and image of the goddess. A knowledge of archaic processes of metal-casting, forging, and hammering of metal is also evident.

The renowned image of the tribal maiden from Harappa, cast in metal and wrongly described as a dancer, is a portrait of a young naked girl with long slender nubile body, bursting with rising sap, with the strength and poise that comes from climbing trees and running wildly through forest glades. Her one hand rests on her hip, the other is stretched by her side, and holds a cup. The young maiden, the *apsarā* of the *Atharva Veda,* modeled with exquisite grace five thousand years ago, stands with easy insolence, one knee bent to better reveal her nudity. The head is thrown back; the hair tied in a knot. The sensuous tribal face is supremely aware of her youth and her power to intoxicate. The arm that holds the cup is heavy with bracelets that extend from the shoulder to the wrist. The cup held in the hand of this young virgin is suggestive, for in the rural tradition the only lady who holds the cup of death is the *grāma devatā,* the ancient, ever-young Earth Mother of village India.

A bronze icon from the tribal heartlands of India captures the magic and sinuous elegance of the beauty from Harappa. The tribal girl is naked and her *yoni* is prominent. The breasts are round pellets of metal encircled. The maiden is slender, long-limbed; her arms are held before her; in her hands are a bowl and a stick. The face is primitive, the mouth is wide, and the lower lip heavy. The body stands proudly in a stance that reveals and affirms her youth and her promise. The tiny image has been exquisitely cast with the precision and detailing of the goldsmith. The age and antiquity of this metal image is impossible to determine: it could have been cast within the last fifty years; it could be as old as the image from Harappa.

In contrast to this is the faceless, sightless icon of the first millennium BC found in the valley of the Gaṅgā, with legs wide apart and arms stretched at the side. The stark geometric form cast in copper has a total austerity. Its sacral nature is evident. Recent finds of massively cast, immensely impressive copper images of the buffalo, the rhinoceros, the elephant, and the herdsman with two yoked bulls of the chalcolithic period c. 1500 BC found at Daimabad in Maharashtra[1] establish the continuity of a sophisticated technology of casting metals and a mature sculptor's art capable of controlling and using the volatile technique of the *cire perdue* processes of casting metal, to produce images of supreme power and vitality.

Primitive metalsmiths in the mountains, valleys, and heartlands of India have through millennia continued to forge ritual metal objects using the ancient processes of hollow and solid casting of metal. The dating of these icons is extremely arduous, as in most instances the technology and creative skills have remained unchanged from the time the metalsmiths of the Indus Valley cast the bronze figurine of the tribal maiden.

In the *cire perdue* process of archaic metal technology, in the casting and forging of these metal icons, earth, fire, beeswax, and metals were used in a transforming alchemy. The process consisted in the molding of a core image of the divinity out of fine clay. Withes or wires were then drawn from wax or wild gum and coiled around the clay figurine, and around details, to outline and accentuate the eyes, the mouth, and the ears. The image was then placed within a womb of clay, the mold, which had openings into which the molten metal was poured. The molten metal displaced and took the form of the melted wax withes, leaving the earthen core intact. The outer clay mold was then broken to release the metal icon. Millennia of inventive knowledge and awareness of form, material, and technique underlay the molding of these three-dimensional forms. Taking shape in darkness, the metal images with inner bodies of sacred earth were later hammered or chiseled into final shape by the hand of the *ghassia,* the tribal metalsmith. The lost-wax process of casting metal predetermined the flow, the weight, and the rhythms of the icon.

A number of the metal sculptures were in miniature form. There were microscopic delineations of vast themes. The reduction in size did not detract from power. By the very nature of the metal-working technique, the tensions of line were angled inwards, towards the earthen heart. In some icons the coiled withes outlined a continuous spiral movement, enclosing and protecting the sacred clay core image, the essence of the divinity in a metal *kavacha,* the armor spell of protection. Some of the images were conceived as pure geometrical structures. The line of the shoulder, the angular elbow, the uplifted arms, the angles of the head established the geometry and the tensions. The concentration of purpose was in the face, the eyes, and lips, which in their grim distortions reflected mood and meaning. Some of the faces were cast with tightened lines, etching the bone formation, to give the appearance of skulls. In others the wire technique of applied eye and lip followed archaic terra cotta forms.

Among the earliest metal delineations of the goddess and her male counterpart are amulets, possibly dating from the first millennium BC, found in the hinterland of Patna, Bihar. The sacred, bird-faced goddess is manifest as a *mantra* or *dhāriṇī,* a spoken spell which means she who upholds and encloses. The goddess stands with two arms outstretched in the universal gesture of affirmation and protection. Her virgin breasts are two tiny round projections of metal. Her genitals are in the form of a round hole, in the manner of Harappa clay figurines. The face has no eyes, no mouth, no ears. Cast as a flat disc, a pure two-dimensional abstraction, the stark simplicity of the sacred form has the chastity of the hieroglyph. A male amulet from the same period has a brooding animal face; the body is shaped like a triangle; rosette-like protuberances delineate the form.

A very ancient form of the bird-headed goddess, from Himachal Pradesh, an inch and a half high and mounted on a pedestal, is cast by the solid process. The head of the goddess is in profile and rests on a long spiral of coiled metal (one of the names of the Mother is "the great coiled one"). The image is in bas-relief and is revealed as emerging from a flat, thin metal background, worn and bruised and with the luster of gold. The body is molded with a fluid elemental simplicity. Two coils join in the curve of a tendril across the chest and form the two arms, or wings. The breasts are rounded, baring their perfection. The goddess is naked save for a double girdle that defines her hips. On her feet are anklets. Though conceived in miniature the image emanates brooding vastness. Serpents, in sinuous movements, flank the central image of the goddess.[2]

In a metal image of considerable antiquity from Himachal Pradesh, the Earth Mother stands under a royal umbrella, symbolizing the sacred power of the deity. The circular protective halo is attached to the head of the image by a heavy metal cone. The ancient head is tilted upwards. The nose is prominent; the mouth is open; the thick lips are widely stretched. The body is a disc of cast and hand-beaten metal, a very pure alloy that glows and is golden with antiquity. Around her neck is a tightly entwined triple necklace. The breasts are young and tender. Around the hips a folded cloth has been tied; the knot appears as a flaming curve around the navel. There is no exaggeration of breast or hip to accentuate fecundity. As in all rural sculpture there appears to be a loss of interest in portraying the legs and feet. Below the hips, the legs and feet are greatly foreshortened. The goddess is two-armed. In one hand she holds the skull of Brahmā, the cup of blood, in the other a flaming dart, a thunderbolt. The concentration is on the savage face of power. The head is massive and elemental. The enormous open eyes, craters of power, create their field of terror and mystery. The compact virile form, two-dimensional and infinitely compact, is taut with forces that converge inwards, trapping and directing the energies of the worshiper.

An early image of the Earth Mother from Nasik is cast as a flat disc of dark burnished metal. The goddess has the untamed face of the ancient one, wrinkled and old as the earth. The hair is drawn off the face and tied in a knot. The thin outstretched left hand holds the cup of death. In another later image from the same region, the two-armed goddess is portrayed as standing within an aureole. In one hand the deity holds the cup; the object in the other hand is an unidentifiable weapon; on the head is the triple crown. At the base of the metal pedestal is a serpent in undulating movement.

The Narmada Valley is the origin of an image of the goddess who rides an unrecognizable animal. The goddess, who wears a crown, necklace, and earrings, with her hair tied in a pigtail, is surrounded by children. Three children cluster around her body. One rests in her arms, another sits on her head, the third stands beside her. She appears heavy with the weight of her young ones. She is two-armed. In both hands she holds the *piṇḍas,* the round cakes offered to the ancestors in rites to the dead. Her face is primitive; the thick massive lips dominate the face and have been separately attached as in archaic terra cotta figures. Her breasts are pointed. Before the goddess are portrayed the sun and the moon and the five *piṇḍas.*

The goddess as Vārāhī, the boar-headed one, is cast by tribal *ghassias* of Bastar as a thin disc of metal from which the arms, legs, and head project. The arms form spirals of thin metal. The boar-faced divinity is benevolent, the mouth stretched in a smile of benediction.

An image of the goddess cast in iron from the northern foothills cannot be identified. The goddess is shown in movement, striding across the earth. A long skirt extends from her waist to her ankles. She is four-armed. In one hand she holds a full-blown flower, in another a club. Two of her hands are held in a gesture of benediction. The face is quiet and indrawn. There is a crown on the head, and a great flower-like halo, punched with holes, frames the head of the goddess. The skirt of the goddess is also punched with holes, and a nail has been hammered in at the level of the waist. It is a strange image. Though the making of images in iron is mentioned in early texts, iron in popular belief is inauspicious and is used in the worship of Śani, the baleful godling, the harbinger of ill fortune. Iron drives away Śakti as power. There is a mention in early texts of iron images of women being used in rites connected with the purging of the sin of adultery. The penance for incest with the *guru's* wife prescribed that the offender, confessing his guilt, should stretch himself on a red hot iron bed or embrace the red hot iron image of a woman. The use of iron, the holes punched into halo and skirt, and the nail that impales the waist establish the use of this image in magical rituals of sorcery.

A goddess with massive breasts shaped like clay water pots stands holding two elephants in her two pedestal-like arms. Here she is Gajalakṣmī. The face is round and earthbound. At the feet of the goddess are three circular spirals, the esoteric symbols of her face and two breasts. A magnificent icon depicting the identical goddess has been cast by a *ghassia* from Orissa. The goddess is four-armed and sits enshrined within an aureole of circular spirals. Two arms arise as poles from her shoulders; in her hands she holds two elephants. The diminutive size of the elephants establishes the massive scale and presence of the goddess. The primitive face is of an intense grace and splendor. The cheekbones are high, the nose pointed, and the neck holds the head with tribal resplendence. The breasts of the goddess are virgin tender. The body is slender; the legs are weak and are left unfinished. Fine metal withes coil round the hollow form of the goddess.

A vast number of metal images illustrate the victory of the goddess over the buffalo-headed *asura.* The delineation of the goddess varies. In many images she appears in the static stance of the ancient one with an enigmatic smile, poised over the body of the vanquished demon; in others she appears in tempestuous movement, her many arms and her sinuous virgin body in juxtaposition with the heavy black mass of the animal, creating endless tensions of space and form.

A slender, finely-boned Durgā from Bengal stands delicately poised. One foot rests on the head of the buffalo demon, the other on her vehicle, the fiercely leaping lion. The eight-armed goddess holds a bow and arrow, a shield, a dagger, and a trident.

Her skirt, stretched tautly to her ankles, is decorated with a finely-drawn design. The pointed breasts of the goddess are bare. Her eyes rest on the human-bodied demon who emerges from the body of the buffalo. The face of the lady is virgin tender; her open mouth expresses the enigma of the sacral female, though the goddess is also a sensuous beautiful woman. It establishes the relationship between her and the standing buffalo demon. The body of the *asura* is animal-born; the stomach is that of the buffalo; the torso is powerful; the image in its proud acceptance of defeat at the hands of the slender one recalls the valor and the ancestry of the *asura.* A beard outlines the uplifted alien face. It is a portrait of a central Asian chief, vanquished, but still supremely virile and unbending, aware of the feminine nature of her who stands before him. This masterpiece of the vernacular arts is an early bronze, possibly of the thirteenth or fourteenth century.

In another image of Mahiṣāsuramardinī from Bengal, she explodes into space, holding the human form of the buffalo demon in one hand; Gaṇeśa dances at her side. A contemporary *ḍokrā* bronze from Bengal recreates the same mood and iconography. The goddess is triumphant and uprising while her lion leaps on the bison; Gaṇeśa and Kārtikeya flank the form of the goddess. An intricately patterned checkerboard cloth drapes her legs.

One of the strangest icons from the tribal areas of Madhya Pradesh depicts the goddess in her role as seer and priestess. She appears standing solemnly holding in one hand a long stick, in the other the severed head of the buffalo demon in a bowl. The goddess is dressed in a long garment which, in front, falls like a pointed apron to her feet. Her hair is tied in a long plait. The face is grim; the eyes recede into the face; the mouth is a wide gash.

In another early image from the Punjab hills, the goddess appears as Hinglaj Mātā destroying the buffalo demon. The iconography is ancient. The form of the goddess resembles the Hinglaj Mātā image worshiped in the village of Mudh, Bikaner, Rajasthan. The face of the bison-horned goddess is not the face of the Mother of the autochthons. Her grim oval faces has a pointed chin; the eyes are like petals and are set back from the nose; a grim smile darkens the somber ancient face. The goddess wears a trefoil crown and the circular halo that arises behind her head is adorned with widely curved buffalo horns, which could also represent the disc of the moon. The divine lady is four-armed. She holds a sword, a shield, a trident, and the head of an *asura* in her hands. A tight bodice covers the top of her body. She wears a pleated skirt, serrated at the edges, stretching to her knees, identical with the ***kannakies,*** the skirts worn by archaic Sumerian clay figures.[3] The alien skirt worn by the lady of the Himalayas is not unique. A number of metal images from that area of the goddess destroying the buffalo-headed *asura* show the goddess clothed in identical garments.

A bronze *grāma devatā* from Puddukottai of a maiden with an excessively slim serpentine body evokes the imagery of the Nāga Kanyā, the serpent maiden of folklore. The body and face are cast as a vertical elongated shaft of two-dimensional metal. Raised surfaces of nose, breast, and stomach reflect light and intensify shadows. The breasts are virgin, the waist is slender, the curve of the hip accentuates the pelvic triangle. The brooding primitive face is the face of the sorceress, ravishing in its otherworldly beauty and mystery. The fish-like eyes are widely spaced; they hold the venom-filled striking power of the serpent. The lips are sensuous and heavy. A trefoil crown, long pendulant earrings, and a necklace ornament the face and body of the *grāma devatā.*

There is a bronze image of Kālī from the Punjab hills in which the devouring goddess, black as the dark night, is depicted with a skull-like face, shrilly gaping mouth, and round prominent bulging eyes. The hair is drawn off the face and tied in a pigtail. The body of the goddess, cast as a thin plaque of metal, is angled to delineate the waist. The breasts are immature, for she is a virgin. She wears no ornaments save for a girdle around her waist. The goddess is four-armed, but in the tradition of rural sculpture the arms and legs are weak and are left unfinished. The savagely lean and gaunt image, open-mouthed, devourer of him who devours, strikes and pierces the heart of the worshipper. The urgent demand for protection, a wild piercing cry, is held in the face of the dark Mother. This is the same cry that echoes through the Indus Valley seals and is heard in the fear-laden spells of the *Atharva Veda* and in the incantations of the tribal magician-priest. It is the poignancy of this fear that creates Kālī. She is conceived of terror, drinks the terror deep, darkens with it, till she is the color of *kalaratri,* the darkest moonless night. Then she devours terror, annihilates it, cleaving through the darkness of terror, in the eternal primordial mystery. Then arising, emerging to sustain and protect, her wild mask of terror is transmuted to the face adorable as the image of all tenderness.

Ram Prasad, the Sakta poet of Bengal, describes the dread procession of Kālī:

> Jagadamba's watchman, go out into the dread, black night, Jagadamba's watchman! Victory (Victory to Kālī), they cry, and clapping their hands and striking upon their cheeks, they shout Ram! Ram! that worshippers may tremble, the flowery chariot is in the sky and in it ride the ghosts, in it too are Bhairavas and Vetalas. Upon their heads is the half-moon crest, in their hands the dreadful trident; to their feet hang [*sic*] down their matted hair. With them first come the serpents strong as death, then follow mighty tigers, monstrous bears. They roll their red eyes before the worshippers, who, half-dead with fear, cry out, no longer able to sit at their devotion.[4]

At Trichur in Kerala, the Marars and the Chakiars reenact the legend of the goddess. On a dark moonless night in the light of flickering oil lamps, an image of Bhagavati Kālī is drawn on the earth with colored powder. In her is the power and glory, the abundance of the earth, its savage ferocity, its tranquility. In one hand she holds a flame. To the thunder of chanting and drumbeats, the magician-priest dances the destruction of the goddess. With his feet he wipes away her limbs, her breasts, her belly, her face, her eyes, till only the fire held in one hand remains. For fire is eternal and primeval female energy has no end. When the form of the goddess finally disappears in the dust from which she had emerged, in the distant darkness, an oil lamp is lit. The fire from the hand of the goddess leaps across space, to light the oil lamp held by a human hand, and then her victory over the demon is reenacted. Drums reach a crescendo; creation, destruction, the cycle of birth and death are transformed in the hands of the village painter and in the human form as Bhadrakālī; in that instant the eternal dance begins.

Glossary

Ābhīr, Ābhīra — An ancient pastoral tribe who lived along the banks of the Yamunā River.

Akhārā — Village square where the life of the village community is centered. Associated with wrestling and the performance of seasonal plays.

Akhatraja — Sanskrit *akṣaya-trtīyā.*

Alaṅkāra — Literally, ornament. Used in literature, poetry, and art.

Amaltāsa — Latin *Cassia fistula,* the yellow laburnum.

Amāvasyā — The fifteenth night of the dark half of the moon.

Angarkhā — A long coat extending to the knees.

Apabhraṁśa — Literally, corrupt or breakaway. Used as distortion in literature or art.

Aripan, alepan, alpona, or *alpanā* — Geometric drawings on floor or wall, made at the time of festivals and to celebrate any auspicious occasion, such as birth or marriage.

Āsā daṇḍa — A double-faced axe carried by the Ghāzī Muslim mendicants of Bengal, to Hindu houses, during *vrata* celebrations, in the month of *Māgha.*

Aṣṭapadī	A stanza of eight lines.
Astra	Literally, weapon. A magical charm to ward off enemy spells, to protect oneself, and to strike the enemy.
Bewar	A form of agriculture practiced by tribes of Madhya Pradesh in which areas of forest are burned down and the harvest is planted in the ashes. When the crop is harvested the tribe moves to a new site.
Bhāng	Latin *Cannabis sativa,* Indian hemp. The seeds and leaves are ground into an intoxicating decoction and drunk with sweetened milk.
Bilva	Latin *Feronia elephantum.* A tree sacred to Śiva and Parvati.
Birahā	Same as *virahā.*
Bol	Musical beat of the drum, the stamping feet of the dancer, and the abstract sound forms sung by the drummer.
Buā	Magician-priest.
Chārana	Bards. A tribe or caste of Western India, attached to royal courts or to the shrines of the goddess. They were held to be traditionally immune from attack, and they traveled from court to court seeking patronage and trade.
Chauka	Square diagram or courtyard.
Cholī	Bodice.
Chūnam	Lime.

Devalan	Village temple or shrine.
Dhotī	An unstitched cloth worn by men as a lower garment.
Dobru	A musical instrument shaped as a long horn; used by tribes of middle and central India.
Duggī	A small drum used by the wandering Bāul singers of Bengal.
Ekatārā	A fiddle with one string.
Geruā	From *gerū,* red earth. The color worn by ascetics of the Śaiva sect of mendicants.
Ghebar	Sweetmeat shaped as a spiral.
Guruvāyur	A famous temple of Kṛṣṇa in the forests of Trichur district, Kerala.
Jamunā	Sanskrit *Yamunā.* The sacred river of the dark waters which rises in the Himalayas and flows through the plains of northern India, till it merges with the white waters of the Gaṅgā at Prayāga (modern Allahabad). The color of the waters—the dark of the Yamunā and the white of the Gaṅgā—are symbols used with infinite nuances in Indian art and literature. The river Yamunā is closely associated with the childhood of Kṛṣṇa.
Jātrā	Sanskrit *yātrā,* pilgrimage or procession.
Javarā	Barley. Used also as a generic word for tender sprouting grain.

Jogan	Sanskrit *yoginī*. A female mendicant, a sorceress and practicer of magic. Also stands for the goddess in her dark magical form.
Jogī	Sanskrit *yogī,* a mendicant.
Kachanār	Latin *Bauhinia parparia.* A tree that grows on plains all over India and bears white, pink, or mauve flowers.
Kadamba	Latin *Antocephalus cadamba.* A deciduous tree with round ball-like flowers and shining leaves. On the branches of this tree Kṛṣṇa played his pranks with the milkmaids of Vṛndāvana.
Kājal	Literally, collyrium.
Kavacha	Literally, armor. Also used as a magical spell of protection.
Khobarghar	The auspicious central room of the village hut, where the bride and bridegroom live and where babies are born.
Kuṇḍa	An altar at which oblations are offered.
Kuṇḍala	An ear ornament.
Laḍḍū	Round sweets made from wheat flour, clarified butter, and sugar.
Līlā	Sport or play.
Mahuā	Latin *Bassia lati.* A tree that grows wild in the forests of central and northern India. Its leaves, bark, and red flowers are used for food, for oil, and to brew liquor.

Maṇḍala	Literally, orb. A geometric diagram with magical significance, drawn to protect, invoke, or harm. Depending on the purpose for which the *maṇḍala* is drawn, spells are chanted and rituals enacted.
Mangalasūtra	A string of beads worn round the neck by women to indicate that they are married and their husbands alive.
Mātal	The Earth Mother.
Mudrā	Gesture potent with magical power.
Muggu	Sacred diagram used as the outer manifestation of the village goddess in south India.
Navrātri	Nine nights of the first half of the moon sacred to the goddess.
Neem	Sanskrit *nimba,* Latin *Azadiracta indica.* A bitter-leaved tree to be found throughout the plains of India. The leaf and stem have medicinal properties. The tree is sacred to Mariammā (Mārai), the village mother of destruction and disease.
Oḍhanī	Unstitched cloth worn by women in central and western India.
Oraon	A central Indian tribe.
Pachita	An ancient game played on an embroidered or printed cloth cut in the shape of a cross. The game is played with pawns and dice.
Pakhāvaja	A drum with two faces, slung round the neck and played with two hands.

Palāśa	Latin *Acacia modesta.* A tree with brilliant green leaves that grows wild in the forests of central India.
Paramparā	From time immemorial.
Paṭa	Scroll painted on cloth, relating a story.
Paṭuā	Caste of painters of scrolls.
Piṇḍa	Round sweets made of wheat, clarified butter, and sugar, used in the rites to the ancestors.
Pīpal	Sanskrit *Pippala, Aśvattha;* Latin *Ficus religiosa.* A tree considered sacred throughout India. The *bodhi* tree under which the Buddha was enlightened.
Pīr	Muslim saint.
Pīṭhā	Sacred site.
Pithora	Gods of the Bhil tribes of Gujarat. Paintings of horses and riders. The composite painting forms of the Pithora Deva.
Pūrṇakumbha	Overflowing pot.
Puṣṭimārga	Sanskrit push to nourish. Therefore, the path of that which nourishes. Also grace or devotion. The teachings of Shri Vallabhacharya.
Rakhāwal	Guardian, protector.
Rudrākṣa	Seeds sacred to Śiva, strung to form rosary.
Śami	A tree akin to the *neem* tree.
Sanjh-ka-koṭ	House of twilight.

Sāraṅgī	Musical stringed instrument.
Sāvaj	A mythical tiger with a human face, symbol used by Kathis, a pastoral tribe of Gujarat.
Sawāj Jawāb	Literally, question and answer. Dialogue form used in songs and peasant theater.
Sūta	A caste of wandering storytellers.
Vāhana	Vehicle.
Vajra	Thunderbolt.
Virahā	Vernacular, *biraha*. Songs of the Ahīr community expressing the pangs of love and separation, of heroes and heroines.
Yantra	Magical diagram or tool to awaken the inner mind.
Yoginī	Same as *jogan* or *joginī*.

Appendix Iconography of *Dasa Mahāvidya* (English Translation)

1. Śrī Kālī

I bow to Kālī, the mother of the universe, whose feet, resting on lotus blossoms, are worshiped by gods and demons, that great Devī, the living face of terror, with dreadful teeth and laughing face, who stands on a corpse holding a sword and a skull in the two hands, while with the other two she makes the gesture of granting boons and of dispelling fear.

Salutations to that Devī, Śrī Daksinakalika, whose body is dry and hard, who is proud of speech, rolling her hungry tongue and crunching animal bodies in her mouth.

Yantra

First write (draw) a triangle, then another triangle outside it. Within it write a *mantra.* Then write (draw) three triangles over it. Around this make a circular lotus with eight petals. Having written (drawn) the circle, write (draw) the *bhupura,* the outer wall with four doorways.

2. Śrī Tara

Salutations to Nīla Sarasvatī, who holds a *vina* in her hand, wearing indigo-colored garments, blue-bodied with matted hair knot, skull garlanded. To that Devī Tara, the vanquisher of all obstacles, I bow.

She, the fearful one, who is in the stance of the archer poised to attack, one foot resting on a corpse, Tara whose laughter strikes fear in the heart, who is born of the *hum bija,* blue-complexioned with matted hair, *jata* entwined with serpents, with scissors held in her hand, she destroys the *tamas* (darkness and ignorance) of the world.

Yantra

Secretly whispering the *mantra, "O Surekhe Vajra rekhe huṁ phaṭ svāhā,* write (draw) the eight beautiful petals and four petals thereafter, then the *maṇḍala* with four doors, afterwards a lotus within six triangles and lastly write (draw) the ground on which the *maṇḍala* rests.

3. Śrī Ṣodaśī

I worship the four-armed and three-eyed Śiva, who with Kameśvara Śiva appears lustrous like the orb of the rising sun. She holds in her hands a noose, a goad, a bow, and arrows. The fruits that are obtained by a man by performing hundreds of sacrifices or giving great alms can be obtained by him who seeks the *Śrī Chakra* of the Devī.

Yantra

Write (draw) a point, a triangle, eight angles, double ten (twenty), an eight-petaled lotus, a sixteen-petaled lotus, three circles, the outer walls, the *bhūpura,* with three lines, in succession.

4. Śrī Bhuvaneśvarī

I pray to Ambikā, the primal seed of the universe, lustrous like the rising sun, wearing the moon in her crown, high-breasted, three-eyed, with a moon-like face. She is four-armed; in two she holds the goad and the noose, while the third dispels fear (*abhaya*) and the fourth grants boons (*vardda*). She is *ānanda-mayī* sound, *Sākṣāt śabda Brahmā:* I worship her who is the granter of wealth. Salutations to Bhuvaneśvarī, the most beautiful, with fair complexion, adorned with gold ornaments, wearing orange-colored silk garments and resting along with lord Śaṅkara.

Yantra

Write (draw) one eight-petaled lotus, circle it with sixteen leaves, and in the pericarp of the lotus write (draw) six angles, four *asras,* four doors, and lastly the circle in succession. Always auspicious is the symbol of Jagadambā Bhuvaneśvarī.

5. Śrī Bhairavī

I bow to that *devī* who is red like the splendor of a thousand rising suns. She is garlanded with skulls, rosy-breasted, her hands held in the gestures of granting boons and dispelling fear. The crescent moon rests on her forehead. Three-eyed, she dwells in the heart of the sun.

I bow to that Bhairavī from whom emanate the fearful thunderous sounds of dissolution and who is surrounded by the white ashes of the cremation ground; she wears garlands of skulls on her breasts and in her ears. She is Narayanī, who helps us to go beyond. She is Gaurī, the quencher of all sorrows.

Yantra

Write (draw) an eight-petaled lotus, with eight triangles and then write (draw) an outer wall with four doorways.

6. Śrī Chhinnamasta

I bow to Śrī Devī Chhinnamasta who, intoxicated with great joy, holds in her left hands her own decapitated head, drinking from the fountain of blood that spurts from the neck of her headless body.

She is red in color, naked, with untied hair, into which are woven varied colored flowers.

She inspires fear, wearing a *yajnopavita* formed of serpents. She is *viparita rati,* adopting the dominant position in union with Kāma, and so she should be meditated upon.

Yantra

Write (draw) a triangle and three circles within it. At its center make a *yonidvara* (doorway into the *yoni* womb). Draw an eight-petaled lotus outside.

7. Śrī Dhumavatī

Salutations to *vidya* Dhumavatī, to be worshiped with black flowers. She is of the color of smoke, colorless, fickle, wicked, gigantic, wearing dusty, smoke-colored clothes, with faded earrings in her ears. She is a widow, an enemy of gross life, granter of happiness to people. She sits in a chariot, in her hands she holds the sun, her flag has the emblem of a crow. Her breasts are shriveled; she is dry-eyed. Her hand is held in the gesture of bestowing boons.

Yantra

Write (draw) an eight-petaled lotus within a house, *grha*, with four doors. In the *bhupura* with Indra and other *lokapalas,* write (draw) the six *angas,* desire of *rati,* hunger, sleep, wickedness, jealousy, and nonforgiveness on the *kesara* petals.

8. Śrī Bagalamukhī

Salutations to that golden-hued *devī,* who sits in a lotus posture, serious, intoxicated, gentle, four-armed and three-eyed. In her right hands are a staff and a noose, in her left the tongue of an enemy and a thunderbolt. She wears yellow garments and is resplendent with youth. Her earrings are golden, the crescent moon rests on her head.

I bow to thee, O Kalyanī, destroyer of the wicked, remover of obstacles, ender of poverty, destroyer of enemies.

Yantra

Write (draw) a triangle and six angles, two triangles, an eight-petaled lotus, sixteen-petaled lotus, and the outer walls with four doors, *bhupura,* in succession.

9. Śrī Matangī

Salutations to that *devī* Matangī, Śiva, whose body is blue-black in color. She is crested with the tender new moon, three-eyed, seated on a throne, adorned with gems, holding in her own arms sword, shield, noose, and a goad. Her blue-black hair hangs loose and scattered; her eyes are the color of the *jivaka* bird, and her lips are red like the *bimba.*

Yantra

Write (draw) a triangle with an eight-petaled lotus; double it (sixteen petals); thereafter write (draw) six angles, an eight-petaled lotus, and the outer walls, the *bhupura,* in succession.

10. Śrī Kamalā

I bow to Śrī Kamalānanā, the lotus-faced one with lotus feet, and hands that grant happiness to her worshipers. I worship Śrī Kamalā, who wears a shining crown and appears like a snow-clad mountain, radiant with the golden light of the sun. Four elephants pour nectar on her body. She makes the gestures of bestowing boons and dispelling fear with her two hands.

Yantra

First write (draw) an eight-petaled lotus, then a beautiful outer wall, the *bhūpura* with a *bīja* at the center, one after another.

Notes

INTRODUCTION

1. D. D. Kosambi, *The Culture and Civilization of Ancient India,* p. 22.
2. Gustav Oppert, *On the Original Inhabitants of Bharat Varsha,* p. 17.
3. William Dwight Whitney, ed., *Atharva Veda Samhita,* "Hymn to the Earth," XII, 1.

THE RURAL ROOTS

1. Sham Rao Hivale, *The Pardhans of the Upper Narmada Valley,* p. 153.
2. *Census of India* (1961), "Fairs & Festivals of Andhra Pradesh," Cudappah district, p. 85.
3. Ibid., p. 94.
4. Rev. Stephen Hislop, *Aboriginal Tribes of the Central Provinces* (ed. R. Temple), Nagpur, 1866, pp. 2–3.
5. *Census of India* (1961), "Fairs & Festivals of Andhra Pradesh," West Godavari district, pp. 115–16.
6. John Marshall, *Mohenjo Daro and the Indus Civilisation,* I: Plate XII, seal no. 17.
7. D. D. Kosambi, *The Culture and Civilization of Ancient India,* p. 48.
8. Many passages in the *Ṛg Veda* hint to prior conquest of Dāsas or Dasyus. See Macdonell and Keith, *Vedic Mythology,* pp. 457ff.
9. H. D. Sankalia and M. K. Dhavalikar, "Terracotta Art of India," *Marg* 23, no. 1: 33–39.
10. K. C. Viraraghava Iyer, "The Sittars—The Study of Alchemy" in the *Acharya Ray Commemoration Volume,* p. 460.
11. Kosambi, *Myth and Reality,* p. 90.
12. Information given to me by Shri Haku Shah, Nehru Fellow, Tribal Research and Training Institute, Ahmedabad.
13. P. C. Ray, *Rasa Ratna Samuchchaya: History of Chemistry in Ancient and Mediaeval India,* p. 129.

Rasaratnākara—There is a dispute about the dating of this treatise. Some writers assign it to as late a date as the eighth century. A confusion possibly exists because of the name of the author, Nāgārjuna.

Tradition relates all alchemical lore to the Buddhist sage Nāgārjuna, who lived in the second century. Another alchemist seer bearing the same name and writing in the eighth century is also possible. See also Ray's *History of Hindu Chemistry,* pp. xciii, 1, wherein Nāgārjuna Bodhisattva is referred to by Huan Tsang as well practiced in the art of compounding medicines so that neither the mind nor body decayed.

14. V. S. Agrawala, *Vāmana Purāṇa: A Study,* pp. 110–14.
15. Ray, *Chemistry in Ancient and Mediaeval India,* pp. 167–68.
16. R. Shama Sastry, "Origin of the Devanagiri Script," *Indian Antiquary* 35 (1906): 280.
17. Ibid., p. 261.
18. Ibid., p. 258.
19. Ibid., p. 285.
20. Ibid., p. 272.
21. Ibid., 2: 211.
22. Mayadhar Mansinha, *History of Oriya Literature,* p. 27.
23. Ibid., p. 25.
24. "The Washerman's Virasena—A Lingāyat legend," *Indian Antiquary* (1876), p. 183.
25. "The Śakti Pīṭha," *J.R.A.S.B.* XIV–1 (1948), pp. 105–6.
26. Kosambi, *Culture and Civilization of Ancient India.* Plate 9. In Kerala, potters in remote villages mold for archaic *yajñas* clay pots with two protuberances, identified locally as breasts, symbols of the Earth Mother. See also V. T. Induchudan—"Kerala yajña with foreign participation," *Illustrated Weekly,* May 25, 1975.
27. Ray, *Rasārṇava*—Śaivite treatise of twelfth century. *Chemistry in Ancient and Mediaeval India,* p. 136.
28. *Census of India* (1961), "Fairs & Festivals of Gujarat," p. 276.
29. Verrier Elwin; The Song of Raja Bijra—*Songs of Chattisgarh,* p. 298.
30. Santal Songs translated by J. W. J. Gulshav, *Man in India,* Vol. XXVI, Notes and Queries, March (1946), p. 67.
31. *Kubjikā Tantra* MS. discovered in Nepal in Gupta characters. See also Ray's *History of Hindu Chemistry,* p. 53.
32. W. T. Elmore, *Dravidian Gods in Modern Hinduism,* p. 55.

THE LEGENDS OF INTEGRATION

1. C. von Führer Haimendorf, in a review of Sham Rao Hivale's "Pardhans of the Upper Narbada Valley," *Man in India* 24 (1946): 231.
2. In Bengal, Orissa, Rajasthan, and in the Kangra HIlls, Mahisāsuramardinī

rides a lion, but in Gujarat, a *śarabha,* a mystical animal with a tiger's body and an elephant's head.

3. Arthur Avalon, *Hymns to the Goddess,* p. 118.
4. D. D. Kosambi, *Myth and Reality* (May 1962), p. 90.
5. H. A. Rose, "Hinduism in the Himalayas," *Indian Antiquary* (1907), p. 263.
6. According to the *Vāmana Purāṇa,* Mahiṣa, the *asura* chief, took shelter in the Himalayas in a cavern within the Krauñcha hill, when he was defeated in battle by Skanda. Skanda, discovering him, pierces with his Śakti the *asura* chief and the mountain. See V. S. Agrawala, *Vāmana Purāṇa—A Study,* p. 117.
7. *Census of India* (1961), Rao Bahadur Tirumalrao Venkatesh, "Account of the Village Goddesses Durgamava and Dayamava," Dharwar Village Survey Monographs, Hulkotti village, Gadag taluk, Dharwar district, Appendix II.
8. Gustav Oppert, *On the Original Inhabitants of Bharat Varsha,* p. 472, fn. 265.
9. Ibid., p. 467, fn. 254.
10. The most ancient shrine of Elammā is at Ugargol in Belgaum district, Karnataka. In a village named Chandra Giri, Karnataka, devotees proceed from home to temple in a state of nudity to worship Renuka-Elammā, the ancient Earth Mother. *Indian Antiquary* (1882), pp. 122–23.

THE *VEDA* OF THE RURAL TRADITION

1. William Dwight Whitney, tr., *Atharva Veda Samhita,* "Hymn to the Earth," 12.1.11.
2. Ibid., 12.1.15.
3. Verrier Elwin, *The Baiga,* Oxford University Press, p. 340.
4. Whitney, *op. cit.,* 10.8.31.
5. Ralph T. H. Griffiths, tr., *Hymns of the Atharva Veda,* 4.20.5.
6. Whitney, *op. cit.,* 7.22.4.
7. The Indus Valley people were known to the writers of the *Atharva Veda.* They are referred to as folk belonging to all kinds of people from Sindhu. See Whitney, *op. cit.,* 7.45.1, p. 417.
8. Whitney, *op. cit.,* 1.24.1.
9. Ibid., 9.2.19.
10. Griffiths, *op. cit.,* 9.2.25.
11. Maurice Bloomfield, ed., *Kauśika Sūtras, Atharva Veda,* with extracts from the commentaries of Darila and Keśava, *Journal of the American Oriental Society,* vol. 24.
12. H. W. Magoun, on the *Āsurī Kalpa. Āsurī Kalpa* is the thirty-fifth pariśista of the Atharva Veda. It is an *abhichāra* or witchcraft practice. *Āsurī Kalpa* is mentioned in the *Māhabhāsya,* IV, 1.19, *Indian Historical Quarterly,* 7: 1–52.

13. Whitney, *op. cit.,* 5.7.8.
14. Ibid., 8.10.
15. Ibid., 15.1–18.1.

THE RITUAL ART OF THE (INDUS VALLEY) HARAPPAN CIVILIZATION

1. In Maharashtra, two breast-like lumps on stone pillars indicate *satī* stone. The customary symbol of the *satī* is the bent arm with outstretched palm. See Kosambi, *Myth and Reality*, p. 87.
2. Madho Sarup Vats, *Excavations at Harappa*, Plate XCVII.
3. John Marshall, et al., *Mohenjo Daro and the Indus Valley*, Plate CXII, p. 333.
4. Vats, *op. cit.*, Plate CIII, p. 304.
5. *Śatapatha Brāhmaṇa,* 2.3.6.7.
6. Sham Rao Hivale and Verrier Elwin, *The Songs of the Forest,* p. 20.
7. Ibid., p. 21.
8. J. H. Mackay, *Further Excavations at Mohenjo Daro,* Plate XCIV (for Paśupati, Mohenjo Daro, 3rd millennium BC), National Museum, New Delhi.
9. Griffiths, *op. cit.,* 11.2.5.
10. Marshall, *op. cit.,* Plate CXII.
11. The magician-priest stands erect between two tigers. See Mackay, *Further Excavations,* Plate LXXXIV, 3rd millennium BC, National Museum, New Delhi.
12. Jagdish Gupta, *Prāgaitihāsika Bhāratīya Chitrakalā,* p. 459.
13. Verrier Elwin, *The Baiga,* Oxford University Press, p. 327.
14. Ralph T. H. Griffiths, tr., *Hymns of the Atharva Veda,* 4.3.7.
15. Vats, *op. cit.,* Plate XCVI.
16. Ibid., Plate XC, p. 23.
17. *Atharva Veda Samhitā,* 8.7.14.
18. Vats, *op. cit.,* Seal no. I. XXXIX.
19. Kalibangan seal. See *Indian Archaeology 1962–63: A Review,* Plates XXIII B and LXIIC.
20. P. C. Ray, *Rasa Ratna Samuchchaya: History of Chemistry in Ancient and Mediaeval India,* p. 133.
21. Mackay, *op. cit.,* vol. II, Plate LXXXIIC.
22. Whitney, *Atharva Veda Samhitā,* 8.5.12.
23. P. Jayakar, "Kathi Embroideries of Gujarat," *Times of India Annual* (1968), p. 73.
24. K. Krishnan in the *Hindustan Times,* 29 March 1970.

THE ORAL TRADITION

1. K. Bharata Iyer, "*Kuttiyatam:* Sanskrit Drama of Kerala," *The Times of India Annual* (1962), pp. 19–26.

2. Ibid.
3. Krishna Misra, *Prabodh Chandrodaya,* quoted by Mircea Eliade, *Yoga, Immortality and Freedom* (Bollingen Series LVI, Pantheon Books), p. 298.
4. George W. Briggs, *Gorakhnath and the Kanphata Yogis* (Calcutta, 1938), p. 238.
5. P. C. Ray, *Rasa Ratna Samuchchaya: History of Chemistry in Ancient and Mediaeval India,* pp. 167–78.
6. Mayadhar Manshinha, *History of Oriya Literature* (Sahitya Akademi publication), p. 33.
7. Haude Gosain, tr., *The Mirror of the Sky* by Deben Bhattacharya. From the original Bengali, with notes, p. 33.
8. K. Raghunathji, "Bombay Beggars and Criers," *Indian Antiquary,* March 1881, p. 71.
9. W. T. Elmore, *Dravidian Gods in Modern Hinduism,* p. 19.
10. Sham Rao Hivale, *The Pardhans of the Upper Narmada Valley,* pp. 66–70.
11. Ibid., pp. 146–47.

THE *APABHRAṀŚA* AND THE *DEŚĪ*

1. *Mahābhārata,* quoted in Debi Prasad Chattopadhya, *Lokāyatas,* p. 166.
2. *Kāmagīta Gāthās:* "None can destroy me. I am the one immortal and indestructible."
3. P. V. Kane, *History of the Dharma Śāstras,* vol. V, part I, pp. 281 and 282.
4. R. Shama Shastry, "Origin of the Devanagari Script," *Indian Antiquary,* 35 (1906): 291.
5. Kane, *op. cit.,* vol. V, part I, p. 257.
6. Nirmal Kumar Bose, "The Spring Festival of India," *Man in India,* VII (1927): 112–85.
7. Kane, "Anaṇga Dāna Vrata," *op. cit.,* vol. V, part I, p. 257.
8. Ralph Griffiths, tr., *Hymns of the Atharva Veda,* 3.29.7.
9. *Baudha Gāna O Dobā,* quoted in Sashi Bhushan Dasgupta, *Obscure Religious Cults* [as background of Bengali literature], Calcutta (1946), p. 105, song 28.
10. M. M. Sastri, *Song by Savara Pāda,* quoted in Dasgupta, *Obscure Religious Cults,* Calcutta (1946), p. 103, song 5.
11. Verrier Elwin, *The Baiga,* Oxford University Press, p. 441.
12. Ibid., p. 440.
13. Ibid., p. 245.
14. Ibid., p. 269.
15. Rai Krishnadas, "Illustrated Avadhi Ms. Laur Chanda, in the Bharat Kala Bhavan," *Lalit Kalā,* Nos. 1 and 2, pp. 66–71.

THE PAINTINGS OF SETTLED VILLAGE SOCIETIES

1. Verrier Elwin, *The Baiga,* Oxford University Press, p. 391.
2. "Some Bihari *mantrams* or incantations," *Journal of the Anthropological Society of Bombay* 9: 500–523.

BHITTI CHITRAS AND THE PAINTINGS OF MITHILA

1. J. C. Mathur, "Historical Cultural Heritage," *Marg* 9 (no. 1): 4–12.
2. Ibid.
3. Ibid.
4. W. G. Archer, "Maithil Paintings," *Marg* 3 (no. 3): 24–33.
5. *Northern Indian Notes and Queries* IV (Oct. 1894): 111.
6. W. G. Archer, ed., *The Love Songs of Vidyapati,* tr. Deben Bhattacharya, song 7.
7. Ibid.

THE *MAṆḌALAS* AND MAGICAL DRAWINGS

1. P. V. Kane, *History of the Dharma Śāstras,* vol. V, part II, p. 1131.
2. Manmath Nath Dutt Sastri, tr., *Agni Purāṇa,* Chowkhamba Series, pp. 1081–82.
3. Ibid., p. 273.
4. Ibid., p. 1183.
5. Kane, *Dharma Śāstras,* vol. V, part II, p. 1134.
6. Sastri, *Agni Purāṇa,* pp. 1263–64.
7. Laksminath Jha, *Mithilā Kī Sānskritika Loka Chitrakalā,* p. 76.
8. Kane, *Dharma Śāstras,* vol. V, part II, p. 1131.
9. Abanindra Nath Tagore, *L'alpona ou des Décorations rituelles au Bengal* (Paris: Éditions Boissards, 1921), p. 45.
10. Jagdish Gupta, *Prāgaitihāsika Bhāratīya Chitrākalā,* p. 464.
11. Rev. Stephens, *Aboriginal Tribes of the Central Provinces,* ed. R. Temple, (Nagpore: Hislop, 1866).
12. Gupta, *op. cit.,* p. 463.
13. Sastri, *Agni Purāṇa,* p. 117.
14. Ibid.
15. Information given to me by Shri Jai Bapa of Dhrangadhara.

THE *VRATA MAṆḌALAS*

1. Maurice Bloomfield, ed., *Kauśika Sūtras, Atharva Veda,* with extracts from the commentaries of Darila and Keśava, *Journal of the American Oriental Society,* vol. 24.

2. During the month of Śrāvaṇa, the women of Gujarat draw Sathi as on the earth in white. On Sunday they draw *sūrya,* the sun; on Monday, *nāgaposh,* the cobra; on Tuesday, *trikoṇa,* the triangle; on Wednesday, *kaśyapa,* the tortoise; on Thursday, *chatuṣkoṇa,* the square; on Friday, *pañchakoṇa,* the pentagon; on Saturday, *dhanuṣa bāṇa,* a bow and arrow. See *Census of India* (1961), "Fairs & Festivals of Gujarat," p. 237.
3. Abanindra Nath Tagore, *L'alpona ou des Décorations rituelles au Bengal* (Paris: Éditions Boissards, 1921), pp. 18–26.
4. Sri Lakshminath Jha, *Mithilā kī Sāṁskṛtika Loka Chitrakalā,* p. 5.
5. Ibid., p. 47.
6. William Dwight Whitney, tr., *Atharva Veda Samhitā,* 7.37.1, 7–361. See Bloomfield, *op. cit.*
7. Tagore, *op. cit.*, p. 74.
8. Jha, *op. cit.,* p. 26.
9. *Census of India* (1961), "Fairs & Festivals of Madhya Pradesh," pp. 87–88.
10. Ibid., pp. 100–103.
11. Whitney, *op. cit.,* 6.72.1.
12. George W. Briggs, *Gorakhnath and Kanphata Yogis,* p. 135.
13. In Kerala serpents are closely associated with Subramania. They are worshiped on the sixth day of the lunar month (*ṣaṣṭhī*). They are also associated with Śā stā, Āyanār, and Mariammā. "Serpent Worship in Kerala," *Man in India,* vol. 26 (March 1941): 53–64.
14. Jha, *op. cit.,* p. 43.

PAINTINGS AS *KATHĀ*, OR STORY

1. G. S. Dutt, "Tiger's God in Bengal Art," *Modern Review* 50 (Nov. 1932): 520–29.
2. Ibid.
3. Mantra of Narasimha: "With thy *chakra* weapon, shower fire and thunderbolts, thou who art clad in living flames." See Sastri, *Agni Purāṇa.*
4. W. G. Archer, *Bazaar Paintings of Calcutta,* Plate 42.
5. Edward J. Thompson, tr., *Bengal Religious Lyrics: Śākta,* song 24, p. 46.
6. In the temple town of Kalahasti, Andhra Pradesh, temple cloths relating the legends of the goddess of the *Rāmāyaṇa* and the *Bhāgavata* are still painted by *chitrakāras* in the old indigo technique of dyed and painted cloths.
7. Joan Erikson, *Mātā ni Pachedi* (Ahmedabad: National Institute of Design, 1968). A book on the temple cloth of the mother goddess.

THE PICTOGRAPHS OF THE WARLIS, THE BHILS, THE GONDS, AND THE ŚAVARAS

1. As told to me by Jivya Somya, a Warli painter from Ganjad village, Thana district, Maharashtra.
2. Information given by Shri Kulkarni of the Handicrafts and Handlooms Exports Corporation of India, New Delhi.
3. Information supplied by Kumari Mohna Iyengar of the All India Handicrafts Board, after a survey of the tribal areas of Gujarat.
4. Sham Rao Hivale and Verrier Elwin, *Songs of the Forest,* p. 33.
5. Information given to me by Shri Haku Shah, Tribal Research and Training Institute, Ahmedabad.
6. Verrier Elwin, *Tribal Arts of Middle India,* Oxford University Press, p. 185.
7. G. V. Sitapati, "The Śavaras," *Journal of the Andhra Historical Research Society,* 14 (1943): 3.
8. Elwin, *op. cit.,* p. 185.
9. Ibid., pp. 187–88.

THE RURAL GODS—SCULPTURE

1. P. V. Kane, *History of the Dharma Śāstras,* vol. V, part II, p. 36, fn. 83.
2. G. S. Ghurye, *Gods and Men,* pp. 19–20.
3. G. V. Oppert, *Original Inhabitants of Bharat Varsha,* pp. 458–59.
4. *Census of India* (1961), "Fairs & Festivals of Andhra Pradesh," Nalgonda district, p. 64.
5. Kosambi, *Myth and Reality,* p. 91.
6. Motichandra, *Ghurye Felicitation Volume,* pp. 262–64.
7. V. S. Agrawala, *Vamana Purāṇa: A Study,* p. 47.
8. Kosambi, *op. cit.,* p. 10.
9. Ibid., p. 121.
10. *Loc. cit.*
11. *Loc. cit.*
12. *Census of India* (1961), "Fairs & Festivals of Andhra Pradesh," Warrangal district, p. 67.
13. W. G. Archer, *The Vertical Man: A Study in Primitive Sculpture.*
14. Oppert, *Original Inhabitants,* p. 304.
15. In a tiny Mhasoba temple at Himganadi, Mysore State, a figure on horseback identified as Bhairava is carved on the walls of the shrine. Kosambi, *Myth and Reality,* p. 122.
16. *Census of India* (1961), "Fairs & Festivals of Gujarat," p. 229.
17. *Dawn of Civilisation in Maharashtra,* Catalogue of Exhibition held in Prince of Wales Museum of Western India, Bombay (1975), p. 1.

THE FACES OF THE MOTHERS

1. F. E. Pargiter, ed., *Mārkaṇḍeya Purāṇa,* Bibliotheca Indica (1904), pp. 439–510.
2. Arthur Avalon, *Hymns to the Goddess,* pp. 142–45.
3. Ibid., p. 155.
4. B. N. Mukherjee, *The Goddess Nana in Kushan Coins.*
5. G. U. Briggs, *The Chamars,* p. 185. For the links of Lonā, or Lonā Chamārin, to rites of agricultural magic, see Crooks, *Tribes and Castes of N. W. Province & Oudh,* vol. II, p. 171.
6. V. S. Agarwala, *Vāmana Purāṇa: A Study,* p. 137.
7. Manmath Nath Dutt Sastri, *Agni Purāṇa,* p. 542.
8. *Atharva Veda Samhitā,* 6.136.1. Ritual used in the *Kauśika Sūtra* for growth of hair. The *sutra* describes the fruit of the plant made into a concoction and poured by a magician healer, who is clothed in black and has eaten black food in the early morning before the rise of the crows.
9. F. E. Pargiter, *Mārkaṇḍeya Purāṇa,* Bibliotheca Indica, Canto XCI, 43.
10. William Dwight Whitney, tr., *Atharva Veda Samhitā,* 12.1.23.
11. P. V. Kane, *History of Dharma Sāstra,* vol. V, part I, pp. 160–64.
12. Ibid., p. 357.
13. B. A. Gupta, "Harvest Festivals of Ganesh and Gowri," *Indian Antiquary* (1906), 35: 60.
14. Sastri, *Agni Purāṇa,* p. 608.
15. Whitney, *Atharva Veda Samhitā,* 3.5.3.
16. Bāṇa in the *Harṣa Charita* writes of the cat-faced goddess known as Jat Harini, who was worshiped on the *sasthi* day. In her worship figures of small children were painted near her feet. The *Vāmana Purāṇa* refers to this goddess as Charchikā, who had her abode at Inglej in Baluchistan. Charchikā was possibly an Indianization of the ancient Nani, under which name the goddess was originally worshiped. See V. S. Agarwalla, *Vāmana Purāṇa: A Study,* pp. 137–39.
17. *Bulletin of the Prince of Wales Museum,* no. 1–2 (1973), fig. 17(a).
18. *Census of India* (1961), "Fairs & Festivals of Andhra Pradesh," Warrangal district, pp. 37 and 45.
19. The Seven *vāhanas* (vehicles) of the goddess Ambā of Gujarat are as follows:

    On Sunday she rides the Tiger.
    On Monday she rides the Nandi, the Bull.
    On Tuesday she rides the Lion.
    On Wednesday she rides the Airāvata, a mythical seven-tusked Elephant.
    On Thursday she rides the Eagle.
    On Friday she rides the Swan.
    On Saturday she rides the Elephant.

    See *Census of India* (1961), "Fairs & Festivals of Gujarat," p. 237.

20. N. N. Bhattacharya, *Indian Mother Goddess,* p. 25.
21. G. V. Oppert, *On the Original Inhabitants of Bharat Varsha,* pp. 150–52.
22. See N. N. Chaudhari, "Cult of the old lady," *Journal of the Anthropological Society of Bombay* 5 (1939): 447ff.
23. Kane, *Dharma Śāstra,* vol. V, part I, p. 260.
24. Bhavaraju Venkata Krishna Rao, *Early Dynasties of Andhra Pradesh,* p. 533.
25. *Census of India* (1961), "Fairs & Festivals of Andhra Pradesh," Krishna district, p. 60.
26. Ibid., p. 51.
27. Henry Wittehead, *The Village Gods of South India,* pp. 122–34.
28. Oppert, *Original Inhabitants,* pp. 171–85.
29. Ibid., p. 281.
30. Whitney, *Atharva Veda Samhitā,* 1.25.2, *Asuri* (meaning sheep-headed) is the forest woman transformed into a healing plant (the indigo).
31. Mohan Khokan, *Folk Dance of Kerala.* The *thiyattam* was originally intended to propitiate the *ammā* that governed smallpox. *Marg* 13: 38–39.
32. K. S. Karanth, "Folk dances of S. Kanara," *Marg* 13: 46ff.

CLAY IMAGES OF THE MOTHERS

1. H. D. Sahkalia and M. K. Dhavalikar, "Terracotta Art of India," *Marg* 22 (December 1969): 33–39.

METAL ICONS OF THE MOTHERS

1. See *Dawn of Civilisation in Maharashtra* (exhibit catalogue), Prince of Wales Museum, Bombay, Plates 43–46.
2. Compare icon of bird-headed deity with Harappan amulet of divinity with bird head in profile. M. S. Vats, *op. cit.,* Plate XCL, no. 255.
3. Andra Parrot, *Sumerians,* Thames & Hudson, Plate no. 33.
4. J. Thompson, *Bengali Religious Lyrics: Śākta,* in Arthur Marshman Spencer, *The Heritage of India,* p. 47.

Index

About the Author

Pupul Jayakar was born in 1915 at Etawah in the state of Uttar Pradesh. She has been a social worker since 1941. She has also been closely associated with the culture and development of handlooms and the crafts of India since 1947.

Arguably India's best-known cultural personality, Mrs. Jayakar has been, at various times, chairman of the Handicrafts and Handlooms Exports Corporation (Government of India), chairman of the All India Handicrafts Board (Government of India), chairman of the Central Cottage Industries Corporation of India, chairman of the governing body of the National Institute of Design, chairman of the Calico Museum of Textiles, and chairman of the advisory committee for the Festivals of India, France, and Japan. At present she is the adviser on heritage and cultural resources to the Prime Minister of India, chairman of the National Institute of Fashion Technology, chairman of the Indian National Trust for Art and Cultural Heritage, chairman of the Bharat Kala Bhavan, Bhopal, vice-chairman of the All India Handlooms and Handicrafts Board (Government of India), vice-chairman of the Indira Gandhi Memorial Trust, vice-president of the Indian Council for Cultural Relations, and trustee of the Heritage Trust of England. She is also the president of the Krishnamurti Foundation of India.

Mrs. Jayakar has published several critically acclaimed books, among which are *God Is Not a Full Stop;*

Indira Gandhi: A Photographic Tribute; The Buddha; and *J. Krishnamurti: A Biography.* She is currently working on a biography of Indira Gandhi to be published in 1990.

In 1967, Mrs. Jayakar was awarded the Padma Bhushan for her achievements in the field of handloom development and the Watumul Award for her contribution to the Indian handicrafts industry.

Pupul Jayakar lives in New Delhi.